OUT OF ISTANBUL

OUT OF ISTANBUL

A JOURNEY OF DISCOVERY ALONG THE SILK ROAD

BERNARD OLLIVIER

Translated from the French by Dan Golembeski

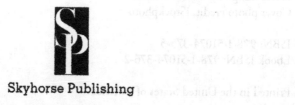

Skyhorse Publishing

Skyhorse Publishing books may be purchased in bulk at special discounts for sales promotion, corporate gifts, fund-raising, or educational purposes. Special editions can also be created to specifications. For details, contact the Special Sales Department, Skyhorse Publishing, 307 West 36th Street, 11th Floor, New York, NY 10018 or info@skyhorsepublishing.com.

Skyhorse® and Skyhorse Publishing® are registered trademarks of Skyhorse Publishing, Inc.®, a Delaware corporation.

Visit our website at www.skyhorsepublishing.com.

10 9 8 7 6 5 4 3 2

Library of Congress Cataloging-in-Publication Data is available on file.

Cover design by Brian Peterson
Cover photo credit: iStockphoto

ISBN: 978-1-51074-375-5
Ebook ISBN: 978-1-51074-376-2

Printed in the United States of America

For Mathieu and Thomas

CONTENTS

CONTENTS

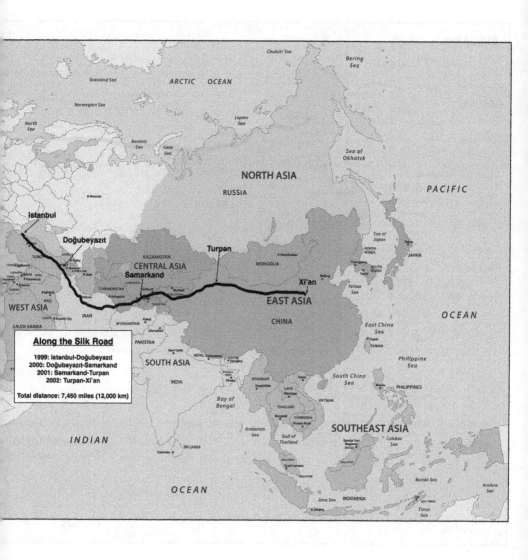

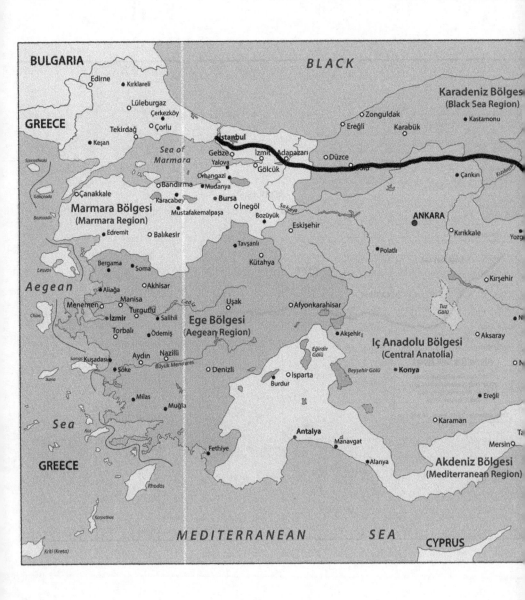

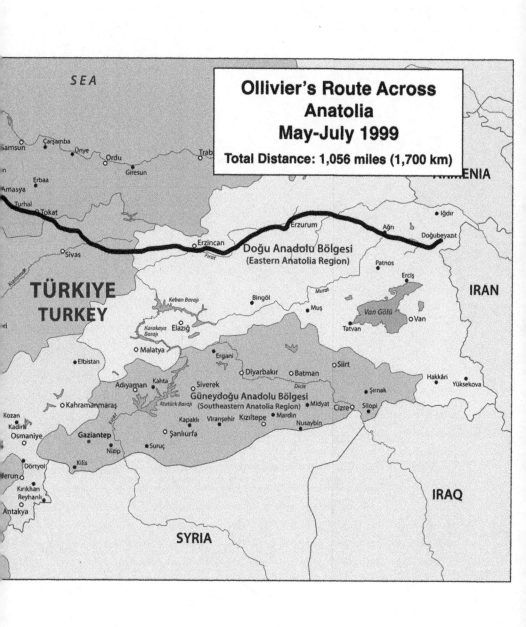

CHAPTER I

THE CITIES WHERE THE ROAD BEGINS

May 6, 1999

My children are out on the platform, waving their last good-byes. The hand of the rail station's large clock suddenly lurches forward: it's time to go. The train pulls me away. The city, with all its noise and light, recedes into the distance. We move through shadowy suburbs, and then into the deep night of the countryside, pierced by fugitive streetlamps. I'm finally on my way. My long Silk Road journey has begun.

As I stare out into space, my nose pressed against the windowpane, my eyes following the fleeting lights, three retirees come alive in our shared compartment. Two are on a long-overdue honeymoon. Thirty-five years and they never found the time. "Business," the woman—a grocer from Brittany—told me a moment ago, "is time-consuming." The other woman, traveling solo, already knows the city. She's back to see the Carnival. In Venice, the season is just getting underway.

I spend a long time in the aisle. I have no desire to talk. In my mind, I'm already out on the road, that incredible road, which has so haunted my dreams. I think about how wise it was to ask my friends not to come out onto the platform with me. Half of them, the ones who are truly upset to see me leave, would have asked me once again: just what is this trip all about? If I were a young man, they would understand: adventure awaits. But when a grown man sets out on a three-thousand-kilometer journey—on foot, with only a pack on his back, in a region reputed to be

1

dangerous—instead of staying home to pamper his peonies in his retirement hideaway in Normandy, it's completely preposterous. And as for the others, those who admire me for what I'm doing or who are simply envious that I'm taking an extended vacation, their presence would have done little to stiffen my resolve. What if I were to disappoint them?

Gazing out into the dark night, never have I had as many doubts about my ability to complete the journey as at this very moment. This is, though, apparently rather common: grand departures are often accompanied by a little bout of the blues.

I explained and reexplained my reasons to them all a hundred times. I'm sixty-one, an in-between age. My career as a journalist, first covering politics and then economics, ended a year ago. My wife and I had been partners in travel and exploration for twenty-five years; then, ten years ago, my heart was broken when hers stopped beating. My sons have begun to lead their lives as full-grown men. They've already experienced the terrifying feeling that, even among others, we are alone. I love them so very much! Together, my sons and I stand before the ocean of life. For the moment, they see nothing but an endless expanse of sea. I, however, have already glimpsed the land where one day I will have to go ashore.

A happy childhood and a somewhat difficult adolescence, then a busy adult life: I've lived two productive, full lives. But why must it all end now? What do "those who wish me well" really want? For me to wait around, lifeless and resigned, reading books by the fireside and watching TV from the couch, so that old age can sneak up and grab me by the throat? No, for me, that time has not yet come. I still stubbornly crave fresh encounters, new faces, and new lives. I still dream of the faraway steppe, of wind and rain on my face, of basking in the heat of different suns.

And then, throughout my previous lives, all too often I was on the run. I never found the time, just like the shopkeepers tirelessly chattering the night away in the compartment behind me. I had to secure a position, work, study, and earn my stripes. Constantly driven by farcical needs in the rush of the mob, endlessly running, dashing about, fast and faster still. Throughout all society, this senseless stampede is still gathering speed. In our noisy, urgent foolishness, who among us yet finds the time to step down off the treadmill to greet a stranger? I yearn, in this third life, for slowness and moments of silence. To stop to admire eyes rimmed with kohl, the flash of a woman's leg, or a misty meadowland immersed in dreams. To eat bread and cheese, sitting in the grass, nose to the wind. And what better way to do this than by going for a walk? The world's oldest form of transportation is also the one that allows us to connect. The only one, in fact. I've had my fill of viewing civilization in boxes and culture grown under glass. My personal museum is to be found in the pathways themselves and in the people traveling them, in village squares, and in a bowl of soup sipped with strangers.

Last year, for my first year in "retirement," I hiked one of the world's oldest roads: The Way of St. James of Compostela, from Paris to Galicia. Two thousand three hundred kilometers (1,430 miles) on foot, pack on my back like a donkey. A marvelous road, full of stories and Histories. I wore out my soles—morning in, morning out—on the selfsame stones of a road that has, for twelve centuries, guided millions of pilgrims, sustained by their faith. For seventy-six days, I was one with the landscape that had seen them all go by, I sweltered on the same slopes, smelled the same smells, and, in its churches, stepped on same slabs that had been buffed by the boot nails of their shoes. Although I did not find faith on the road to Compostela, I returned home elated, feeling closer than ever to those who, from the earliest of times, had left their mark along the way. As I neared the end of my journey, drunk on the fragrance of Galicia's eucalyptus forests, I promised myself that, for as long as my strength would allow, I would continue to walk the world's pathways. And what path could be more inspiring, more impassioned, more infused with history than the Great Silk Road?

At the end of the road to Compostela, I found my new road. That well-known road of men and civilizations. So it was decided: I would walk the Silk Road, from Venice and ancient Byzantium, all the way to China. One foot in front of the other, taking my time. Since I didn't want to be endlessly apart from family and friends, from life as it flows along, I decided to tackle the journey in long stages, hiking three or four months each year, that is to say, from two thousand five hundred to three thousand kilometers (1,550 to 1,865 miles) at a time. For the year at hand, 1999, I planned to go from Istanbul to Tehran.

But before strapping my pack on my back in Istanbul, I felt a need to take in the air of Venice—musty though it is—and catch my breath, looking out at the city's oyster-colored lagoon. Tomorrow morning, I will be in the very city that, over seven centuries ago, saw a young man of fifteen head off to the outer limits of the known world: Marco Polo.

Everyone is fast asleep when I finally slip into my couchette. My gear is here, beside my head. It will be my only companion. I am headed out onto paths of silence and dreams. For the past three months, I have thought only about this. Maps, stopover points, equipment, visas, reading material, clothes, hiking boots. I am hoping to leave as little to chance as possible. This road-before-the-road has, for some time, robbed me of both my nights and my days.

I finally fall asleep, lulled by the soft whoosh of the wheels, my mind filled with visions of caravans advancing across the steppe at the slow, rocking pace of a thousand wooly camels.

The sun is coming up as the train glides silently over the still-sleeping lagoon. At first, only the campaniles break through the soft light of early morn. Then, suddenly, the whole city is upon me. A fairy city, a sorceress city, a city for walkers, a Christian city, a pagan city whose grandeur came from commerce and from, above all, the invention of a form of democracy, albeit quickly snuffed out, it's true, by the patricians. A major breakthrough since, at the time, it was commonly believed that empires were only established through force.

Venice's fortunes came by way of the Silk Road. At the start of the thirteenth century, as the age of Byzantium was drawing to a close, the golden age of La Serenissima was just beginning. There were now no limits to the city's merchants' desire for ever-greater riches. To conquer new trading posts and establish themselves along new roads, they were in an exceptional position, between the mythical land of China on one hand and the wealthy West on the other, hungry for spices, silk goods, paper, and precious stones. A powerful fleet gave them control of the Mediterranean.

One more stroke of good luck: a new route to the East, one that six centuries later would be called "the Silk Road," was now open. The "Pax Mongolica," set up by Genghis Khan's successors, made the route a safe one. Was it not said that a young virgin, bearing a golden cup on her head, could cross the territory from the Caspian to modern-day Korea unafraid for either her virtue or her fortune? On roads built by Alexander the Great and secured by the Tartars, business boomed and fortunes followed, hidden in bundles strapped on the backs of camels and yaks.

To get to know Venice, one option is to take one of the vaporettos of the Grand Canal, but she surrenders herself most readily to those who stroll her shaded side streets. Heading into Venice is like traveling back in time. I get lost in the piazzas, dreaming of one of the first and most amazing adventures that the Silk Road has ever known: that of the Polo Brothers. Perhaps they traversed this very square, built of solid marble and crumbling brick, before venturing out one morning in the year 1260. They set off seeking riches beyond the borders of the known world.

They came back nine years later, having sojourned at the court of the great Kublai Khan. They had convinced the Mongolian emperor that their religion was superior. And so, Kublai gave them safe passage back home. No sooner had they returned than they wanted to head back out, this time to convert the Mongolian barbarians to Catholicism, but also—and chiefly, no doubt—to round out their wealth. They knew what extraordinary riches lay hidden in the Far East. So the two men were back on the road in 1271, accompanied this time by Nicolo's sixteen-year-old son, whose mother had died. First by sea, and then on horseback: the grand voyage was underway.

It wasn't until twenty-five years later, in 1295, that the three men finally returned home to Venice. Venetians were dumbfounded. The trio had been presumed dead, and their inheritance had already been divvied up. Marco, who had a talkative streak, told of the splendors he'd seen twelve thousand kilometers away, cities where, he said, there were inhabitants *by the milioni*, and he bragged that the emperor had given him gold pieces, *by the milioni*. It all seemed so incredible, so extravagant, that no one took him seriously; and so, in jest, he was given the nickname of *Il milione*.

As I stroll through the city, I notice how Venice unabashedly celebrates its doges, musicians, painters, and poets. But for Marco, I find nothing. Not a single *vicolo*, no *campo*, not the least plaque to call to mind the name of the most famous of all Venetians. Very recently, the city made up for this by renaming its airport *Venice Marco Polo*: tempting us to other forms of travel. When the house where he lived burned down, just a step or two from the Rialto Bridge, a modest little brick building was rebuilt on the site. But I search in vain, on the *piazzetta*, for some sign of the most famous of early travelers to the Orient. I keep looking, and finally, yes indeed, I find one: the place itself is called the *piazza del . . . . Milione*.

It's early May, and tourists are pouring into the city. They walk in circles among the pigeons in St. Mark's Square, hardly noticing, for the most part, the incredible equilibrium of the place: religious power symbolized by the Basilica, civil power epitomized by the Doge's Palace. Would we, in the civilizations we live in today, be able to represent that kind of dualistic power so harmoniously? I find myself wandering about, feeling rather giddy, savoring these moments on the eve of a grand departure. I wander through the Museo Correr, whose treasures I had the occasion to admire on an earlier visit. And then I finally explore the maritime museum, which I missed on my previous journey. But the city's magic that so gripped me on my first visit has somehow worn off; to tell the truth, in my mind, I am already out on the steppe.

The *Samsun* is a large Turkish ferry providing weekly service between Venice and İzmir. Docked at the wharf, the enormous white ship juts out over the roofs of a city built at sea level. The immense forward gates are wide open, gobbling up a host of powerful German vehicles lined up single file on the wharf, loaded with packages, some even on the roof. They are driven by Turkish workers headed back to their hometowns for the summer, who would never think of simply leaving their cars in garages in Frankfort or Stuttgart. In their home villages, such vehicles provide concrete proof of their success.

I share my cabin with two Armenians headed home with two large Mercedes, bought in France. For the entire three-day voyage, the only time they leave their berths is to eat. They make sure the sink is constantly stocked with a few cans of beer, kept cold by letting the tap run nonstop. I don't quite get it: why travel so far to pick up a couple cars? The youngest one, who speaks a little slang-laden French, tries to prevent me from coming to the wrong conclusion: don't get the idea, he tells me, that they're involved in trafficking cars that have been *chouravées* (stolen). The next day, as we talk, I discover that he learned to speak our language in the fair city of Lille . . . in one of its prisons, that is.

Slouched in an armchair on a part of the deck where a bar has been set up near the ship's stern, I try to make out the Croatian coastline, not far off. The war in Kosovo serves up its daily dose of horror. That evening, while we are at dinner, one of the waiters suddenly yells out. We look in the direction he's pointing: in the night sky, a long trail of fire, followed by a column of smoke, informs us that a missile has just blasted off from one of NATO's ships on its death mission to Serbia.

On board, I meet three French nationals, white-haired adventurers, like me. Louis, a former industry executive, and Éric, a dentist, are both retirees. Long-time companions, they have been through a thousand adventures, traveling each year with friends, from the Tropics to the high Arctic. This year, they're cycling a series of stages that should take them from Gaillac—Louis's home village in the Aveyron department in France—to Jerusalem in the year 2000. They have, at the ready, a treasure trove of colorful anecdotes from their earlier adventures; they have explored half the world but want nothing more than to roam the other half. Their stories bring me back to my own fears. Like all travelers, Louis and Éric remember their journeys solely in terms of the trials, catastrophes, and accidents that toughened them up along the way. As if we could reduce travel to only its troubles and torments, its particular way of putting us through the paces that, later on, makes us laugh all the heartier. The narrative, most often, goes like this: "My travels were amazing, and to prove it, let me tell you about the three times I came *this close* to dying." A few years ago, Éric was stricken with a horrific foot infection, picked up while on a train on his way to the Far North. (In my head, I say to myself: I sure hope my own feet hold up.) Another time, the two rascals got lost in the fog on a glacier, such that just one misstep would have sent them to spend the rest of their lives at the bottom of a crevasse. (In my head, I imagine myself lost in the deserts of Central Asia; as for sheer drops, in Anatolia and the Pamirs, I will see a thousand of them. But there's a difference between their story and mine: *I will be alone.*)

The other Frenchman, Yvon, a solid, stocky, square-jawed Breton, walks up and down the ship poking about like a veteran seafarer. He spent his entire life working on offshore oil rigs. He, too, has knocked around a lot and wants nothing more than to keep on going. He's headed to Turkey, to the city of Çorum *(cho-room)*, where he will assume ownership of a sixteen-meter (52-foot) sailboat that he was finally able to buy for himself, realizing the dream for which he slogged away for forty years: to stand at the helm of his own ship. I like this partner in madness who—alone, like me—is going to cross the Mediterranean, then head up the Atlantic to his native Brittany.

Roused by their stories, I talk about my own dream, too: to walk, step by step, from Istanbul to Xi'an—Xi'an, the former imperial Chinese city that became world-famous when a "buried army" was discovered there some years ago by a man digging a well.* Yvon, taciturn like a true Breton, listens to my story without saying a word, but the two others admit that they're astounded by my plans, a reaction that succeeds in rekindling my own fears. If globetrotters like these consider my trip reckless, then perhaps my own plans should be little less ambitious. Perhaps I should stop acting, head high and heart hopeful, as if I were invulnerable to the wicked ways of the world.

In earlier times, travelers in the Occident were mostly moneyed young men out to sow their wild oats, intent on having a taste of the exotic

---

* Translator's note (TN): in 1974.

before settling down into a career, one that was most often prearranged. They had time for themselves. Today, the fact that people live longer and retire at sixty has produced a new generation of adventurers. They have furrowed foreheads, and their hair has turned gray. They are bold, resilient, headstrong, and keen on fulfilling their childhood dreams. Previously, family life, professional obligations, and financial concerns prevented them from actually doing it. Retirement brings freedom.

The *Samsun* is an ideal place for meeting people. It is also, in its countless nooks and crannies, a haven of solitude. Lying low, I ponder my impending solo trek. I am fairly familiar with the route I will be taking. As for my muscles, I am on my game. But what am I to do with my mind and thoughts during the long, oh so long journey? In what direction will they go? Should I try to keep them under control or allow myself to be carried along by them? Before my departure for Compostela, I drew up a list of questions to guide my thoughts: Who am I today? How did you turn into the man you've now become? Did things go the way you planned? Did you maintain course, or, instead, did you betray your dreams? What were the compromises, which of my aspirations were abandoned during the journey? Which stone should I set in place and on which wall should I set it before the final bow? Taking that daunting mathematical calculation—I subtract my pains, multiply my gains, divide the result by my joys and *voilà!* there is proof positive that I exist—and then applying it foolishly to questions of an ontological nature was, in any case, one of the last vestiges of that cursed habit of ours to attempt to understand everything in terms of an equation. But Compostela changed me. Although I still have a long way to go before I can hope to close in on true wisdom, I am leaving lighter this time, emptier, more *undone.*

Walking stirs us to dream. It is not very compatible with structured thought. The latter is more at home in contemplation, eyes half-closed, the body resting on a soft cushion of fine sand, lounging about in the shade of the pines. Walking is action, momentum, motion. While the body is hard at work, the mind, constantly solicited by imperceptible variations in the landscape—a passing cloud, a gust of wind, puddles on the path, a rustling wheat field, the purple hue of cherries, the fragrance of cut hay or of flowering mimosas—begins to panic, unable to bear the unrelenting work. So thoughts set about foraging and harvesting; reaping images, sensations, and scents, which are then set aside for later on, when, back at the hive, it will be time to sort through them and give them meaning.

Soothed by the drone of the engines and the gentle to-and-fro of the ship, I could easily doze off, perfectly content. But no, a sense of apprehension suddenly slips in, capitalizing on the empty space that forced inaction has carved out within me. Inevitably, instead of daydreaming, my mind pores over the catalog of a thousand questions to which, just maybe, I will find answers along the way. Will I, by journey's end, come to know the source of the force compelling me to head out all alone, for three or four months at a time, into the unknown? Although I more or less know why I choose to walk, I have no idea why I choose to get lost while there are so many marked, well-known, and risk-free trails out there, anywhere from the Alps to my own backyard in Normandy. What if this is just some comical attempt to relive my long-lost youth? If my body fails me, I'll have an answer to that question, at least. The mind may go along with a lie for a while, but it's much harder for the muscles.

And the solitude that lies ahead, will I manage to defeat its dark valleys and keep its pleasures under control? And above all, will I be able to make the most of it? For this solitude is not the result of fleeing something; I am choosing it freely. It is the blank slate on which I plan to write the next chapter. A garden where I will plant thoughts like flowers—some will be soft as silk and others thorny to the touch—and they will only fully bloom when I return home.

But who says that I will return? I am not so naive as to embark on this adventure without at least giving some thought to my death. Until quite recently, it was enough to simply imagine that one day I might die. Today, I know that I will. Will death allow me to see this journey through? I know that many dangers lie in wait: sickness, accidents, violence. In groups, people support one another, help one another, comfort one another, carry one another. There is room for error, or a momentary weakness. Malfunctions are relative, temporary. For the solo traveler, however, second chances are rare.

Whether I am sitting in a dark corner of one of the bars, standing at the edge of the ship, my elbows resting on the railing, or looking out to sea seated beside an airshaft on the forecastle of the *Samsun*, these are some of the vague worries that take hold of me, and I do nothing to stop them. I know that as soon as I take my first step out onto the road, they will let go, waiting for a more favorable opportunity to grab hold of me once again later on. And when my little bout of blues, so characteristic of these eves before battle, starts to seem too much, I go rambling around the ship's passageways and decks for a few new encounters or to rejoin familiar faces.

As night falls, we—the four gray-haired French adventurers—are standing in a row with our noses in the air, gazing up to admire the spectacle of the ship's passage through the extraordinary Corinth Canal. Its steep walls and narrow channel have drawn everyone out on deck. The ship's Turkish passengers have already settled back into the habits of home. Conversations resound, teacups parade back and forth. There is little or no alcohol. Those with a taste for strong drink retreat into the two small bars tucked away in the vessel's side. Alcohol is easier to savor in the scant light seeping in through the portholes.

I am one of the very few foot passengers. All the others, whether alone or in family groups, have brought their car with them onto the *Samsun*. I talk for a long time with a Turko-Swiss couple going on vacation in the husband's hometown. He's a retired engineer who, after attending a Swiss institute of technology as a young man, spent his entire career disfiguring French-speaking Switzerland with roads and bridges. But since childhood, he has had a strong attachment to his hometown. Though the couple resides in Switzerland, he doesn't let a year go by, not a single summer, without making the trip home.

Yarup, a young businessman who, with his family, started a clothing business in the suburbs of Paris, is taking his car back home for good. With so much competition in France, he decided to rebuild the company's workshops in Turkey—in his hometown, of course. "For just one person's salary in France, I can pay ten workers in Turkey," he explains. He will fly back to Paris for work and to visit his family who has settled down . . . in housing that recreates the feel of a village. In order to stay together, all the brothers and cousins bought apartments in a single building, which they now own from the basement to the rafters.

In İzmir, Yvon, Éric, Louis, and I wish one another the best of luck. That very evening, I board a bus that drops me off early the next morning in Taksim Square, Istanbul's business district. I make a quick stop in the Turkish bank where I had opened an account while still in Paris. When I walk in, the women at the counter elbow one another, chuckling. They've all heard about the slightly madcap Frenchman planning to hike the Silk Road. The risk of being mugged is real. To be on the safe side, I want to avoid carrying large sums. They provide me with a plastic debit card so that, in larger cities, I can use teller machines to withdraw Turkish liras. Can (pronounced like the English *John*), the bank's manager, and Mehmet, his assistant, both speak my native language, which they learned in Istanbul's *écoles françaises*. Though they are astonished at my endeavor, they are mostly worried. "You are going to need a lot of luck," Can tells me, shaking my hand as I head out. Words I will often think back on along the way.

I walk across the square and go to have my passport stamped at the French Consulate, just around the corner. If something nasty happens to me, a threat I take seriously, at least the French authorities in Turkey will know who I am and what I was doing. I do not know if it's the classic pusillanimity often attributed to government employees in their cushy, well-guarded offices, or because they've been conditioned by the line of business they're in, but the consulate's employees do not mince words in warning me of potential catastrophe. They tell me there's danger everywhere. According to them, the only hospitable places are along the coast in Turkey's south popular with tourists, or Cappadocia. And they list off, one by one, all the risks I may face: Turkish drivers, who pose a real threat to pedestrians, as well as thieves, snipers belonging to the PKK party (the Marxist-Leninist Kurdistan Workers' Party), and of course Kangals, the fearsome shepherd dogs of eastern Turkey. Were I to take these warnings seriously, I would immediately reboard the *Samsun* and go back the way I came. The only risk a tourist runs in Venice is having to pay too much for a cappuccino.

This is my second trip to Istanbul. Earlier this year, I did some research on the Silk Road and met Stéphane Yerasimos, director of the Center for Anatolian Studies. He compiled, annotated, and prefaced reeditions of several works on the Silk Road, most notably The *Description of the World* by Marco Polo[*] and *The Voyages of Ibn Battuta*.[†] He also edited the two volumes of Jean-Baptiste Tavernier's memoirs.[‡] Tavernier, a seventeenth-century French trader in precious gems, kept a meticulously detailed journal of his travels through Turkey and Persia. And he took scrupulous notes on the cities and the caravansaries in which he stayed. I will be following, from here to Erzurum, one of his best-chronicled caravan routes. That road, a major thoroughfare for commerce with the Orient, led straight east out of Istanbul and all the way to Armenia, via Erzurum, then turned directly south to Tabriz, in Persia. From there, one branch continued on to Baghdad. The other, skirting the south shore of the Caspian Sea, headed up toward Bukhara, Samarkand, and China. That's the section that I plan to hike next year.

Before my grand departure, I've given myself twenty-four hours. Is it to get a good a running start, or simply to tour the city? I don't really know. Today, Istanbul is an immense metropolis of 13 million people. It's the economic and cultural capital of the country, having begrudgingly relinquished the leading role in the political sphere to Ankara. It is still, however, the most European of Turkish cities. In these first few days of May, the city's weather is mild but wet. I have lunch at the *Lades*, a restaurant in the Beyoğlu (*bay'-oh-lu*) district, directly across from the small mosque of Galatasaray. I rehearse what will be the case all along the way: it's always a good idea to first do a quick tour of the kitchen to check for any questionable cooks. There's no need to speak Turkish or to know

---

[*] Marco Polo, *Le Devisement du monde*, Paris: La Découverte, 1998.

[†] Ibn Battuta, *Voyages*, 3 volumes, Introduction and notes by Stéphane Yerasimos, Paris: Maspero, 1982.

[‡] Jean-Baptiste Tavernier, *Six voyages en Turquie et en Perse* (Six Voyages in Turkey and in Persia), Paris: Maspero, 1981.

the names of the dishes. I simply point with my famished index finger to a variety of hot and cold *meze*, which I always enjoy, as well as some eggplant, looking perfectly slow-cooked, another one of my favorites. By the time I take a seat, my food is ready. Turkish chefs, whose cuisine often includes ragout dishes (*etli sebze*, literally, "vegetables with meat"), are true masters at combining culinary excellence with lightning-fast service.

After lunch, I stroll through the old city. I need to finish breaking in my new hiking boots, which I must have so far only hiked in for at most three hundred kilometers. At the consulate, a secretary warns me about elusive young individuals, fluent in French, who often target tourists traveling alone. They come up to them, in the street or on public transportation, wearing a friendly face. They then offer their victim a drink or pastry laced with some drug. The victim immediately falls asleep, only to wake up later on stripped of all his or her belongings. The "spiked drink" technique is not new. It was often used by bandits to steal from merchants on the Silk Road. The drink was usually laced with tarantula venom, and the merchants never woke up.

In the small streets behind the bazaar, a poor neighborhood where people live in unhygienic conditions, I run little risk of encountering tourists or those who seek to steal from them. I see that some of the old wooden Ottoman-style houses are finally being restored, and none too soon. Until now, the focus has been on monuments only—such as the Topkapı Palace*—and religious buildings. To be sure, Istanbul—or

---

* The Turkish and Latin alphabets are very similar. There are, nevertheless, several differences that make Turkish somewhat difficult to transcribe in English, most importantly the dotless *i*—*ı*—pronounced like the English schwa (such as the *a* in *about*), but with the mouth slightly opened and top and bottom teeth closed. Although one often sees the word spelled *Topkapi* in English, the Turkish pronunciation of the final letter is different, closer to *Tohp'-kah-puh*, and is spelled *Topkapı*. The letter *ö* is also similar to the English schwa, although it is pronounced with rounded lips. Other tricky transcriptions include: Turkish *c* is pronounced *dj*, the *ç* like *ch* and cedilla-s, *ş*, is pronounced *sh*. Should I transcribe the name of my banker in Turkish as *Can*, or phonetically, as *John*? TN: In this English edition, Turkish spellings have been used unless there is a common English equivalent. An approximation of Turkish pronunciation has been provided if it differs considerably from what an English speaker might expect. Tonic accents, if unusual with respect to English, are indicated by an apostrophe following the stressed syllable.

Constantinople, to be exact—did not have a monopoly on the Road and was never but one link in the chain. It was a kind of storehouse with an adjoining tollbooth. On the other hand, Byzantium had political control of all the Mediterranean cities, from Antioch to Alexandria, and each city was a departure point for its own caravan trail. There was not just one, but many Silk *routes*.

I also have a little time to spend with my friends: Dilara and Rabia, two young women who studied in Istanbul's *écoles françaises* and who roll their r's delightfully when speaking French; and Max, a musician from Paris who came to Istanbul to study, as well as to learn how to play Eastern musical instruments, in particular the *Saz*. Having lived here for two years, he finds it hard to imagine ever returning to France. The four of us enjoy a wonderful dinner together that feels to me a little like a *veillée d'armes*: a final evening of camaraderie before I dive head-first into my adventure and the solitude of the long-distance walker. We talk about everything other than my trip. With my departure imminent, the die is cast, and so I'm thankful that my friends choose to talk about something else. Particularly since Rabia informs us that she is going to be married to Rémi, a Frenchman who moved to Istanbul for work. If they decide to tie the knot quickly, I won't be able to make the wedding.

On the night of May 13 to 14, I sleep very little and rather poorly. I have no need for an alarm clock; I jump out of bed early that morning all on my own. The sun has only begun to rise over the Bosporus and the Golden Horn as I hurry out, pack on my back, into Istanbul's still-deserted streets. I scurry down the steep thoroughfare linking the İstiklal—the *Champs-Élysées* of Istanbul—to the port. Along the way, I salute the ancient Galata Tower overlooking the famous bay. And in no time at all, I'm standing on the pier, ready to cross the Bosporus strait, going from Turkey's European shore to its Asian shore. When I step off the ship, I will be in Asia and at the zero-kilometer mark of my journey. With just under three thousand to go to reach Tehran.

CHAPTER II
THE PHILOSOPHICAL WOODSMAN

The *Suhadyne*, a small ferry linking the two banks of the Bosporus, scoots away from the European shore and quickly heads out amid a flotilla of fishing boats. At this hour of the morning, there are only a few passengers. One portly fellow avails himself of the ten-minute crossing to catch a few more z's, his head comfortably propped up by his triple chin. The sun is struggling to break through the mist. On the European side receding into the distance, only a few islands of greenery have survived the unbridled urbanization busily attacking the city from all sides. The novelist Pierre Loti, who was madly in love with Istanbul at a time when it was known simply as "Stamboul," would probably not appreciate the modern metropolis it has become.

Above us, on the immense suspension bridge linking the two continents, cars and trucks process back and forth like ants to and from an anthill. The bridge is off-limits to pedestrians, so if you want to get from Europe to Asia, you have to get your feet wet. The official explanation is that too many hopeless souls have climbed the bridge's parapet and jumped off into the Bosporus. In reality, it is because the army, which has guardhouses at both ends of the bridge, is worried that the Kurds might try to sabotage one of the premier symbols of Turkish modernity.

The mosques on the opposite bank, along with the sumptuous Topkapı Palace, have vanished into the mist by the time the ferry lands in Üshküdar. The neighborhood is one gigantic bus depot. This is a simple continuation: it has always been a travelers' district. In fact, from time immemorial until the early twentieth century, Üshküdar was the gathering place for caravans traveling to Central Asia. When the convoy's leader determined that enough merchants and animals had arrived to ensure that profits would be worth his efforts and that the convoy would be safe—in general between eight hundred and one thousand animals and one hundred individuals or so—he would give the go-ahead, and the caravan would depart.

And so that's where I've decided to begin to walk, allowing myself, however, a first deviation from the old caravan route. The ancient camel path, which starts in this district on the Asian shore of Istanbul and heads east to Adapazarı, hugging the Sea of Marmara, became a road in the early twentieth century, and then a highway. Hardly interested in starting my trek amid so much engine noise and the foul smell of exhaust fumes, I opt for a detour, following the Bosporus upstream. Although I wish to keep to the route of the caravans, it goes without saying that I'm more interested in honoring its spirit than its exact course. Far be it from me to attempt to do the work of a geographer or historian. Rather, as I go along, I hope to share some of the thoughts, feelings, and perhaps even perils that were part of the everyday life of caravanners and traveling merchants. I expect that it will be in the villages, and not in the cities, that I'll come closest to the atmosphere, traditions, and way of life of those who once traveled these routes. I therefore intend to avoid major thoroughfares. But in the original stopover points, I'll make a point of ferreting out any vestiges of the ancient road and especially of the caravansaries, the wayside inns that housed men, merchandise, and animals and provided for their rest, food, and safety.

The road that runs along the Bosporus—a kind of slender canal connecting the Black Sea to the Sea of Marmara—is not a highway; what a pity, though, that it carries just as much traffic as one. I'm straightaway in the mad rush. Turkish drivers are maniacs. Zooming along at top speed, gesturing, honking; zigzagging to avoid potholes when there are some, and zigzagging all the same when there are not: they're a constant threat. It stems from a general consensus: in this country, pedestrians survive only by categorically recognizing that drivers *always* have the

right-of-way. Last night in Istanbul, I saw an old man get knocked down
by a motorist. The driver cursed his victim profusely, and the old man
couldn't seem to come up with anything to say in his own defense.
That's how it is here: drivers reign supreme, so pedestrians are always
wrong. Of course, the street is no place for pedestrians. But Istanbul's
narrow and impractical sidewalks are really no better. So, where is one
supposed to walk?

For the time being, I've decided to walk against the traffic, so I can
see danger coming head-on. I slowly press on along a kind of parapet,
the base of which is being splashed by waves from the strait. I'm ready
to jump into the water should a car come too close. Trucks and cars
brush past me, racing by in a roar. It's forbidden to walk under the two
suspension bridges. The first arch is a military zone. Barbed wire and
soldiers guard it: stone-faced men, each holding an assault rifle across
his chest, one hand near the trigger. Warning signs proclaim: *No cameras allowed.* I will come across warlike scenes like this a thousand times.
Occasionally, the road veers somewhat away from the bank, and in
those places, it's lined by opulent-looking houses protected by walls and
warning signs that all walkers recognize without any need for a translation: *Beware of the Dog.* The residents of these houses must be deaf; the
loud rumble of the vehicles is unbearable. On my guard, hemmed in by
cars and trucks, I'm not really able to enjoy the scenery. I walk slowly,
heedful on this first day of my feet, which seem to be holding up, and
of my shoulders, which are starting to burn where the straps of my pack
cut into them. All perfectly normal and expected; my skin just needs to
thicken a bit.

Yes, I'm carrying a little too much weight. In Paris, I lightened my
load ten different times. But how much lighter could I go when the
container itself weighs only two kilograms (4.4 pounds) and I've got
nearly three kilograms (6.6 pounds) of books, documents, and maps
to bring? Everything else is small potatoes. Aside from the clothes on
my back, I've packed two T-shirts and a pair of boxers, an extra pair of
socks, and a pair of pants made of very thin, lightweight material to help
me cope with the heat. I'll come to find out—too late, of course—that

the fabric is slightly transparent, but when wet from perspiration, it becomes perfectly see-through. So I only wear them in the evening at stopovers. I have a sleeping bag and a bivvy sack as well as an emergency blanket. Pocketknife, toothbrush, and ultralight camera, I weighed everything twice before cinching the straps. But I couldn't get under twelve kilograms (26.4 pounds), on top of which I must add a two-liter jug of water and a little food: bread, cheese, and fruit. All in all, a total of fifteen kilos (33 pounds).

On the opposite side of the Bosporus, plowed by rumbling cargo ships, the city's old fortifications are still in good condition. But the view of the strait—its name means "cow-passage"—is worse off with its two suspension bridges and a high-tension power line, which spoil the panorama.

After about fifteen kilometers or so, I have to make a right turn in the village of Paşabahçe (*pa-sha-ba'-chuh*). There are no road signs anywhere, not even the smallest signpost. No directions for roads, cities, or villages. I will have to ask the locals. At 1:00 p.m., I stop in a small, working-class restaurant, a *lokanta*. It's my first opportunity to put my Turkish to use without my Istanbulite interpreters beside me. The result must not be very convincing, since the owner interrupts me with a wave of his hand and goes off to get the dishwasher. The short-statured fellow washes his dishes wearing a two-piece suit, a crisp white shirt, and a tie. He tells me in English that he used to be a math professor in Albania. He hoped to immigrate to France but was denied a visa. He makes much more money here as a dishwasher than he did as a professor back home. After a cup of tea offered by the owner—in Turkey, tea is always included with a meal—I set off again.

Much like an athlete before an important event, I'm very attentive to my body. A small pain in my side, another in my knee, a cramp in my foot, and I start getting worried, although I'm aware that these are, in fact, proof that I'm in shape. On the *Samsun*, I inspected my feet nearly every day. No concerns at all. But even so, my mind is hardly at ease. After these first few hours on my feet and as I head back out onto the road, I remain vigilant, on the lookout for the least sign of fatigue in my body and especially in my feet, the walker's most precious possession. In

Paris, going over my map, I planned to take it easy for the first few days, doing only short stages. There are only six or seven kilometers to go this afternoon, since I plan on stopping in Gümüşsuyu (gu-mush'-soo-yuh), twenty-five kilometers into the journey. For my first day, that's a reasonable distance.

But where, oh where is that road on the right? I ask two walkers, who, very kindly, offer to take me there themselves. They lead me a few hundred meters down the road . . . to the bus station. I had, however, been very clear about asking for the *road* to the village, not the *bus*. But they would never expect, even for a second, that I would want to *walk* those seven kilometers! Somewhat to rouse them, I tell them in my rudimentary Turkish that my final destination is Tehran. They are dumbstruck. I'm not really sure whether their stunned incomprehension is because of my limited vocabulary, or because of my plans. I rephrase what I said, and this time, I think they've grasped it. Now there's no doubt whatsoever: they are dealing with a madman. I can read in their eyes such disbelief, combined with pity and mistrust, that I decide to abstain from casually telling people about my undertaking in the future. I set off once again, and as I do, I can feel the weight of their stares on my back.

Having made very little progress, I keep walking in circles. No matter whom I ask, no one has ever heard of the village of Gümüşsuyu. I'm reminded of ventures into Paris's outlying suburbs, when I was looking for the *Rue de la République* or the *Rue du Président Fallières*, which no one, ever, has even heard of. My success rate is headed down the tubes. And then, all of a sudden, there it is, passing between a warehouse and a bottle factory. The road makes a steep climb out of the Bosporus trench. Halfway up, I realize that I've lost my pedometer. Too bad. From now on, I'll just have to estimate the distances I travel. Its little tick-tock mechanism annoyed me anyway whenever I went for jaunts in the countryside. On top of it, it wasn't very accurate, probably from never having been properly calibrated. It was by no means essential, so good riddance.

On either side of the road, hundreds of single-family houses are going up. Protected behind walls or gates, they are being erected in "compounds" resembling fortified villages; ghettoes turned inside out—islands for the well-off—which, in the United States and Africa, are designed to protect the privileged from the rank and file. Here, like there, the entrance is flanked by a guardhouse, complete with guards. Their outfit, of the same color and cut as that of the police, is designed to scare off troublemakers. Higher up on the hill, one can see the concrete skeletons of towers and high-rise blocks that will soon house ordinary folk. Istanbul's metropolitan area and surrounding province, home to thirteen million souls today, will grow even more in coming years, and developers are delighted at the prospect.

In various places, the houses remain unfinished. Their owners typically reside on either the first or second floor. Above them, the walls have only been started, concrete pillars with rusty metal arrows pointing up toward the sky. I later find out that this is done on purpose: housing tax is due only when construction is completed. So they are left unfinished.

I finally make it to the top of the long climb. The Bosporus has disappeared. At the summit, along the roadside, there is a *büfe* run by a little old man and his wife. It's a modest shop: four wooden stakes covered by a plastic tarp. Beverages are kept cool in a refrigerator hooked up to two wires that illegally tap into lines on a nearby electric utility pole. I drink the first Coca-Cola of my life. What other choice do I have when that's all there is in the refrigerator, and my two-liter water jug is empty? At 3:30 p.m., I've made it to Gümüşsuyu. The village has no hotel. I'm assured that there is one in Polonez, a little burg, ten kilometers down the road. Since I don't feel the least bit tired, Polonez it is.

It's only day one, but this is a typical illustration already of what I ran up against in preparing my trip. On the map, I planned out theoretical stages based on the distance to be traveled, the altitude, and the presumed historical interest of the area. But I'm well aware that in Turkish villages, hotel infrastructure is nonexistent. Inns, designed for those traveling in vehicles, are located only along major thoroughfares and are spaced great distances from one another. Having opted to journey through villages, I knew that almost every day would bring its share of surprises.

There are fewer and fewer houses, and I enter a dark forest of fir trees, which progressively give way to more friendly-looking oak trees.

The road heads directly east, jumping from one hill to the next, and the view from atop each looks out over a vast expanse of green. Upon arriving in Polonez, I stand confounded before a gate topped with a cross. A Christian cross in Muslim lands? It's a cemetery and the doors are locked. The *Polska* hotel is full, but several families open their homes to travelers in exchange for a few shiny coins.

Krisha, a young blond with jade-colored eyes, runs the *Lora Pansiyon* and offers to provide me with dinner, a bed, and breakfast for ten million Turkish liras. I have to admit that I'm still astonished to see people handling bills in denominations of five million. But in a country where a cup of coffee costs four hundred thousand liras, you soon get used to such fantastic sums, the result of double-digit inflation over many years. Ten million is the equivalent of the modest sum of one hundred and sixty French francs (about US $25). On this first day, I've walked thirty-two kilometers (20 miles), ten (6 miles) more than I intended with respect to my hiking schedule. I feel vaguely tired. But it's already nighttime, and that should take care of it.

A gold cross glimmers around Krisha's neck. She's wearing neither scarf nor chador, and her lightweight garment has a chic, yet modest neckline. Never again, throughout my travels in Turkey, will I encounter a woman dressed so freely. She speaks Turkish, but, like almost all the village's inhabitants, her first language is Polish. She tells me the town's history. In 1842, the Sultan Abdulmejid, after a war with Russia, granted a group of Polish citizens the right to build a village in a forest belonging to Istanbul. For over a century, they were a community of woodworkers living in isolation from the outside world while maintaining traditions of their homeland. Apart from the *Polska* hotel, nearly every business in the village has a Polish name. Its inhabitants were formerly all Catholic and spoke the language of their ancestors. Over the past fifteen years or so, however, a few Muslim Turks have begun to move in. The Polish residents have maintained the right to practice their religion. They have their church. But since education became compulsory, Turkish is the only language taught in the village school.

The bed is comfortable, and the half-Turkish, half-Polish breakfast quickly fills me up: bread, tomatoes, cucumbers, a hard-boiled egg, and a very salty *fromage blanc.** All washed down with tea, served in little tulip-shaped cups. I already had the opportunity to see how Turks prepare tea, a method that yields a most amazing beverage. I watch Krisha as she prepares mine. She uses a two-stage urn, the *çaydanlık* (*chai-dahn'-luhk*), which works on the same principle as the samovar. The large lower level holds the boiling water. The upper level, the *demlik* (*dehm'-leek*), contains a large quantity of tea and very little water. The tea is thus kept at the right temperature by the steam from the large vessel. By skillfully operating the two, she can draw tea at the desired strength; but make no mistake, doing so is an art. People drink tea everywhere, at any hour of the day. The tea urn is kept continuously hot, from early morning until bedtime.

The sun is high in the sky when I bid Krisha farewell. With a twinge of regret. I always find it difficult to leave a place where I've received a warm welcome. I think about the traders who preceded me, long ago, on these roads. They didn't have misgivings as I do. For them, what good were the stopovers? Arriving at their destination, finalizing some gainful deals, and then returning home—as quickly as possible and in one piece—were their only concerns.

Will the second stage be difficult? My muscles are sore from the distance I covered yesterday. But the day is bright, and before too long they start to warm up. I cheerfully head out onto a road as straight as if a saber had sliced a path through the oak-covered hills. Once again, as a precaution, I walk on the left, but the traffic is lighter than yesterday. The cars, which are considerably fewer than the trucks, are visible from a distance, since their sound is amplified in the tree-lined passageway. Drivers make it known how surprised they are to see a hiker, especially one loaded down like a donkey. Most of them slow down and wave, which I take as a sign of friendship, and so I wave back. Others, less frequently, authoritatively motion me to walk on the berm, furious that

---

* TN: A kind of curd cheese.

a lowly pedestrian would dare encroach on their turf. They make no attempt to move over and give me some room. Since I don't want to go head-to-head with machines weighing ten or twenty tons, I politely move aside. During the day, several trucks coming toward me slow down and indicate that they'd be happy to give me a ride. Two privately owned cars stop and invite me to get in. I decline the invitation each time with a smile. I'm not about to forego the pleasure of hiking along what has been, for several months now, the road of my dreams! I come upon three men on horseback. Farther down the road, an elderly countryman with a white mustache and a black hat is rolling along, slumped in his seat, in a cart pulled by his son. We say hello to one another: we are the slow ones, the meanderers, those who lag behind. The father and son are clearly consumed with curiosity but are not so bold as to stop to find out more. As for me, my Turkish is so minimal that, at least for now, I avoid initiating any conversations.

After two hours on the road, my muscles have warmed up to the extent that I don't even think about them, but my thighs and buttocks now sting where my pack rubs against them. I still have too much fat in all the wrong places. I'm used to giving my body time to adjust to the conditions I impose on it, and I can typically tolerate some pain without a fuss. If I drop a few more kilograms and pick up a few more kilometers, my hide will toughen up all by itself. Even so, I anticipate a difficult first week. Then, after the stress of the first few days, my body will adjust. My long-distance walking muscles are not yet performing at the level I will soon require of them. Before they let me forget about them, my feet will have to struggle with my boots; my shoulders, hips, and back will have to endure the battering from my pack; and my thighs and buttocks will have to suffer a little. A day like yesterday amounts to nearly forty-five thousand steps and just as much rubbing. We lead sedentary lives, and so, at the outset, our skin isn't ready for such physical demands. Mine is going to have to get used to it. The pleasures of walking are never simply ours for the taking. They have to be earned, and that means abiding by a few simple rules. Initially, the human body is caught unawares. You must therefore, as gently as possible, help it become attuned to sustained activity. Going too quickly at first only results in pain, stiffness, and inju-ries, and those will take much longer to heal, since, each day, the hard work begins anew. Our ability to gauge the right level comes from within, in all our fibers and joints. But although it is weak over the first few days, our body doesn't simply accept our inabilities. It doesn't just whine: it sets about making repairs and begins working harder. Is a particular muscle atrophied, shriveled, or starving? Then the body will nourish it, smooth it out, and oxygenate it until it reaches a level of equilibrium. When such a state is finally achieved, the body blossoms and there's a sense of phys-ical fulfillment. Hiking creates and instills harmony.

Back in Paris, I had planned that, on the second day, I would stop in the village of Sırapınar, after a short, eighteen-kilometer jaunt. But with yesterday's ten extra kilometers, my schedule has shifted, so I get there by noon. Heading out of the village, I spot a restaurant where a few tables have been set out under the oak trees. A fire pit promises tasty grilled meats. I walk over to take a seat, but before I can, the manager, thinking I look rather strange, intercepts me and leads me to a table far away from his other customers.

There's no question that—with my red backpack, my blue, wide-brimmed canvas hats, my misshapen vest with pockets full of everything but the kitchen sink, and my shorts with gusseted pockets—my outward appearance is, to say the least, out-of-the-ordinary. My unusual look, almost shocking in a country where less-than-careful attention to one's dress is frowned upon, is exacerbated by the fact that I hold a walking stick. I carved it yesterday upon entering the forest from a branch of hazelwood. I carry it not so much for walking, but to help protect me from dogs—every hiker's worst nightmare. And in Turkey, people have told me a great deal about Kangals, a breed of ferocious dog popular among shepherds, who use them to protect their flocks from wolves and bears. The customers seated at this outdoor restaurant all seem to be sporting the same uniform: dark pants and a white shirt, and most are wearing a tie. The more venturesome—in anticipation of the summer, which has yet to begin, and given today's glorious sunshine—have put on short-sleeved shirts. These fine people like conventionality, normalcy, conformity. Each one has a car parked in the shade of the lot next door. Since I don't, some of them look over at me inquisitively, others in disapproval.

As I finish eating some lamb ribs roasted to perfection, the manager, having softened up, comes over to talk. I saw him in conversation with several of his customers who were looking me over indiscreetly. They must have asked him about me, and he wants to be able to satisfy their curiosity. I delight in taking revenge for his initial disdain by pretending not to understand his questions. In reality, the few words that he pronounces, such as "*Nerede?*" (Where from?) or "*Nereye?*" (Where?) are quite clear. But he will not know where I come from or where I'm headed. I later regain my ability to speak Turkish to ask whether, in the villages I show him on the map, there are any hotels. "Yes," he says, "in Kömürlük."

My stomach full, I strap my gear back on and leave behind the busy Istanbul-Şile (*shee'-lay*) Road that I had taken for seven or eight kilometers (4 miles). Almost immediately, even though there's no signpost, I find the small dirt road that disappears into the forest, heading east. Spotting an inconspicuous grassy area, I go over and lie down, out of view. What a relief it is to unload my pack, since not only are the straps slicing into my back but, due to the sweat, the back-and-forth of the wide waist belt is chafing my hips. The hot spot I felt before breakfast is now a much more precise pain, my muscles having cooled down during the break. A quick check reveals that the top layers of the epidermis are gone. The skin is red and stings. After an hour-long nap, I set off again. My hips hurt, but by adjusting the tightness of the straps, I'm able to prevent any rubbing on the sensitive spots.

I head down a hill with a bird's-eye view of an ocean of dark thickets when, farther down, an army jeep suddenly emerges from a side road. It begins to take the road off to its right, but then comes to a sudden stop. I see the occupants' faces turned toward me. Everything I have read and everything people have told me over the past few months, the numerous army zones and barracks that I saw on my way out of Istanbul: it all reinforces the idea that the Turkish army is indeed very powerful, even omnipresent. I was told not to be surprised if soldiers were to prevent me from traveling certain roads, and if I were frequently stopped and asked for my papers.

The jeep's engine goes silent. The passenger riding shotgun steps out and takes up position at the front of the vehicle, just to the right of the hood, eyeing me all the while. From the position of his arms, I can tell that his weapon is aimed in my direction. His finger is no doubt on the trigger. A false move on my part, and he has only to raise his machine gun slightly to have me in his line of sight. I do my best to look as relaxed as possible, which probably robs me of whatever remaining naturalness I have left. There are six of them, their faces tense. I try to smile, but it probably appears strained. Ever so cautiously, I head toward the other side of the road, preparing to walk past the soldiers at a distance, when suddenly, one of them, seated behind the driver, opens his door and motions me to come over. He's the only one not wearing a helmet, and he has a pistol on his belt. The men are all in camouflage. They each hold either a machine gun or an assault rifle. I cross back to the other side of the road. The commander, cold as ice, howls, "*kimlik!*" (papers), and then, since I'm obviously a foreigner, he adds another, more international word, "*pasaport.*" I take it from my pocket and hand it to him.

One of the soldiers asks, "Do you speak English?" "Yes," I answer and begin to explain where I'm from. But that one question was apparently all the English he knows. He doesn't catch a single word of my reply. It's up to me, then, to call upon the full extent of my Turkish. "I am French," I declare in the language of Atatürk, "and I am walking along the Silk Road from Istanbul to Erzurum." Surprise replaces suspicion. Where did I start this morning? Where am I going this evening? They want to know everything. "Polonez, Kömürlük." They know these places, and that reassures them. Finally, when the commanding officer reads on my passport that I live in Paris, he beams a broad smile. One of the soldiers, swooning, repeats "*Pa-ree, Pa-ree.*" The soldier positioned to the right of the jeep's hood lowers his weapon and, without waiting for a word from his commander, climbs back inside the vehicle. In the rear, obeying a gesture from the officer, a soldier scoots over. Pointing to the open spot, they invite me to hop in.

They're heading to Kömürlük. I decline the invitation with a wide grin: "Thanks! But I'll walk!"

Incomprehension. They drive off. I watch them leave, then sit down by the side of the road, rump on the ground beside my pack. The May sun is delightful, and my first contact with the terrible Turkish army really wasn't so bad. Later that afternoon, I spot the jeep on patrol two more times; the soldiers wave their arms at me in recognition of our special bond, and I wave back.

By the time I arrive in Kömürlük, it's five o'clock. Surrounded by forest, the village is composed of squat, grimly painted houses roofed in faded red tiles. In the dirt streets, piles of petrified cow dung hold the imprint of tractor wheels. Trickles of water flow here and there. It's a drab scene, broken only by the figure of the white mosque. As soon as I enter the village, kids come running up and encircle me. Looking up at this odd foreigner, they waver between curiosity and fear. Past the mosque, on the small square, I make my way to a sad-faced shop. From behind a plank on which stand several bottles of fruit juice and a handful of cucumbers, a man sporting a three-day-old beard and who's as grubby as his shop sits watching me. Above the door, the word *bakkal* (grocer) is scrawled in clumsy white letters. He returns my greeting, a little wary:

"Where is the hotel here?"

"*Otel yok.*" (There is no hotel.)

The manager of the restaurant this noon, in telling me a fib, has succeeded in giving me a taste of my own medicine. Here I am, all alone in this village, my legs shot after thirty kilometers, with nowhere to spend the night. However much I tried to prepare for eventualities like this, it comes as a hard blow. Where will I eat? Where will I sleep? The weight of my pack was a determining factor: I brought along neither tent nor cooking gear. Too heavy. Dictionary in hand, hemmed in by an increasing number of kids buzzing around me like flies, I ask:

"Is there a hotel in a village nearby?"

"*Hayir.*" (No.)

Two or three men come to my rescue. One of them tells the children to give me some breathing room. They back away about a millimeter and a half. A discussion ensues, and everyone has something to say. There's a lot of jabber of which I catch nothing, and then one of the men tells me that there's a hotel in Şile on the Black Sea coast.

"Is it far?"

"No, close by."

I take a look at the map: it's thirty kilometers to the north, in other words, a full day's journey. As a longtime hiker, I'm not very surprised. Ever since the car became king, our sense of distance has been skewed and is now expressed only in terms of kilometers per hour. The walker has to know how to reinterpret expressions such as "not far," "close by," or "in ten minutes." They are statements made from a motorist's point of view. "Ten minutes," upon scrutiny, translates as ten or twelve kilometers, or two hours on foot. That a person on the street in France should respond that way is understandable, but in Turkey, where owning a car is still the exception not the rule; well, that's something for lovers of slowness to think about.

When I explain that I can't get to Şile, the men's distress kicks up a notch. I'm a hot potato, how can they get rid of me? The grocer declares that he has to tend to the sale of a handful of cherries and loses interest in the question. The other adults suggest that I push on to the next village.

"Is there a hotel there?"

"*Otel yok.*"

Out of the flow of children, which has now reached high tide, I hear "*What is your name?*" in bursts, like gunfire. It's an expression kids try out on tourists the world over and is followed up by "*My name is*" Mehmet or Mustafa. The adults start conversing again. What are they going to do with me? A man who had disappeared a few minutes earlier comes back and tugs at my sleeve, smiling. He has the sunburned skin of a man who works in the fields, a short white beard, and bushy eyebrows so black you'd think they were colored with kohl. A smart-looking lace skullcap doesn't quite cover his bald spot. He tells me his name, Zeki, and asks me to follow him. I don't understand much of what he says except that he has solved my problem. So I follow in the footsteps of his massive frame, and I, in turn, am followed by the entire village, both young and old, all circling and chattering. In all humility, I do believe that I've become the day's main event. As we approach the mosque, a man steps toward me, his hand extended, a large smile on his lips.

"*Welcome,*" he says, in a generous voice.

I answer in English, but he stops me with his hand. His vocabulary must be as limited as that of the soldier I met at noon. He's a strong man, his hair, brows, and beard like coal against a swarthy complexion, and the skin of a healthy baby. Ibrahim is the imam of the mosque. He guides me to a stairway in front of which the entire village gathers, loudly discussing the affair. Ibrahim, myself, and an old man go up to the second floor. They remove their shoes with a quick motion of the foot since they're wearing slip-ons, or at least shoes whose heels have been so crushed that they're like open-back slippers. It takes me a long time to unlace my boots, as my new friends look on. With my pack still heavy on my back the entire time, it's quite a feat.

We enter a rather large room with a view of the village through large bay windows. A carpet on the floor, a few books on the shelves, a table, and a sofa bed; the place is minimally furnished. This is, Ibrahim explains in a mix of English and Turkish, the classroom where he teaches religion to the children. And it will be my room for the night.

Zeki, who had disappeared once again, returns with cold meat dumplings, tomatoes, a cucumber, and a large bowl of yogurt. I say that I cannot thank him enough and take out my millions, but they beg me to put them back. Someone brings Ibrahim one of those "practical" Turkish-English phrasebooks, intended to facilitate international conversations. He thumbs through it for a long while as I eat, but all he comes up with are those silly stock expressions whose use is always highly improbable, such as "*How long will it take to repair my car?*" or "*I would gladly have a second helping of this delicious dessert,*" which, in the present circumstances, will probably do little to further dialogue between the imam and myself. When he finally gives up, we fall back on sign language and consult my pocket dictionary as needed.

I tell him I would like to visit the mosque. Ibrahim agrees, but first he motions to a young man, who disappears, only to return a few minutes later with a pair of sweatpants, which he hands me. I don't understand. Ibrahim points to my bare legs. There is no way I can enter the religious building dressed like that. So out of my pack I pull a pair of leggings that zip to my shorts, and I slip my boots back on . . . which, five minutes later, I have to pull off again. I do have a pair of light sandals that I brought to give my feet a break during stopovers, but there wasn't enough time to dig them out of my bag.

The mosque is huge. The floor is covered in carpeting from one wall to the other, featuring a motif of small rectangles. Like the alveoli of a beehive, they designate the spots where the faithful are to take up their positions when the building fills with men for Friday prayer. The women, who clearly participate in far smaller numbers, have their place on high, in a small balcony overlooking the main room. The imam, very proud of his domain, shows me the *mihrab*, a kind of niche in one wall, oriented toward Mecca, from which he leads the faithful in prayer five times a day. Next to it is the pulpit, which he climbs up into by way of a long wooden staircase and from which he gives the Friday sermon. Not very familiar with Muslim religious practice, I express my astonishment that women are not allowed to worship alongside men. With a show of great patience, Ibrahim explains to me that if women and men were in the same area, then when the women bow toward Mecca, the men behind them might be disturbed by unwholesome thoughts. My vocabulary is too limited, and so I hold off on the question that I'm dying to ask for some other time: aren't the women, high up in their gallery, disturbed by the countless rear ends of which they have a fine view from their gallery? Further on, in a tiny room, the imam of Kömürlük shows me the sound system he uses to broadcast the call to prayer five times a day without having to climb the steps of the minaret. Given how stout he is, he would benefit from the workout, and so I find it rather unfortunate that technology lets him off the hook.

They lead me back to the building where, as village guest, I'll be spending the night. Before taking leave of me, Ibrahim volunteers that he is Kurdish. Then he shoos away the remaining kids blockading my stairway. I roll out my sleeping bag on the sofa, go back down-stairs to quickly wash up at the spigot used by the faithful to perform their ablutions before prayer. As a large crowd watches on, I wash—or rather, rinse—the undergarments I wore today: T-shirt, boxers, and socks. Having opted for parsimony, throughout the journey, one set will have to dry while the other is getting drenched in sweat. Back in my "bedroom," I once again examine my hip, dabbing the sensitive spots with Mercurochrome so that the wounds dry more quickly. My feet hurt a little. There is some redness around my toes, but I don't give it a second thought: possibly a mistake. I lie down and fall asleep straightaway.

That is one of the virtues of walking: in Paris, it takes me two hours of quiet time before I can fall asleep. Here, when Ibrahim's amplified call to prayer blares at 11:00 that night, I have no problem going right back to sleep. The Islamic sound system is also what wakes me at 5:30 the next morning. I get dressed, go down to the tap, where I splash cold water on my face and shave. The T-shirt I washed in the evening is still cold and wet. I pin it to my bag; it will dry along the way.

It is 5:45, and the sun is coming over the horizon as I head out. On the square, I meet one of the village patriarchs as he's leaving the mosque. I don't understand everything he says, but his gestures and talkativeness speak a good deal for themselves, and so I interpret his little speech as follows:

"What is this all about? If you really want to travel, buy a car like mine." He points to it and then continues: "You are too old to be walk-ing. All right then, come have a cup of tea . . ."

I beam him a big smile and head off toward the rising sun, which has set the minaret's aluminum roof afire in glimmering red light. The first village that I traverse, still very much asleep, is called Kervansaray, but there is not (or is no longer) a single caravansary anywhere in the area.

As I exit the village, I notice an impromptu campground set up by the roadside in an empty field. About ten people are busy at work sur-rounded by three tents, two of which are constructed out of a clear sheet of plastic stretched over some logs. Out in the middle, an old woman is attempting to rekindle a fire. One of the men catches sight of me and beckons me:

"*Gel, çay!* (*gal, chai*)" (Come, tea!)

I walk over. The man in charge of this group smiles, showing all his decayed teeth. He goes to get a cushion, which he places on a rusty old metallic mattress, and invites me ceremoniously to have a seat. His son helps me take off my pack. Off to one side, a stockpile of partially assembled brooms reveals what the clan does for a living. There are three men, four women, and a baby. In addition to the baby's mother, three unmarried women live here. They are young and attractive, wearing scarves covering only their hair, and they are cleanly dressed despite their precarious living conditions. They are, from the looks of it, treated as the men's equals. The head of the family, out of that sense of fraternity that exists among travelers everywhere, tells me how honored he is to have me as his guest. I spend a pleasant half-hour drinking tea with them, and I take a few photos of the group. Unfortunately, they have no address where I can send them.

The sun is already high in the sky. Every so often, I have a hard time figuring out which way to go, given that my map is not very detailed and, as a rule, there are no signposts at crossroads. After hiking for two hours through a dense forest, I'm completely lost. I haven't the slightest idea where I might be. I ask a countryman I run into how to get to Darlık (*dar'-luhk*). In my mind, it must be to the north, but he motions me to go south. He then launches into a long monologue of which I understand absolutely nothing. And now, when I go back to my map, I can no longer even find where I left off. How could I have gone so far off course?

I arbitrarily continue going north and walk for about another hour before I come upon a group of picnickers from Istanbul. They invite me to join them for lunch. The women, in European dress without headscarves, take two large tablecloths and some edibles out of the trunks of their cars. We eat in two groups, the men in one, the women in the other. They are charming, but they are of no help to me in finding my position on the map, nor can they tell me how to get to Darlık. So I blindly wander back into the forest.

In a clearing, woodsmen are cutting logs with two circular saws and then loading the cut wood onto trucks. "The road to Darlık, please." The man begins to reply but, noticing that I'm not catching much, heads over to another lumberman hard at work a distance away. The man stops what he's doing and approaches, wiping the sweat running in rivulets down his mostly bald brow. He introduces himself: Selim, and the friend who came to fetch him, he tells me, is Mostafa. In true Turkish fashion, conversation taking precedence over everything else, they shut off the saw whose loud whine would have forced us to shout. We sit down in the shade of the beech trees, and Mostafa yanks out a few ferns that he arranges for me into a comfortable seat.

Selim speaks English fairly well, and he has a soft, calm voice. As soon as he sees my map, he chuckles to himself, revealing a toothless mouth except for one decaying canine. He tells me my map is very old. A large reservoir has since been built to supply Istanbul with drinking water. And the three villages that figure to the north have been moved fifteen kilometers to the south but have kept the same names. That, then, explains how I "drifted" off course this morning. But the rest of what he has to say is less amusing. The change also affected the roads. The one that headed east is now cut off, which means I will have to make a detour to the south or the north of fifty kilometers or so before I can reach the village of Değirmençayırı (day-heer-men'-cha-yuh-ruh), which is where I had planned to stop this evening. Not a very pleasant prospect.

"Of course the forest road is still there," Mostafa mentions, Selim translating. "But you will get lost, the forest is huge . . ."

"Is there someone in the village who, for a fee, could guide me through?"

The two men exchange a few words, and then Mostafa, striking his chest with his powerful hand, says: "I can guide you through, and it will cost you nothing. But first, I have to finish loading my truck, which will take at least an hour."

He gulps a great swig of water and goes back to his logs. Selim, with whom I can chat a bit, continues to astound me. He's forty-four years old and was in the army for nearly ten years. He gave it up to become a woodsman. With his receding hairline, his wide nose, and sparse mustache, there's something calm about him, something warm and friendly, communicative and serene. Before answering a question, he pauses quietly for a few seconds. He makes fun of himself, and each one of his statements is prefaced by a big silent laugh, revealing his one, yellow-stained tooth.

"I like the woodsman's life. Yes, I like nature, but I mostly like that I can spend the winter months reading. I have always been fascinated by philosophy. So, from January to March, I read as much as I want, and in the evening, I go to the teahouse and try to win my friends over to the joys of esthetics and logic." His eyes twinkle, revealing a bright mind and its partner in crime, a kind heart.

"I envy you, you are a true follower of the Peripatetics. I have to be satisfied just reading Aristotle."

Now that he has started talking, he tells me pell-mell about Nietzsche, Descartes, Plato, Hegel, and Heidegger. I goad him on a bit: "But there is more than just philosophy in life, there are women . . ."

"Yes, Joan of Arc, for example. She is my feminine ideal. I want to learn French to be able to read all that has been written on her, to see all the films that portray her, and to read Aragon in the original."

I'm astounded.

"Do you have children?"

"No, I am not married. I am the only single man in the village."

"Why?"

He laughs: "Perhaps because I have not yet met my Joan of Arc . . ."

Mostafa finishes loading the truck. I'm sad to have to say good-bye to Selim. He returns to his work, waving his arms in a big farewell as Mostafa and I disappear into the forest. Spending a little time in the company of these two men who radiate a sense of simple happiness has fully reinvigorated me. Mostafa, leading a way, has slipped on a T-shirt highlighting his colossal torso. The forest is absolutely gorgeous. The logging road glides through hills that rise and fall as far as the eye can see. My guide stops from time to time to point out a particular landscape. This is his domain and he is proud of it. At a spot where we have to ford a small river, a few people resting in the shade of the poplar trees on a Sunday outing ask if we want to join them for refreshments. They, too, live an unhurried life. These are magical moments. I close my eyes and I am the master of time.

We finally arrive at the southernmost tip of the reservoir. As Mostafa is saying good-bye, a group of soldiers pulls up in a jeep out of nowhere. This time, they are *jandarmas (zhan-dar'-mas)*, a police force specialized in the fight against terrorism. The young officer in charge, with the inscription *komando* on his pea jacket, asks for my papers and then questions me at length. He is very intrigued and wants to know more. Mostafa, making the most of Selim's translations earlier on, explains my itinerary to him, both past and future. We sit down in the grass, and, at the officer's request, I take out my map to show him the route I plan to follow. The others, meanwhile, each holding a machine gun or rifle, stand guard near their vehicle. The presence of these armed men is strange on a day like today, surrounded by a welcoming forest bathed in springtime sweetness. I head off again and then stop a short distance down the road to rest. Looking up, I discover a tortoise at the top of the embankment, watching me with its round eye.

Hello there, friend! Just so you know, this is no race.

CHAPTER III
MISAFIRPERVER

Although the village of Değirmençayırı is rich in syllables, it has only a few houses, the mosque, and a grocery. While I stock up on dried fruit at the *bakkal*'s shop, a rising tide of children gathers at the door to see the foreigner. Where can I spend the night? The grocer thinks for a long while, scratches his head with conviction, and then finally tells me that there is no solution. Giving in to fatalism, I have tea in the adjoining parlor. Probably alerted by some kid, a young man, introducing himself as the schoolteacher, sits down at my table. He has, he tells me, a solution to my problem and invites me to follow him. We traverse the village under the inquisitive eyes of its inhabitants and escorted by a throng of chirping children. This is, I sense, something I am going to have to get used to.

In another teahouse—read, a Turkish "bar"—the teacher introduces me to Huseyin. He's a retired employee of the military police. About sixty years old, he has a salt-and-pepper mustache and a massive frame, wears a gray hat and brown suit, and is a man of few words. He gestures us to sit down next to him. My guide lays out the situation. The former cop is not about to give us a speech, that's not his style. Can he take me in for the night?

"*Evet.*" (Yes.)

The customers, who were waiting for my problem to be solved so they might ask a hundred questions, are finally able to give free reign to their curiosity. Making exaggerated facial expressions and heaving sighs of pleasure—in lieu of conversation—I try to slowly empty at least some

37

of the many glasses of tea that, one by one, they offer me. Huseyin has disappeared to prepare the meal. He comes back to get me, shows me the bathroom, where, to my great delight, I see that I will be able to take a shower, rinsing off two days' worth of sweat. Dinner with Huseyin, the schoolteacher, and one of the latter's colleagues who joined in the meantime, is a joyful event. The younger men display great respect for the old man. When they leave, my host, in spite of all my protests, sets me up in his own room. He will sleep on the sofa in the greeting room.

In the morning, after having groomed, I buckle my pack and knock on his door. He has gone out. He is probably over at last night's teahouse. I go out, slamming the door closed behind me. But he's not there. I go back and wait a few moments for him. Then I scribble a word of thanks on a piece of paper and slip it under the door along with a banknote, worth five million liras, in payment for my lodging.

Later that afternoon, a Turk explains to me that in so doing I committed a gross error, that Huseyin will be outraged. What I did was contrary to the traditions of Turkish hospitality. In the Islamic world, to welcome a traveler in one's home and treat him as best as possible is the believer's duty. To be hospitable (*misafirperver*), he explains, means that for you, a good Muslim, it is your duty to treat your guest (*misafir*), the traveler, with the utmost respect. Your house is his, and you must share your food with him. You will reap the rewards of such kindness in the kingdom of Allah. To bar your door to a traveler is the worst crime a believer can commit. Those of us happily living in the world's wiser regions would do well, I tell myself, to follow their example.

A misty, soothing rain is falling. My feet hurt. And what happens to the soul when you're busy giving your toes so much attention? Very little, truth be told. The redness I noticed yesterday morning has grown worse. Yesterday evening, in the shower, I observed some chafing on the top of my feet. This morning, a small, pus-filled blister has formed on each of my big toes. If an infection sets in, it would be a serious setback for my walk. But I have nothing to treat them with; all I can do is cover them with bandages. I feel some discomfort for about an hour. Then it passes.

The landscape reminds me of the Haute Loire region in France.* The road dives into vertiginous valleys, at the bottom of which meanders a shimmering river. When the climb is too steep, and the grade aggravates the bend in my shoes, the pain returns. Around noon, in the shade of a thicket of hazelnut trees, I take my shoes off to find that the two small bubbles have burst and are now oozing yellowy pus. The skin around them, having suffered under the pressure of the leather with each of the thousands of steps I've taken, is red, puffy, and abraded. I cut away the dead skin with the small scissors on my tiny Swiss knife—can enough ever be said about how useful that portable arsenal is?—and I clean the wounds with what I have at my disposal: two pieces of cloth good enough to work as a compress and a little remaining Mercurochrome.

Once again, I have tremendous difficulty finding my way. The 1:500,000-scale map I have with me is not very comprehensive. But worst of all, it's quite inaccurate. And yet, going by the caption, it was apparently produced collaboratively between a German firm and the Turkish Ministry of Defense. This is unquestionably one of the Turkish army's war tactics, meant to prevent attempts at invasion. Certain indications are simply dead wrong. And so, thus equipped, I head in the direction of a small village that my map tells me is on my route, and that has the distinct privilege of having a signpost pointing the way. In reality, it turns out to be located at the end of a cul-de-sac. I've walked two kilometers for nothing and have no choice but to go back the way I came. But the detour turns out to be well worth it, since I converse for a moment with Ahmed, the carpenter. His eyes are full of laughter, and he tells me that he makes wooden forks and spoons for a living. While speaking, he whets a kind of small adze, running his thumb from time to time along the blade to check how sharp it is. He could probably shave—he has a short beard—with the tools he makes, for their edges are razor-sharp.

In the forest, I discover huge piles of wood, two stories tall, that are to be transformed into charcoal. I walk all around, but the charcoal makers

---

* TN: Located in the mountainous Massif Central region in south-central France. The chief city is Le Puy-en-Velay.

are nowhere to be found. I would have liked to hear how they go about it. A heavy rain forces me to take out my poncho. In a small village that I traverse, a young man comes over to me, strikes up a conversation, and begins to follow me. I expect him to give up as I leave the village, but he continues to walk by my side for one, two, five kilometers. He doesn't say much. We traverse another burg: will he stop following me here? No, he presses on, even though his vest has been sopping wet for a long time now. Out of the blue, he asks me what I have in my pack.

I begin to understand what he's all about when he takes out of his pocket a small flask, which, he assures me, contains a miracle cure-all. Just a few drops and I will no longer feel tired. Despite waving his hands all around to get me to take a sip of his magic potion, he's not very persuasive. He's clearly having a hard time just keeping up with me, even though he has no load on his back—and mine is soaking wet—so I tell him he should drink some himself. I think back to what I was told in Istanbul about thieves who use drugs to rob tourists. There's no way I will so much as touch his vial. First of all, because I'm leery of this fellow's shenanigans, but also because I abhor stimulants of any kind whatsoever, for they are the instruments of delusion. When we reach the small town of Kargalı (*kar'-ga-luh*), I spot a pharmacy and suggest that he go in with me. I tell him that the pharmacist would be very interested in his vial, since it's a miracle cure-all. Lo and behold: is it possible my words have some magic power themselves? They sure do, since the chap, like a jinn, suddenly vanishes. I'll see no more of him.

The druggist is horrified when he sees the state of my feet. The infection has indeed progressed very quickly. On my right foot, two more toes are starting to fester. He and a colleague attend to my feet, and the result is everything I could possibly hope for: my toes have been transformed from beggars in rags to little nicely aligned, mummified dolls. I'm ecstatic, give them my thanks, and ask if I can buy some 90 percent rubbing alcohol, but the druggist has only half-liter bottles. I would prefer a small, lighter flask to slip into my pack. A nearby shopkeeper, who is enlisted to help, finds a small bottle for me. After hearing my story, he presents me with a gigantic loaf of bread, a large hunk of cheese probably weighing nearly a kilo, and a jar of honey, just as heavy. I wear myself out trying to turn him down. He can't understand why. Having exhausted all my arguments, I finally invite him to pick up my gear himself. Realizing how heavy it is, he agrees to give me just one large chunk of bread and a quarter wheel of cheese. The man skilled in the art has prepared a small flask of alcohol for me, a second containing tincture of iodine, and some compresses. He won't allow me to pay and, as if he hadn't already shown enough concern and kindness, draws up a detailed map of the road that I need to take to get to the village where I plan on spending the night.

My feet like new, I head back into the countryside under a bright, springtime sun. In a beautiful green valley beside a lake, I stop to converse with an old, very old, country dweller by the name of Ahmed, his skin leathered by the weather and baked by the sun. All year round, he leads his only cow—his one treasure—back and forth along the byways so that she can graze as much as she wants. We exchange a few words, and he lets me take his picture.

Doğancılar (*doh-an'-djuh-lar*) is a sorry town of cob houses crowded along a single street. The successive downpours of the past two days have saturated the soil, creating a pitch-like mix of dirt and dung. The villagers are curious and follow me about. I take a few snapshots of a mud-block, corbelled house falling into ruin. The construction materials—wood, straw, and dirt—are the same as for the traditional, half-timbered houses of the Pays d'Auge or Pays d'Ouche regions of Normandy. As soon as they see I have a camera, the locals want me to photograph their barn, or themselves. In these villages, cameras are rare, and to have one's photo taken is a special event. That is why I've vowed to take pictures of the people who put me up and send them a copy once I'm back home. It's the only way I can think of to thank them for their hospitality, since they refuse money and the weight of my bag prevented me from bringing along any gifts. For the children, though, I did bring a hundred or so little lapel pins. The first time I took out the bag they're in was to give a few little gifts to a half-dozen kids. I spread the "treasure" out on the table so that they could take their pick. Twelve hands were suddenly all over them, and I had a very hard time recovering any of them at all.

Ever since, I hand them out them one at a time, giving away only the one pinned to my vest.

Leaving the village, I stop in a gas station-teahouse-grocery store. A man wearing a cap and large, strong-prescription glasses with thick, coke-bottle lenses is seated at a table reading a newspaper. Does he know anyone in the village who might have a room where I can sleep? He looks over, scrutinizes me for a second, replies, "me," and then goes back to his reading. I'm a little flustered by his invitation, so quick and devoid of warmth. I sit down, too, and order a cup of tea. The young man who brings my order is also the grocer in the store next door. I buy a box of chocolate cookies from him. Although a bit late, this will be the lunch I had no time to eat. The man who is supposed to put me up gets up from his seat and, without a word, walks out. I'm increasingly confused. Did he go home? Was his "invitation" sincere? The teahouse manager comes over and sits down at my table with another, slightly older man. They ask a thousand questions, and I answer them gladly since they're so nice; they want to see my passport and the map on which I've charted each stage.

"Who was the man reading the paper a moment ago, and who just left?"

"That's our father, Zekai (zay-kah'-ee). Let me introduce myself, I am Recai (ray-djah'-ee) and this is my younger brother Sezai (say-zah'-ee). As we speak, Zekai is making dinner for us, and for you, too."

A third brother, the youngest, and answering to the name of Mehmet, joins us. When their father comes in with the meal, his children sum up our conversation for him. They may even be adding to it. My understanding is that, believing that it would be impolite to question a traveler who's his guest, and yet somewhat wary all the same, Zekai has instructed his sons to find out about this odd pilgrim who stumbled in off the road and into his home. He speaks in a deadpan tone. The dinner is joyful. Mehmet shares his room with me, which has two beds. Before falling asleep, I tend to the wounds on my feet, which have become larger. Once again, I have to cut off the dead skin. I try to let my poor feet air out as much as possible to stimulate the healing process. But in the morning, a kind of transparent layer has formed over the wounds, and pus-filled blisters have reappeared. I break open the abscesses, dab them with rubbing alcohol, and bandage them before I head back out on the road in the rain.

I walk taking small steps. With each one, the bend in my shoe presses on the infected areas. The pain is made even worse because the gauze I used to wrap my feet means there is even less space inside the shoe. I take it off, but that doesn't seem to help. To soften the leather, and since Zekai did not have any special lotion that might have worked, I rubbed my boots with tractor grease that I collected from an engine in the yard. I can't get my mind off the pain as I walk, blind to the surrounding scenery. I notice, however, that the sun has returned, slowly drying the drenched and slippery ground. Finally, after walking for an hour and a half, little by little, the pain disappears, neutralized by the endorphins that my body must be churning out now in phenomenal amounts. I can once again contemplate my surroundings, which have changed. Yesterday, the soil was red and the vegetation sparse, somewhat like that of the highland plateau in the Aveyron region in France's southwest known as the Causses. Today, there are vast cultivated hillsides. When I reach the summit of one of them, I discover, for as far as the eye can see, geometric plots of freshly plowed black dirt, and the soft green of wheat and rye. Since morning, I've also noticed an increasing number of hazelnut groves.

I lose my way two more times. There are few signposts, if any. And when there are, they're illegible. Turkish road signs are made of painted sheet metal, and city names are written in blue letters on a white background. I should say "were written," for hunters—and there must be quite a few in this country—apparently find them ideal for target practice. And most of them must hunt with bullets. These unfortunate signs remind me of the griddle I use to roast chestnuts every fall. Peppered with holes, rust has eaten away at whatever information remained between the impacts. Turkish road signs are, in fact, good only for reading the signs in the sky that can be glimpsed through the holes. I can hardly rely on the villagers that I run into, either. This morning, I met two young boys roughly twelve years old who had never even heard of a village located just eight kilometers from where they lived.

I leave dirt roads behind and head out onto a small road suitable for vehicle traffic. My unusual appearance makes drivers of tractors and cars curious, and so they stop. With looks of incomprehension, the palm of their hand turned up toward the sky, no doubt in the hope that some information will fall from above, they ask me about my journey. Then they offer to give me a lift. When I turn them down, they rummage around in their trunks and present me with apples, cherries, cans of Coke or fruit juice, and chocolate bars that I either eat right away or throw out, out of fear they'll melt in my pockets.

Around 5:00 p.m., I'm closing in on the destination I've set for the day: Ambarcı (*am-bar'-djuh*). According to my map, I've covered thirty-five kilometers, and that's the distance I record for the day's leg. But in reality, having been lost twice, I'm sure I covered over forty. Which is probably why, with the finish line in sight, my endorphin factory has decided to go on strike. I limp along, gaining no ground. To make matters worse, the burning sensation on my hips from my backpack's waist belt has come back to life. I take it all philosophically. I had prepared myself for what I call the "breaking-in period" of a long walk. The first few days, the body strengthens overworked muscles, and severe aches and pains make it hard to get going again. In addition, areas subject to a lot of rubbing —the feet, the thighs, the buttocks, and points in contact with the pack— heat up. This leads to either open lesions or blisters. All of this amounts to nothing more than superficial wounds that will disappear in ten days or so. The sores I'm suffering from are also payback for not having kept to the very manageable walking schedule that I laid out for myself in Paris. I had planned short stages, between eighteen and twenty-five kilometers per day (11 to 16 miles). Foolhardy, I pushed ahead, and have averaged over thirty-five kilometers (25 miles). I'll be in Sakarya tomorrow evening, two hundred and two kilometers (126 miles) from my starting point, and will have taken six days. My schedule called for eight.

I should therefore walk for shorter periods of time, less in the sun, less in the rain. You can't cheat when you walk. You have to give it your all. I carry everything myself: my body, my souvenir-bag, my medicine-bag, my clothes-bag, my food-bag, and my bed-bag. Each and every miscalculation comes at a cost, on the spot or the next day. I walk alone, and so I have nothing and no one to fall back on. I'm isolated by language, by my lousy map, by the road I've chosen. The only indication of modern civilization are the two small plastic rectangles in my pocket. One, a phone card, reconnects me with the world; the other lets me withdraw money. But in both cases, I can only use them in cities. Out in the middle of the prairie and hazelnut trees, atop mountain passes, they are, at best, out of place. What I eat, where I sleep, and my personal safety do not depend on international phone calls or paper money. Those things are in the hands of my fellow human beings—so much like me and yet so different—the very people I'm walking toward now as I stir up these bleak thoughts.

The village of Ambarcı is almost deserted. Alone in the small square in front of the mosque, a young boy is playing with a rusty old bicycle wheel. The grocery is closed. Out front, a wooden bench invites me to sit down. The morning rain has let up, and a hot sun has begun to dry the sweat making my T-shirt stick to my skin. The boy, who says his name is Recep (*ray-djep'*), comes over and sits down beside me. I settle in on the bench, in the sun, and rest for a few minutes. Since the *bakkal* is nowhere in sight, I go off to visit the village. An old woman, out behind her house, is readying an oven to bake bread. She doesn't seem particularly surprised by this stranger in shorts, who has come over to watch her work. But as soon as I return to my bench, she approaches, acting as though she were going for a walk, while looking me over out of the corner of her eye. She must be dressed in the same way women dressed here a thousand years ago: a long, black skirt hanging down to her ankles, a shawl, and a scarf to cover her hair and neck.

Shelves run the length of the window serving as the grocery's storefront. They are piled high with packets of cookies and candy, looking all the same under an ancient layer of dust. Between the packets, little piles of mouse turds are artistically scattered on the newspaper pages covering the bare wood. Recep points to a man crossing the square with a sickle in one hand: the grocer. He's a dry old man with a purposeful step. His short, white beard softens his face, and his eyes sparkle under thick, deep black eyebrows. He's wearing a firecracker-blue knit wool skullcap and a plaid shirt. His skin is surely bronze from the hours he spends out tilling his field, not in his shop, and the stoop in his back cannot be ascribed to long hours tending his till.

He apologizes for being late, opens his store, looks in a cardboard box for a can of fruit juice, and asks if I want to sit down on one of the two benches that take up most of the floor space. At Mostafa's, more time must be spent engaged in conversation than in business, and more energy must go into business than housekeeping. Surprise, then disbelief, transforms him into a statue upon hearing where I come from. Since the front door is wide open, some bold, cackling chickens jostle their way in to peck away at grains of rice under one of the many sacks, the one that mice have chewed holes in. Worried that I might be annoyed, Mostafa repeatedly waves his arms in an attempt to shoo them away, but to no avail. You get the sense that the real masters here are the birds. But the man is concerned for my comfort, and so he keeps at it. As I describe my odyssey, he interrupts me two or three times to ask me if I'm all right, whether the sun, now winking at me from an angle, isn't in my eyes, and whether I'd like a cushion. Fatigue must be written all over my face.

Too exhausted to find the right words to ask for accommodations, I take out a short paragraph I had the two young Turkish women I know in Istanbul write out for me. With all the appropriate conventions and using much purer language than my own usual babble, it explains my itinerary and states that I'm looking for a place to stay for the night. Mostafa reads it attentively, slowly, and then looks at me, smiling widely. Just like Mostafa the woodsman, he points to himself. He himself will host me. And, as it turns out, that makes him very happy. Me too, since I positively like the fellow.

The first people alerted by Recep—who has been combing the village, announcing, as if with a bullhorn, the presence of a foreigner in shorts—finally show up. This is no doubt a first in this out-of-the-way hamlet, whose only link to the rest of the world is a small dirt road full of ruts left by tractor wheels. Every last inhabitant will parade by. They stand in the doorway, say something to Mostafa, then sit down on a bench, ask a few questions, hang around for a moment, and then go back out. As the flow of visitors grows, my host increasingly quivers with pleasure. Visibly, in the eyes of the entire village, it is a considerable honor for him to host a foreigner. Every five minutes, after a sentence or two to his friends, he turns to me, concerned, asking if I'm hungry or thirsty, if everything is okay. His cheeks are red from the excitement. His little, sunken eyes twinkle with delight. From time to time, a mouse or two sprints across the grocery's double ceiling, but I think I'm the only one to hear it, despite the loud pitter-patter. In a brief lull, a woman comes in to buy eggs. Mostafa looks over at me with a look of remorse, for he has to take care of a customer, and apologizes, uttering one word: "business . . ." That's the only time, during my entire stay, that I'll see him work.

I've been in the spotlight now for over an hour and a half, and I'm ready to drop. The next time my host comes over to ask if everything is fine, I seize the opportunity to suggest that I should carry my pack to the room where he'd like me to sleep. In reality, I need to look after my painful feet, which are feeling feverish. Mostafa quickly gets up, tries to pick up my pack to carry it for me; upon seeing how heavy it is, however, he gives me a look of surprise and leaves it to me to deal with. Mostafa is my host, not my porter. We climb a steep staircase with wobbly steps and walk out into an attic. Through holes where the roofing tiles don't quite touch, I can see the sky. On an old scrap of cloth, a big tomcat throws us an annoyed look. In a corner of the garret, a sleeping room has been set up. It's comfortable. A bed sits on a large rug against one wall, and a couch along the opposite wall. Between the two, there's a window out of which I can see girls in chadors who, since they hadn't been allowed to meet the stranger in the grocery, now try their luck at the window, hoping to at least catch a glimpse of his profile. I stand at the window so that they can see me, and I smile at them. They run off, laughing. As much as I was annoyed by all this fame at Kömürlük, I'm now actually starting to enjoy it. Mostafa takes a tray from the bed, on which pumpkin seeds were drying out, and places it on a table: my room is ready. He then vanishes, telling me once again to let him know if I need anything.

I appreciate everything there is about this man: his smile, his face, his voice, the extraordinary way he cares for those around him. There is an uncommon harmony about it all.

Alone at last. I have just begun to tend to my feet when the door opens partway. A young boy's nose appears out from behind. He then opens the door all the way and comes in, followed by three other children. All four of them, silent and attentive, head over to the couch across the room, never taking their eyes off me, and then, like a troupe of well-rehearsed ballet dancers, sit down all at once. Their curiosity is so intense that they're adorable. I break the silence:

"Hello, my name is Bernard."

They tell me their names and then there is silence once again. They look so much alike that I immediately mix up their names. Their hands placed between their thighs, resting on their forearms, leaning slightly forward, they are like statues. Their big eyes, full of amazement, wander from my feet to my pack, from the clothes on the bed to my sandals, and then to my bottles of ointment. I resign myself to their silent contemplation, and, with the sense that I am their Muse busily sprucing himself up, I go back to caring for my feet. With respect to the latter, the situation seems stable: the wounds have not grown in size, but they're still weeping quite a bit.

After about ten minutes, the boy who came in first gets up, immediately followed by the others, and they all leave the same way they came, in single file, with bashful smiles and a silent little farewell bow. The door closes on the last one who practically runs out, so afraid that he might find himself alone with the foreigner. A minute later, three youths about twenty years old come in next. I suspect that Mostafa is at the bottom of the stairs, organizing visits for the latecomers and sending them up in batches. What a delight it is to make people happy simply by existing! Without having to say anything, I start to really enjoy it. The newcomers are more talkative. My Turkish improves. One is a mechanic in the neighboring village, the other is doing his military service, and the third is a college student. They look me over, answer my questions, and head back out a few minutes later. Between two visits, I manage to take off my shorts. This is no easy task, for here, no one knocks before entering. And having seen how extremely modest Turkish people are, I don't want to shock anyone. Mostafa accompanies some of the groups. Rejuvenated, exhilarated, he is full of happiness, overwhelmed by this unexpected honor. These young people clearly adore him.

At long last, the visits come to an end, and my host returns all alone with a platter of food. We dine just the two of us, sitting cross-legged on the carpet. It's a position I have a hard time maintaining, as it's so uncommon for Westerners, and my spine and legs protest.

With the help of a dictionary, Mostafa wants to know what I do in France. I describe myself once again as a retired elementary school teacher. But he could care less about my profession. He wants to know about my family and where I live. I have a photo of my children, but he doesn't have one of his. So that he will have one of himself, I take his picture.

After dinner, I wander slowly around the village, now completely deserted. A community television is crackling in a small shack. It's a black-and-white set with a picture so blurry that viewers spend more time guessing—than watching—what's on. It looks like an encrypted channel. A single viewer ensconced in his chair in the darkness seems to be catching everything. The set is located in an iron cage with its door wide open. It's the duty of the last villager to make sure it's locked up for the night. My little after-dinner walk is not particularly interesting: I decide to head home and go to bed, which I do with a limp.

It's a noisy night. Around 3:30, an insomniac rooster greets the dawn. Two hours later, the imam, over his electric sound system, calls the faithful to prayer. Then it's the birds' turn to sing, since, in the time zone chosen by the Turks, day gets a very early start. The sun rises at 5:15. The next to join this bucolic concert are the sheep, demanding their daily portion of the prairie. They make so much noise that they wake up the cows, causing them to start mooing impatiently at 6:30. That's when I get out of bed, too. Mostafa must be watching for me to stir, because, as soon as I set my feet on the ground, he tells me breakfast is ready. The yogurt mixed with milk and sweetened with honey tastes of childhood.

My host, on the grounds that I'm going to walk a great deal today, serves me a big breakfast and wants me to finish everything.

When I head out all strapped up, he insists on going with me to make sure I find the right road. In the morning sun, the village enjoys a magnificent view. It's perched high atop a hill, and, whichever way you look, you can see far off into the distance. "Beautiful, isn't it?" Mostafa declares, telling me that he loves his village. He left it twice. The first time was to go to İzmit to visit his three sons, two of whom are married; the second time was to go to Sakarya, the city where I'm planning to sleep tonight. Two trips, forty kilometers each, in all his seventy-one years. But he has no complaints. The old man, wearing some kind of rubber slippers over bare feet, walks slowly, shuffling along like Charlie Chaplin, with toes out and stiff knees, swaying from left to right with each foot forward. The slow walking pace and sheer joy of conversing with him take my mind off the pain of the day's first steps. A kilometer on, we stop. We have to go our separate ways. Both of us, I believe, are rather choked up. I shake it off and hold out my hand. Taking it, he then draws me to him and gives me a hug. A tractor is headed into the village. He climbs aboard, and I just stand there for a few minutes, watching as this friend-for-a-day recedes into the distance.

This evening, I'll be in a city. The road is easy. For once, my compass and map are in agreement. I have the feeling that this is going to be a good day. Late in the morning, I walk past two men chatting away by the roadside, seated outside a teahouse. They wave their arms for me to come over:

"*Gel, çay, çay . . .*"

Tea? And why not? It's nice out, and I'm walking without too much trouble, now that my endorphins are back at full strength. As he pours my tea, the server's curiosity gets the best of him:

"Where are you from?"

"Istanbul."

"You didn't walk, did you?"

"Why yes, I walked!"

He goes back inside the watering hole and trumpets the news so that all can hear. Almost as if choreographed, the twenty or so people inside come out on the patio and surround me. An avalanche of questions ensues.

"What country are you from?"

"Did you really begin your journey in Istanbul?"

"Where are you headed?"

"What is your occupation?"

"Are you married?"

"How many children do you have?"

The Turks are endlessly curious and unafraid to show it. One of the customers, a tall, dapper-looking man, somewhat portly, sporting a thin mustache and a three-piece suit, introduces himself. A former schoolteacher, he left the profession, as it did not allow him to make ends meet, and so he started a business. He makes chess pieces that he sells in Europe.

"Would you like to see my workshop? It's just across the street."

We head over. Children are running the machines. They must be somewhere between ten and twelve years old. I tell this "industrialist" how surprised I am by this. He has no qualms.

"I am training them for a profession," he says, very teacher-like.

I cut the visit short, pick up my gear, and turn down with what energy I have left the chess set that the industrialist-teacher eagerly wants me to accept.

In Sakarya, also known as Adapazarı (*ah-dah-pah'-zah-ruh*), I appreciate the anonymity of being in a big city. I can finally look around without drawing everyone's attention. Plenty of soldiers crisscross the streets. On the sidewalks, girls—who always walk in groups, or at least in pairs—are, for the most part, in Western dress, and nearly all are not wearing a chador. No short skirts, though: they hide their legs under long dresses or in pants.

Starving for a bit of comfort, I delight in a hot bath after having dropped off a few pieces of clothing to be laundered at the three-star hotel where I checked in. Since I didn't first inquire about the price of this service, they charge me as much as the room. This is a lesson I must not forget: in villages, I find hospitality; but here, I am just another tourist to be gouged.

There is nothing graceful about the city of Sakarya. Farther south, the river of the same name was the scene of a violent battle against the Greeks during the War of Independence. Before launching a massive counterattack, Mustafa Kemal, the future Atatürk, used a sneaky tactic. He needed to bring together his high command in preparation for the attack but feared that spies might catch wind of their plans. To prevent anyone from knowing what was going on, he gave his generals their orders during . . . a soccer match. He also made each general lead his own troops into battle and not remain behind back at headquarters. It was a victorious counterattack, the enemy was caught off guard, and half the Greek army was taken prisoner.

Having eaten and slept, and my wardrobe like new, I get back on the road, walking at a good pace. After Sakarya, the countryside changes. A vast plain of vegetable fields is bounded on the distant horizon by a chain of mauve mountains trembling in the hot, hazy air. My next stop is Hendek. I expect to find a few vestiges of caravan traditions there. I take a small road parallel to the highway linking Istanbul to Ankara. A beverage salesman's truck passes me from behind as I head out of town. A little farther on, I see it parked, waiting for customers. It passes me once more, and then I come across it yet again, farther down the road. Our little game goes on two or three more times. When I enter a small village, the salesman is standing in the middle of the street, having called together virtually every woman, man, and child, as well as any of the able-bodied elders. It's a bona fide welcoming committee. And they are all very curious. Smiling and intrigued, they come running over. By now, I know the questions by heart and can provide the answers with ease.

Around noon, I have lunch in a small nearby restaurant. The owner, who heard my story, only charges me a third of what I owe. A little later on, I have tea with an astonishing eighty-six-year-old man still mourning the recent passing of his mother, who was over one hundred. Old in his mind, he is nevertheless physically young, and I'm sure that, given how fit he looks, he could follow me with unfaltering energy. A little before Hendek, I take a short rest at the foot of a monument honoring those who've died in accidents on the road. In light of the way Turks drive, this probably concerns a significant percentage of the population.

Etymologically, Hendek means "inn." It's the first town where I stand a chance of finding a few reminders of the Silk Road. In the seventeenth century, it was an important stopover point with no fewer than four caravansaries. Ahmet Muhtar Kirval, a medical doctor and author of a monograph on the city's commercial history, confesses that no buildings from the old days remain. The last one was destroyed in 1928, and a bank was proudly put up on the spot where it once stood. A few years ago, having looked into the question, a German researcher managed to locate the path that the caravans once followed. It was demarcated with stones that he had unearthed. Shortly after his discovery, the stones were stolen. With the exception of mosques or religious structures, the Turks clearly don't give a hoot about the architectural remains of their extraordinary history. The caravansaries, just like so many pretty Ottoman houses, are at risk of succumbing to wrecking crews.

Although I don't feel all that tired, I force myself to take a day off and stay in a comfortable hotel. In this small city's central square, young men are dancing to the sound of a drum and bugle. They are conscripts who've just received word that they're fit to serve. The army enjoys enormous prestige in Turkey. Performing one's military service is considered an honor. Any man who makes it past thirty without having fulfilled his military obligations will have a lot of trouble finding a job.

A day off from walking has been restorative, and my wounds, which I've been tending to with dedication and commitment, have begun to dry out. My morale is as high as ever the following day as I head out to face the usual difficulties. I spend nearly an hour looking for the little road to Yeşilyayla (*yay-shee'-lee-eye-lah*), which I had located on my map. No one, at this early hour, has even heard of it, and I cannot find a city map anywhere. After two or three attempts ending either in people's yards or in the middle of a field, I tire of the game and head for State Road 100 that crosses Turkey from west to east with insane traffic. Noisy cars and trucks force me to hug the ditches for ten kilometers. I finally find a small road running south, toward the peaceful countryside.

At noon, a peasant farmer approaches me and offers to give me some water to drink. I'm happy at the idea of a break especially since the gentleman seems to want to chat. We go to his house. He tells me about his trade. He grows hazelnuts and harvests a hundred tons a year. He tells me many other things, but I think I quickly lose interest, because I'm no longer able to make sense of what he's saying. Meanwhile, his brother has made lunch. We eat outside, on the patio. The weather is gorgeous, although a little hotter than I like. I thank my kind hosts for their country hospitality, but I need to be on my way. For whatever reason, I get lost once again. I've gone five kilometers too far. I have to double back.

To switch out of my sweat-soaked T-shirt, I drop for a few minutes into the shade of a bridge under the railroad. A minibus with six soldiers on board suddenly pulls up out of nowhere. They spot me after overshooting by fifty meters or so and throw the vehicle into reverse. Three soldiers sporting bulletproof vests leap from the vehicle, weapons in hand, and surround me. They each hold a maching gun pointed at my feet, a finger on the trigger, and for them, this is clearly no laughing matter. I'm not laughing, either. A young, chubby man in civilian dress, stinking of cheap cologne, suddenly bursts out from behind them.

"Papers!" he says, as though looking for a quarrel.

Speechless, surprised, and startled, I hand him my passport.

"You're coming with us," he tells me, before even opening it.

He seems very jittery, mean-spirited. In a sudden burst of anger, I protest: "I'm a tourist, my papers are in order, you have no right to stop me."

He wavers, heads over to his vehicle, and phones his higher-ups. In a long, painstakingly slow exchange, he explains the contents of my travel permit, which he angrily flips through in every direction, no doubt looking for some indication that I am, in fact, a terrorist. They must be calming him down. I don't understand a word he says, but the attitude of the other soldiers is telling. Two of them get back in the vehicle; the third remains in front of me but rests his machine gun on his forearm, his index finger no longer on the trigger. Their leader finally hangs up, hands my passport back to me, and asks what I'm doing. He adds that people called them about me, saying I looked suspicious. In this country at war, both civilians and soldiers are afraid. And everyone is suspicious of everyone else.

Reliable indicators of my psychological state, my aches and pains all come alive at once. The road seems endless, and I crawl along miserably at four kilometers per hour. In a field, keeping an eye on two meager cows grazing in an equally meager hollow, a mother is seated in the grass, her little girl on her lap. The child is clutching her, one hand on her mama's thigh, while the woman picks lice out of her child's long black hair. I'm tempted to sneak a photo of this enchanting scene, decide against it, and instead wave my camera up and down to let her know that I'm going to take a picture. With a smile and a graceful back-and-forth of her head, the woman tells me "no." Too bad, I won't get the photo, but in my mind's eye, even today, that heartwarming scene is still as clear as ever. My memory of it is likely even more vivid for having failed to get the picture.

A little farther on, two men are mowing a prairie by hand. They follow each other, slightly staggered, working the blades of their scythes together in one motion. As if they were driven by the same clockwork. I haven't seen men cut a field by hand since my childhood. A short distance away, sitting barefoot in the grass, a third man is pounding his scythe in an attempt to restore its sharp edge. These two scenes of rural tranquillity, which call to mind a world of a distant past, frozen in time, perk me up a bit.

There are no restaurants to have lunch in along these small country roads. I nibble at a piece of bread bought the day before yesterday. Once again, I'm lost. The sun is beating down hard. My feet and hips are painful, and my back is dripping with sweat. As if that weren't enough, I've reached a point where dirt roads head off in all directions to provide access to the hazelnut orchards. None of them, of course, appear on my map. I advance blindly, vaguely heading east as indicated by my compass. I finally arrive at a village, and an old man comes up to me.

"What country do you come from?"

"From France."

"Our two countries are friends. Come have a drink. Where are you going?"

"In the direction of Hacıyakup (*ha-djuh-yah'-koop*)."

"This is the wrong road; my son will put you back on the right one."

He offers me a chilled drink, *ayran*, a mix of yogurt and water. Never have I had such a refreshing drink. So I give in to the moment, in the presence of this generous old man, savoring old-fashioned pleasures that only walking off the beaten path can provide. His son, Hassan, starts up a motorized cultivator, hitched with a small trailer. Three kids, delighted to go for a ride, hop in with us, and suddenly we are rolling along through plantations of hazelnut trees. The trailer bounces over the ruts. The children laugh. Then we make for a hill covered in low-cut grass bursting with the vibrant colors of wild rhododendrons. Hassan drops me off on a knoll and points down below to the road that I have to take. I had been advised against walking after five or six o'clock in the evening, but time is passing quickly, and I'm still far from any possible layovers.

I head down into a very damp valley planted with thousands of poplar trees. Tired and achy, I ponder the thought that if things aren't soon on the mend, I'll have to stop for several days until my wounds are fully healed. It's after seven when I arrive in a small town called "Gölyaka" but which, on my map, is strangely renamed "Gülkaya." Another army ploy to throw off the enemy. There's no hotel. Another town, Hacıyakup, appears on my map six or seven kilometers farther. I'm going to try to make it, too bad if at this hour ambushes are possible. Heading out of Gölyaka, I come to a fork in the road. Is it to the right or to the left? Some young people playing soccer in a field come over and form a circle around me.

"You're going all the way to Hacıyakup? But that's far, at least fifteen kilometers."

"My map says seven."

"It's wrong."

As far as that goes, I'm hardly surprised.

"Is there a hotel in Hacıyakup?"

"No, I don't think so. But it's late. We would be honored if you would be our *misafir* . . ."

And they seem so pleased at the idea, and I'm so tired and depressed, that I agree. They live in a hostel for students of various disciplines, funded by a religious foundation. The students are all devout believers. The daily schedule is austere. When class is in session, rise and shine is at 5:30 a.m. In the evening, studies until 10:00 p.m. It's a spacious building, and, since school is currently out of session, many students have returned home. Thrilled, my hosts show me to an empty room.

While I take a shower, the cook, who had already put away his pots and pans after the students' supper, prepares a meal for me. As I eat, the students bombard me with questions. There are quite a few rough patches in our discussion, but between my imperfect Turkish and their rudimentary English, we manage. We then spend some time in the large common room, delving into topics that get the discussion going again. They lavish me with their attention, pampering me, and I go along with it all. The most obliging one is Hikmet, a management major, who serves as house supervisor here. He's twenty-four years old and has three years left before two years of military service, as required by a militaristic, warlike culture.

Hikmet, as much my protector as Mostafa was in Ambarcı, has his companions ask their last questions, saying that I need to get some rest. In the morning, when I wake up, he is already busy getting everything ready so that I can make an early start. We all have breakfast together. Hikmet walks with me into town to help me explain to the pharmacist what I need: some healing powder so the wounds on my feet recover more quickly. Then I heave my load onto my back, and my host accompanies me all the way to the road. He's endearing. When I'm ready to go, he gives me a hug, and in English, he says:

"Thank you, Uncle Bernard."

Thank you for what? All of Turkey can be summed up in those words. Imagine if we were to shift this same scene to some small French town, like Vesoul or Montauban. Would you ever hear: *"Merci, tonton Hikmet"*?

From there, I think of Ibn Battuta, the famous Arab voyager, who speaks in his journal of the Akhiya. The Akhiya was a sect that specialized, six centuries ago, in accommodating travelers: "Nowhere on Earth," he writes, "is there a people more concerned for the well-being of foreigners and more ready to provide them with food, and satisfy their desires."* And he tells how, in a city not far in advance of Antalya, two groups of Turks offering accommodations to foreigners actually took up scimitars and prepared to do battle just to have the honor of welcoming the voyager and his companions. Through arbitration and drawing lots, it was finally decided that the travelers would spend four days in each of the two abodes where they had been invited.

After Cırcır (*djur'-djur*), a village where I'm invited to spend the night, a schoolteacher tells me that, in the old days, every village maintained a house or room just for visitors.

Although this tradition is today a thing of the past, the warm welcome I've received in villages since leaving Istanbul by no means does injustice to the legend as it is told.

---

* *Voyageurs arabes*, translated into French from the Arabic by Paule Charles-Dominique, "Bibliothèque de la Pléiade," Paris: Gallimard, 1995.

CHAPTER IV
DOUBTS

I have to travel east on an unpaved road, but I come to a fork in the road. I hate forks in the road. Near a bus stop, there are two men sitting on a bench, under an awning. I greet them.

"Is the road to Beyköy (*bay'-kuh*) to the right or to the left?"

The two men, both perfectly self-assured and with comic effect, point in opposite directions at exactly the same time.

"They both lead to Beyköy?"

"No," they both say simultaneously. And then they argue, each one claiming to be pointing in the right direction. Two cyclists out for a ride join in—in Turkey, as soon as a conversation gets underway, everyone rushes over to join in—and set the gentlemen straight.

"We are going to Beyköy," they tell me. "Come with us."

The road to the left was the right one. The cyclists are charming. One of them hitches my bag to his bike rack. I suddenly feel light and the sun seems glorious. In a village, the sound of accordions playing for a country wedding attracts our attention. A dozen men are dancing in a circle in the middle of the farmyard, to the strains of a small orchestra. Orchestra is perhaps an overstatement, since there are only three musicians, but what virtuosos they are! A fat, beefy, mustached man is sweating water and blood as he coaxes throbbing notes from his *Zurna* that a short, quicksilver accordionist grabs from the air and uses to embroider a dancing tune, tempered by a maudlin violin. I'm entranced. Is this a special piece, just for marriages? It is far more than just oriental; the music is above all universal, the transcription of all that comes into play on a day when two destinies

59

join forces. The carefree days of youth are about to give way to a life of responsibility and hard work. But, if it is a ponderous moment, it is also a joyous one, for what could be more cheerful than two hearts beating as one? A short distance from the men, a few girls spin around in circles, their hands stretched out toward the sky. Are they praying for it to send down to them, too, the man of their dreams? The bride—a serene young girl who seems almost surprised that all this should be happening to her—no longer has that to worry about. She has been made to sit on chair from which she reigns, like an empress, over a court of ancestors dressed in somber clothing, planning, no doubt, to give yet her a few final words of advice. Advice from the wise is indeed vital when one is still little more than a child. All the others are busy stuffing themselves with sweets. An ice cream salesman has dropped by the square on his tricycle. We are asked if we want to sit down and have something to eat, but we turn them down.

At the entrance to Beyköy, the cyclists continue on without me. It's Sunday, and, just as they do every Sunday, after their bike ride, they return to their families. My bag comes off the bike rack and back onto my shoulders. I drink a cup of tea seated out on a teahouse terrace and I wonder: should I press on, or should I spend the night here? Beyond Beyköy, a vast forest awaits, and the terrain is rugged. It's already late afternoon, and to leave now might be risky. Two taxi drivers chatting away at the next table assure me that the road is easy. They draw me a map. I would have three turns make. They estimate the distance of each leg of the journey: five kilometers, then two kilometers, and finally three kilometers. After that, it's a little complicated, but people will tell me what to do. Reassured by such detailed explanations, off I go.

I'm still feeling the previous day's fatigue and am not in the best of moods. Above all, I'm worried about my feet. It's a contest, and either my boots are going to learn to get along with my feet, or my feet are going to have to get used to my boots. For the moment, the boots are winning. Whenever I can, I walk in water, hoping to soften up the leather. All of my agony is coming from the stitching on the lower part of the tongue, which is too low. The fold in it feels like a guillotine, slicing into my toes with every step.

In the very deep, narrow valley that follows the course of a mountain stream, families have come out to enjoy a Sunday picnic. Children are barefoot in the water, catching crayfish with their hands. The adults are cooking them over fires on makeshift pits between two rocks. The sky has clouded over. I'm creeping along. The taxi drivers gave me good information regarding directions, but the distances are completely unrealistic. For the last leg that they said would be about three kilometers, or a forty-five-minute walk, I've been hiking for over an hour and a half, and the end is nowhere in sight. Suddenly, the road abuts the stream and turns right, heading steeply up between the hills. I follow it for about a half-hour before coming upon some woodsmen. They tell me that I should have forded the stream. My taxi drivers left that detail out. I turn around, take my shoes off, cross, dry my feet, reapply my bandages, and get back underway. I'm starting to regret not having stopped in Beyköy.

What is it that constantly pushes me to keep going farther than planned? Common sense and caution told me I should stop. I'm angry with myself. But I can't seem to help it. Just a little more effort, just a little farther, I don't know how to hold myself back, as if the initial momentum were uncontrollable. I'm very critical of myself in this respect, as I'm always the first victim. What is this furious impulse to walk, and then keep on walking, that propels me onward? Is it vanity? Pride? The desire to test my limits? To break some record? I honestly have no satisfactory answer. But it's a feeling I know well, ever since I took up walking; that is to say, some twenty years ago.

Long-distance running is unlike most sports in that, aside from a few professionals, it isn't about beating one's competitors. When, after having run for thirty-five kilometers, the body screams for mercy and a complicated chemical process forces it to convert fat into a form of nutrition that starved and painful muscles can use, the runner has to dig deep into the mind and heart to muster new energy, replacing all that has been lost. It's in that complex combination of the mental and the visceral, and in a burst of pride, that the runner is able to nibble away at those last few precious seconds. After kilometer forty-two, the finish line crossed, muscles cramping, the runner turns around to glance at the clock. And therein lies happiness: in those few instants that have been shaved off a previous time. The marathon runner has but one opponent worth competing against, and whom, one day, it will be impossible to catch: him- or herself.

As for walking, the need to outdo myself cannot explain everything. Yes, of course, the grass is always greener a little farther on, behind the hill, just past this village, or over that mountain pass. But mixed in with this uncontrollable momentum pushing me forward is a fear I find hard to quell: that of not reaching my destination. So, like a miser stockpiling his coins, I hoard each and every kilometer, fearing that I might come up short. With such focus on my destination, I walk and I walk, for as long as I still have strength to put one foot in front of the other and carry my pack. It makes even less sense when you consider that my only imperatives are the ones I set myself. I have no deadlines to keep, no daily targets to meet, no minimum distance to travel. I must, of course, get to Xi'an in four stages, one per year. But if it were to take me an additional year, what difference would it make? For now, I have only one constraint: to reach the Iranian border before my entry visa expires. As it stands, I'm in step with the timetable I set for myself back in Paris. I'm even a little ahead. So relax, I tell myself. Just relax.

After fording the river, on the forest road that climbs through the fir trees, for a good hour, I don't see a living soul. Then a couple with a child—the child riding on a strange little cart built by his father— reassures me: I'm going the right way. Fifteen minutes later, I come to a fork in the road. To the right or to the left? Damn you, fork in the road! My map is of no help; the path isn't even on it. My compass vaguely indicates that the east is to the right. So I go right. Night is quickly falling. Five hundred meters on, in front of a cabin next to a sawmill, a white dog is barking ferociously. There's a light on inside. I call out. A man steps out: he's albino. I have to admit that seeing the milky white dog alongside this opalescent man with night falling seems very surreal, and for a moment, my head starts to spin.

Once again, I went the wrong way.

His hot-tempered white dog yapping away, the alabaster man tells me that I should have gone left at the fork in the road. Sazköy is indeed the next town, two or three kilometers distant.

This time, I'm hobbling, making miserable headway. Night has fallen. It comes early, around 8:30 p.m., even though the summer solstice is not far off, and the air cools quickly. An hour later, still without any indication of a village, I unenthusiastically come to terms with the idea that I'm going to have to bivouac for the night. I'm a little uneasy about sleeping out in the cold without shelter in the middle of an unfriendly forest. I should probably have asked the albino man whether he could put me up for the night. This is what I get for being so stubborn. As luck would have it, I come to an opening, telling myself that, why yes, this would make a cozy spot to sleep in, when, all of a sudden, the electrified call to prayer of a muezzin blares off to my left. I'm saved! Fifteen minutes later, I'm walking past the first houses. It's 9:30 p.m. I've been on the road for at least eleven hours.

I find the largest and most beautiful house and knock at the door. The old man answering it looks me over with a wary eye. I try to explain who I am and where I'm going, but I must be too tired, and my Turkish vocabulary has flown the coop. In desperation, I take out my little "open-sesame" letter and hand it to him. He reads it, stares at me, taking his time, and then, with his index finger, he strikes his forehead several times: you're nuts! His reaction is so unexpected, and I am so happy to have made it to where I wanted to go and freed from my fears, that I make no attempt at formality: instead, I burst out laughing. He smiles, steps back, and invites me in.

Nevzat is a peasant farmer. He's seventy years old and lives here with his sick wife and his daughter Şükran (*shu'-kran*). They are of Caucasian origin, as are all the inhabitants in this village, and they've maintained the language and culture of their forebears. The spacious, two-floor house is comfortable, and the shower that they suggest I take washes away some of my fatigue. But like I said, as a hoarder of kilometers, I want an accounting, a calculation of just how exhausted I am. Rich with Nevzat's insights and my bad map, I can now estimate how far

I've walked today: I must have covered between thirty-eight and forty kilometers (24 and 25 miles) . . . not counting the times when I went off course. It's an impressive total.

After dinner, the master of the house ushers me into a large room, which he methodically fills with smoke, puffing on one cigarette after another, and after that he finally focuses his attention on the mystery I represent for him and that he wants at all costs to make sense of. Why did I embark on such an adventure? No, as much as he tries to wrap his mind around it, it simply makes no sense. Then suddenly, in a triumphant moment, he smiles, rubbing his thumb and index finger together:

"*Para!* (Money!) It's for money, isn't it? *Çok para?* (*chok pah-rah*) (A lot of money?)"

"No, not at all!" I try highlighting some of the points of interest: The Silk Road's HIS-TO-RI-CAL significance, the IN-COM-PAR-A-BLE joy of walking, and the MIR-A-CU-LOUS pleasure of meeting new people. My host doesn't buy a word of it and sticks to his version. For him, I'm driven by money. I get tangled up in explanations that my limited Turkish vocabulary prevents me from making sound persuasive; I furiously page through my dictionary, but to no avail, his mind is made up. He asks me to step out of the room for his evening prayer, and then we call it a day.

I have a hard time falling asleep as I grapple with serious doubts over just how my adventure is going. Am I going to be able to keep going? Are my injuries finally going to heal? Will I have to stop for a while to let the wounds heal over? How am I going to navigate across this country? I should have brought along a GPS unit, an instrument that would let me find my way based on a satellite positioning system. Should I change shoes? No, the cure would be worse than the malady. The infection that has already set in wouldn't necessarily heal, and I would have to break in the new boots, in the hope of finding "a shoe that fits" (an appropriate expression), which is dependent moreover on whether I can even find any in this region——which, in fact, is highly improbable. Fatigue knocks me out cold.

I awake to a mouthwatering scent. In the kitchen, Şükran is making fritters: lovely, triangle-shaped *börek* (*buh'-rek*). She tells me that she was a designer for a firm in Germany. She returned home to take care of her mother. She gives me a crunchy fritter and encourages me to go take a look at the garden, of which she is very proud. There, seated on a bench, my bare feet in the morning sun, I contemplate the dawn of the world. The rose bushes that she planted are flowering, and their sweet smell fills the air. Did Beauty chase the Beast from the kitchen so that she could work in peace, or because she didn't want to give rise to any rumors? In these little villages, in light of religious and social rules, is it possible for a man and a woman not joined in holy matrimony to simply spend a little time alone in a room together without people talking?

Her friend, a correspondence school professor, joins us. She stuffs a bag of carefully stacked fritters that she made for me into my pack. When I'm ready to leave, alone with Nevzat, I try to express my gratitude by offering him a little money. Of course he refuses. But then Şükran, coming out of nowhere and catching me with banknotes in hand, purple with rage, turns to her father and doesn't hold back: "I hope you didn't take his money!"

Of course not, dear lady, fear not: even though your father cannot grasp who I am, he would never think to profit from the situation and transgress the sacrosanct tenets of Turkish hospitality.

Sazköy, like Polonez, the village where I stopped at the end of the first day, are non-Turkish enclaves in the country's interior. As I walk, I ponder how, in the countries of Central Europe and Russia, minority groups tend to maintain their distinctiveness. This is quite different from France, where immigration policy seeks to integrate the many waves of foreigners who've come to live there. A few years ago in Romania, I was able to visit villages where some Germans had successfully maintained their language and culture for centuries. Nevzat and Şükran are proud of their ancestry. And in Hendek, Dr. Kirval readily shared with me, and not without some pride, that his father was Georgian and his mother Laz, which is a small tribe native to the shores of the Black Sea.

I head back out onto the trail at a snail's pace, the pain in my feet requiring a determination and acceptance of suffering typically associated only with the saints. More than an hour goes by before I can press on without moaning. I've promised myself not to exceed twenty kilometers today. At the foot of the mountains I glimpsed while leaving Sakarya, I have no choice: to get past them, I'll have to abandon the small roads and take State Road 100. Turkey is a stairway that climbs out of Istanbul, which is at sea level, and culminates at Erzurum, at an elevation of more than two thousand meters (6,500 feet). The Bolu dağı (*boh-loo dah'-uh*) (or Mount Bolu) that I have to climb today is the first step up, and it's dreadfully steep. Here at the base, my altimeter reads three hundred meters. It will read one thousand meters (3,280 feet) at the summit, barely seven kilometers (4 miles) away.

There are hundreds of them, bumper to bumper, two lanes across in both directions. These legions of trucks, make no mistake, are the harbingers of hell. Their engines whine, spewing thick, oily black smoke. Their motors wail as they head downhill in second gear. Their brakes chirp and their engines sputter from the release of compressed air, piercing my ears. Swirls of partially burned diesel oil foul the air, no doubt rising so high as to pollute the mesosphere, as well. A minuscule pedestrian amid these belching steel monsters, battered by the blazing sun, I begin the climb under the truck drivers' disapproving—or perhaps perplexed—eyes. I feel small, fragile, threatened. I walk on the left side of the road, so I can see trucks coming toward me. The space between the guardrail and the cliff is so tight that I cannot safely walk there. So I have to squeeze my way between the steel retaining wall that forms a barrier and the trucks that brush past me, some so bold that they graze my backpack as they go by. I'm seriously starting to shake in my boots. After all, whether I get crushed against the railing or my body free falls to the bottom of the ravine, who would care? One truck driver, furious to see part of his territory encroached upon by some cockroach, delivers a burst of compressed air that explodes in my ear as he drives past.

From the very first kilometer of the climb, I start sweating like a rookie sherpa. Once my T-shirt is soaked, the sweat starts dripping down my back, is channeled by my buttocks, trickles down my legs, and pours into my shoes, giving an unforgettable acid bath to . . . my feet, which can bear no more. To my left, the view is magnificent. A dizzying drop-off draws the eyes down, planted here and there with unexpected flowering rhododendrons in a landscape of scrap metal, smog, and rock. Adorning the downslope, I notice the rusted remains of trucks that really did take the plunge. I notice, moreover, that in several spots the guardrail is twisted or flattened by vehicles whose drivers must have had the fright of their life. The place is gigantic, dizzying, inhuman. Below, at the very bottom of the valley, just under my feet, bulldozers, angledozers, and other machines are on the move. They've been working—for the past five years now—on the last leg of the highway linking Ankara and Istanbul. This is a gargantuan undertaking: they have to cut through the mountain and build colossal bridges to span the ravines.

A song would seem to evoke some of the difficulties facing the traveler on this road, this "Bolu" road, as it is so deservedly called in this famous old Turkish folk song:*

The island road leads straight ahead, Oh! A graceful young girl is heading out:
That girl is on the wrong road—By the grace of God—I hope she'll come this way.
The Bolu island road is formidable, Mount Bolu is clouded in mist,
Play your Saz, my friends, Oh! 'Tis a time to celebrate!
There are chestnuts all along the island road, Oh! They fall one by one,
The girls are all in a row along the road, Oh! Let there be one for each of us.

When, at long last, I reach the summit, my T-shirt has become see-through from the sweat and sticks to my skin, and my shorts are dripping wet. In the lavatory of a restaurant set on a rocky outcrop, I don a

---

* Based on the French translation by Ayhan Erdal.

new shirt, but everything else will have to dry while I wear it. I find a
table out on the terrace overlooking the valley and have lunch. Beyond
the reach of the traffic's roar, heartened by a copious serving of *mercimek
çorbası* (*mehr'-djuh-mek chor'-bah-suh*)—the name of that invigorating
red lentil soup has finally come back to me—I dream of the caravans
that, long ago, must have climbed the mountain in silence, the animals
advancing in single file through the clumps of tall grasses. In those days,
before the existence of bulldozers, certain paths were so narrow that the
animals could only get through one at a time. These were the places that
local lords, the *paşas* (*pah'-shah*), chose for their customs offices, and
where they set up their tax collectors to levy a duty on the merchants'
camelids loaded with packages. In the seventeenth century, Jean-Baptiste
Tavernier tells us the price of passage: a half Reichsthaler for camels, a
quarter Reichsthaler for packhorses. Riding animals passed duty-free.
Each caravan driver could have up to three. I've tried in vain to super-
pose those centuries on my own, telling myself that a truck is well worth
a dromedary, and a Reichsthaler one hundred million liras, but I can't
keep track of it all; the lenses through which we interpret the world have
changed, the musical notes have been altered along with the key.

From my bird's-eye view high above the valley, I can more easily understand why Turkey chose to build roads rather than rails.
Historically, ever since the invention of the harness, nations have had
to decide whether to transport merchandise by pulling it or by carrying
it. It could be pulled by cart, chariot or wagon; and today by train. It
could be carried by Bactrian camel, dromedary, or horse; and today by
truck. In the United States, the train won out. Given its topography,
Turkey hardly had a choice. Trains have a hard time rolling through
lands that rise like a stairway! Rail transportation requires huge capital
investments. On the few rail lines that have been constructed, most of
which are single-track, Turkish trains travel at a snail's pace, whereas on
every road, ultramodern motorcoaches whiz by at full tilt. Whichever
urban center they come streaming out of, these large, comfortable buses
slip silently over the roads, crisscrossing the entire country. As for trucks,
there are thousands upon thousands of them, transporting anything and

everything on each and every road, fully loaded with all the utensils, food products, odds and ends, tools, and paraphenalia that every nation regards as its pride and glory.

I had promised myself not to walk more than twenty kilometers today. But the thought of sleeping in this hotel atop the Bolu pass—that is to say, at the gates of Hell—amid a Dantean din of trucks, buses, and screeching loudspeakers with messages for those stepping out of them is hardly enticing. My feet seem to be sufficiently content in their sweaty sauna, and I've stopped thinking about them. So it's settled: I'll push on. After the pass, a short descent brings me back to an elevation of nine hundred meters (2,950 feet). The plain, extending out as far as the eye can see, has supplanted forest. Far off, tens of kilometers distant, the horizon is obstructed by a mountain chain painted in a surprising medley of blues. I find no other hotel along the way, and so I finally wind up in Bolu, having walked thirty-five kilometers since morning.

The city is surrounded by a wall of apartment towers and high-rise blocks into which commercial developers pack the common people. In a country with so much space and frequent earthquakes, what could possibly prompt architects to build housing projects skyward? Is it to draw a little closer to heaven?

In Bolu, I wash off the day's perspiration by sweating it out in the very beautiful Tarihi Orta Hammam, built in 1321. Natural daylight floods the bathhouse's rooms, diffracted through blocks of glass set in the domes. As the sun's rays pass through them, they become iridescent in the floating steam. I partake of this soothing, golden mist. I finally relax.

And then I decide to go sightseeing and visit the caravansary. It's a *Taş-han* (*tash-han*): the term *han* refering to a city caravansary, the word *taş* meaning "stone." The construction is relatively recent, as it dates from 1804. This is not surprising, since previously the caravans followed a route that took them north of the present-day city. The *han* is very well preserved and the obligatory "tearoom" in its rectangular courtyard is a great place to unwind and share secrets in the cool shade of the arcades. The cells, formerly intended for travelers, are now occupied by artisans and small shops. In its inner recesses, there's a bookstore run by a blond, curly-haired man with small, thick-lensed glasses and an athletic build: this is Mustafa Açıkyıldız. He and his wife Emine lived in France for twenty-one years. He was in the French Foreign Legion. He tells me that he rarely has the opportunity to speak French, except with an engineer from Lyon who works for a local company. I ask him a few questions about his life in France, and the kind of commitment he made with the Legion. He brings up something else, changing the subject. When I offer to take his picture, he flatly refuses. It's an awkward moment, and we bid each other good-bye.

I make use of my stopover in this city to reconnect with civilization—to send messages over the Internet, among other things, so as to catch up with my family and friends and reassure them that I'm doing okay. I've noticed that nearly every Turkish city, even medium-sized ones, have Internet cafés thronged with people passionate about communicating, both young and old.

Is it the sweat bath or the healing powder that I purchased with Hikmet? The next morning, I notice that my wounds have begun to heal over. So as to further accelerate the healing process, I opt for a very short stage. But I remain cautious, having finally decided to nip in the bud my damned habit of always overshooting the reasonable decisions I already find so hard to make. I hold off until 3:00 p.m. to leave the city; that way, I won't be able to walk more than three or four hours before the fateful onset of night and the risk of danger.

The sun is shining brightly. A minibus packed with passengers comes to a stop, and the driver invites me to hop in. He's disappointed when I tell him no. An hour later, as I'm walking by a courtyard that has been converted into a parking lot, he comes out running, beckoning me: "*Gel, çay!*"

He and his friends make quite a fuss over me, consumed by curiosity, as they had all seen me, either earlier today or yesterday, along the road. Nationality? Where do I come from? Where am I going?

I gladly answer the usual litany of questions as we sip cups of very sweet tea. It makes me laugh to see how these men—whose only physical activity is to downshift, brake, and accelerate—can be so fascinated by someone who walks; it's as if I were a man from Mars. There is, in their eyes, a mix of admiration for what I'm accomplishing, a tinge of condescending irony, and a certain degree of disbelief. Why walk when you can go by car? Of course, once again, many of them ask whether they can drop me off a little farther on down the road. But this time, they're not put off when I turn them down.

Is it for lack of vocabulary or because I'm afraid of sounding pedantic? I give up trying to explain. But then, isn't our leisurely conversation over a cup of tea the perfect answer to their incomprehension? If I were traveling by car, or had climbed up into their vehicles as a fare-paying rider, would this conversation have ever even taken place? No. Motor vehicles confiscate our words. They go too fast and make too much noise. Stops are predetermined; exchanges are strictly limited to payment of the fare. And if I get into a vehicle and find myself next to another passenger, there's simply no guarantee that he'll even want to talk, or that, since he's getting off at the next stop, he'll see the point of starting a conversation. Walking is freedom and exchange; vehicles are prisons of steel and noise, places of unsought intimacy. And how can I get across to these men, the descendants of nomads—whose virtues they love to extol—that they've become motorized, legless cripples, no longer capable of getting about on the strength of their own muscles, which are wasting away through lack of use?

In the hours that follow, I continue to ponder the parallels between nomadism and the Silk Road. In Central Asia, this mythical road was created by Arabs and, later on, by Muslims. In Arab culture, travel and commerce are linked. Mohammed, a descendant of nomadic tribes, followed in the footsteps of merchants and, during his exile, journeyed extensively. His successors continued to do as he had. Nomadic Arabs conquered a large geographic area before they were finally halted—in France at Poitiers, and elsewhere. The Ottomans, themselves descendants of Mongol nomads, conquered present-day Turkey by force. Once the Muslim faith had unified the steppes of Central Asia, both groups capitalized on their dual heritage: commerce and travel. Through to the tenth century, Muslim trade flourished, merchants enjoyed considerable prestige and enormous wealth, until military forces portioned out fiefdoms for themselves at the merchants' expense. Buying and selling continued on nevertheless for nine more centuries along the roadsides of Central Asia and China.

The Arabs are indisputably the inventors of the literary travelogue. At the end of the ninth century, Abu Dulaf Mis'ar provides an account of his expedition to Central Asia, Malaysia, and India. Another great traveler, Abu Hamid al-Gharnati of Toledo, relates his exploration of the world in the twelfth century, one hundred years before Marco Polo. Whether they were traveling for business, out to discover the world, or simple pilgrims, by the time Europeans were only beginning to set out on their great journeys, Arabs and Muslims had already crisscrossed the globe. Three Arab travelers, the three *Ibn*, described the known world in great detail: in the tenth century, Ibn Fadlan visited Bulgaria and Russia nearly three hundred years before the first European, Jean du Plan Carpin, would head out on his diplomatic mission in 1245 to visit the great Khan. At the end of the twelfth century, leaving Arabized Spain on his pilgrimage to Mecca and back, Ibn Jubayr depicted the Mediterranean basin in what was extraordinary detail for those days. But it is Ibn Battuta of the fourteenth century who stands out, beyond any doubt, as the greatest Arab traveler. Thanks to him, Arabia, Asia Minor, Russia, India, China, Spain, and the Sahara—just a handful of places!—would no longer be, for the curious, *terræ incognitæ*.

All these mental incursions back into the past have taken my mind far from the road before me: without thinking, I've just passed through the village of Çaydurt, fifteen kilometers from Bolu, and I unhappily note that State Road 100 and the Istanbul-Ankara Highway are drawing nearer to each other so as to make it over another gap, the Fakilar Pass. At the foot of the valley, in between these two roads barely one hundred meters apart, stands a dirty, gray, rectangular cement structure: an inn, used primarily by truck drivers. The dining room I enter is dimly lit, probably so people don't notice that the floor hasn't been swept since the place opened. One of the kitchen staff, shuffling his feet, shows me to my room one floor up: it's a minuscule unit with a window looking straight out over the highway. Two one-person beds take up all the space. The sheets have probably never been washed since opening day, either; they're stiff as cardboard from all the dirt. The boy goes out, leaving the door open behind him, letting me share in the blissful sleep of another hotel guest, snoring like a diesel engine in a room across the hallway.

I have a bathroom, but it's unfortunately rather dark. Someone unscrewed the only bulb intended to brighten a place reserved for hygiene, light, and cleanliness. In the shadows, the first thing I hear is the sound of a waterfall. A pipe is broken in the ceiling, and water is loudly spilling down onto the tile floor. A noisy leak in the toilet's flush mechanism is unsuccessfully trying to drown the other one out. The sink has no hot water, and the cold water tap that I finally manage to break free is already stuck such that I can no longer shut it back off. My pocket lamp, which is about to give up the ghost, throws enough light, however, for me to notice that no one would ever guess the shower basin's original color, as it, too, is covered in a thick layer of slimy filth. A nauseating odor tops it all off. I walk back out, closing the door. There will be no shower tonight, not even a cold one: I'm too afraid of getting dirty.

Fearing that the one in charge of housekeeping might also be the cook, I make do with a cup of yogurt for dinner. In my room, I lay out my sleeping bag on one of the beds, but so much intimacy with all the dirt is overpowering, and so it will be a short night. What's more, a truck-hating dog howls every time a motor roars by on the highway; that is to say, whenever the old dog feels like it. When, exhausted and voiceless, he finally quiets down, an army of toads, probably inspired by the sound of water coming from my "bathroom," begins to serenade me with a chorus of a thousand dreary voices. Howling trucks, a barking dog, the stench of filth, mourning toads, and the splash of water pouring from gargoyles: I stare out at the highway swept back and forth by the bright beams of the passing vehicles, sleep drags its feet, and anxiety disrupts the shadows.

As on the *Samsun* two weeks ago, or two days ago at Nevzat's house, the questions once again raise their ugly head. Will I make it through to the end? This evening, I have my doubts. The pain on the top of my toes has, little by little, eroded my optimism. To this has been added an enemy that I had completely underestimated: linguistic isolation. While walking alone, I don't suffer from the solitude. The images I amass, the dialogue I have with myself are enough. It's during the stopovers, in restaurants, and with the people I meet that I feel stranded on my linguistic desert island. The vocabulary I learned before my departure and what I pick up here and there along the way are simply not enough. This insurmountable barrier—this prison cell of words—is unbearable, and I can think of no solution to the problem. And what will it be like when I'm in Iran, since I haven't learned a single word of Farsi?

The Turks, devilishly chatty, sometimes speak to me at length, and I can't understand a thing. On television, omnipresent in restaurants, teahouses, and peoples' homes, faces flash by, and out of the mouths pour sounds that, for me, are entirely incompehensible. I wasn't very pleased to find out, several days after my departure, that the trial of Öcalan (*Oh'-djah-lan*), the Kurdish leader of the PKK, had begun. Television networks are broadcasting special coverage. People are riled up and there is a lot of debate, but I understand nothing. What worse form of torture can there be for a journalist? A manager of one establishment, in response to my question—"How long is the trial going to last?"—replied with a satisfied smile by simply sliding his index finger under his throat. That language, sad to say, is universal.

Late that clamorous night, in a hotel room reeking of goats and grime, I make a cursory assessment of my journey. It has been twelve days since I left Istanbul, and I've walked three hundred and sixty kilometers (220 miles). But there are still over two thousand five hundred (1,550 miles) to go before I reach Tehran. From here to there, will I be able to hang on, both mentally and physically? Am I going to solve the difficult problem of finding my way? And will I be able to brave the many calamities that people here and there have warned me about: Kangal dogs, PKK gunmen, highway bandits, and of course some nasty hole in the ground that will cause me to stumble and break a leg (or two)? In the wee hours of the morning, overcome by fatigue, I finally drift off to sleep for a few minutes, unable to answer the one question that encompasses all the others: will I see this journey through to the end? If I had the choice right now, I wouldn't stake my money on it.

When I wake up, I'm happy to note that my feet feel better. And, for one who walks, when the feet feel fine, everything's fine. Yesterday's shortened stretch and the healing powder have worked wonders. And so, with a lilt in my step, I head over the Fakilar Pass, which rises to an altitude of twelve hundred meters (3,900 feet). To improve my vocabulary as I walk along, I make a game of translating superlative-packed billboard advertisements, cleverly positioned in between these two heavily traveled roads. And every day, I make myself review what I've already learned, while adding five new words. I'm a tenacious walker and a conscientious traveler. But still, my main difficulty is understanding. Turks speak very quickly, and the structure of their sentences is far removed from ours. Even words I know are camouflaged under a profusion of prefixes and suffixes, making them seem unfamiliar. When I don't quite catch a sentence and ask for it to be repeated, my interlocutors, mostly simple folk, think I'm hard of hearing. So they repeat the same thing at the same speed, only shout.

A short distance after cresting the hill, the Ankara Highway turns southeast. State Road 100 also splits in two. The section heading east, emptied now of a good deal of the traffic, becomes bearable once again. In order to discourage vehicles from trying to pick me up, I walk on the left side of the road. There must not be many walkers in Turkey, and the thought bolsters my ego: I'm seen as a veritable curiosity, a rarity, a national phenomenon. However fleeting our encounters, the road hogs and I communicate through sign language. Our dialogue consists of a succession of sound and light signals, gestures, and facial expressions that in and of themselves express the different reactions I give rise to. They can be classified as follows, from hostility to enthusiasm:

– A honk of the horn accompanied by a hand gesture brushing me away: "Get outta my way!"

– A simple honk of the horn: "Let me get a look at that face." This happens most often when I'm heading up a steep incline, looking down at the pavement. It's also the way trucks call out to me when they're coming up from behind. They spot a pair of legs over which there is a rucksack, in turn topped with a hat, and, quite understandably, they want to see whether or not there's a head.

– A honk of the horn with a hand in the air, palm turned up toward the sky an an inquisitive facial expression: "What the hell is this? Nationality? How'd you get here? Where are you going?"

– A honk of the horn, hand in the air, palm turned out in my direction as Romans would do: "Hello, friend!"

– A honk of the horn and a military salute: "Nice job, buddy!"

The most demonstrative are those who, headed in either direction, have passed me previously and who greet me as they would an old acquaintance. From a distance, they flash their headlights and then honk as they pass me by, with wild gestures and an open smile. When there are several people up front, the passenger closest to me leans out the door and shouts a word of encouragement. Later on, toward the end of my journey, I come to find that, in cafés along the highway, many drivers have already heard of me and come over to tell me so, wanting confirmation of the incredible story: A MAN TRAVELING FROM ISTANBUL TO TEHRAN ON FOOT. They know better than anyone that, depending on their load and the engine's horsepower, it would take them an exhausting two- to four-day journey to cover that same distance.

The bus drivers who've already seen me, or who've caught wind of the crazy Frenchman, are especially friendly and make an announcement to their passengers. Then all the passengers spur me on. I always respond. To the most aggressive ones, I raise my middle finger to the sky. The others receive a Roman salute and a smile. For the nicest ones, those who flash their headlights from a distance, I metamorphose into a kind of windmill, waving my arms and walking stick to the extent that my load allows. But sometimes, after fatigue has set in, I put on much less of a show.

Around noon, a van coming toward me zooms past, does a one-eighty, passes me in the other direction, and then comes to a stop a hundred meters on. The driver gets out, walks over to me, and starts asking questions.

"Nationality?" "Where are you from?" and so on.

He looks at his watch.

"I've got two hours. Hop in, I'll take you a hundred kilometers or so."

In the face of my amused rejection, he scratches his head, assuring me that he would love to help me out. He's truly disheartened that I've turned him down, and I feel awful. How hard it is to be free!

High atop Fakilar, my altimeter reads 1,200 meters (3,940 feet). The landscape looks rather swampy in spots. At Yeniçağa (*Yeh-nee'-chah-ah*), they are mining the peatlands. The deciduous trees have disappeared, but on the summits of some hills, fir trees have been planted. Everywhere else, plowed fields and meadowlands blanket the gentle slopes, warmed by a spring sun. The road continues to gradually climb: 1,360 meters (4,460 feet). Herds of russett cattle watched over by young shepherds pepper a prairie landscape painted in every possible shade of green. There are no walls, no fences, no ditches; the plain would be endless were it not for the ever-present chain of mountains obstructing the horizon. Although it's nearly the end of the month of May, the altitude here has slowed the walnut trees' progress, such that their first leaves are only beginning to open out. Out on the plain in advance of the Bolu Pass, not even fifty kilometers away, the leaves were fully open and nuts had already formed. At the edge of a pond, children are fishing with makeshift poles while keeping an eye on their animals. These young people seem to be from another era! And yet these are scenes from the world I knew as a child. Could I possibly be that old?

I stay at the only hotel in Gerede (*gay'-reh-deh*), a small city with an old quarter filled with tiny shops. The merchants appear to be busier entertaining friends than handling customers. The sight of teacups and sugar on trays set out on a workbench, table, or chair makes these shops feel more like sitting rooms. Two men suffice to fill one. Who are these people, prattling on while the shopkeeper is busy sewing, sharpening, or whittling? A friend? A client? A supplier? A relative? They are all endlessly babbling away . . .

Nowhere is it announced, and so it is by sheer luck that I discover, straying beneath a worm-ridden portal, Şehit (*shay-heet'*) ancient and marvelous caravansary. A short thin man with a scanty mustache, Şehit gets up from his seat at a neighboring teahouse as soon as he sees me, a camera-equipped tourist, standing in the courtyard of his architectural marvel. The man is no less venerable than the building itself, and he's delighted that someone has taken an interest in what is no doubt the focal point of his life. He gives me a guided tour. The paved, rectangular courtyard is framed by a structure two stories high, comprising countless cells that once housed caravan travelers. The wood used to construct passageways and staircases, worn by the elements, has turned various shades of amber. To prevent accidents, fencing has been added to reinforce wood balusters that have rotted over the passing years. The walls, whitewashed in times past, now bear innumerable black bruises. There are holes above some of the cell doors, where it seems likely a stovepipe was installed at one time.

Perhaps all the wrinkles of the place are what make it so magnificent. Şehit opens a door and makes his way down a staircase, inviting me to follow. The former basement stables, built for an entire cavalry, now house only his small horse. He caresses the animal while speaking in a soothing voice. Poor old Şehit can do nothing but watch as his caravansary falls into ruin. For two years now, he has been requesting financial assistance to repair or preserve the roof at very least. He still hasn't received a reply. It's a sad thought that, in only a short while, this remarkable testimony to the Silk Road will, like so many others, simply disappear.

Of course, while we were talking, a group of men left the teahouse and came over to join us, eager to take part in our conversation. I ask when the caravansary was built. Şehit doesn't know but speculates that it might be six hundred years old. An old man, Mehmet, who has said nothing up to now and to whom everyone listens with respect, offers a more precise answer. Deliberately, trying to find simple words, writing in my notebook and thumbing through my dictionary, he explains. This caravansary, or rather this *han*, predates the Ottomans, which means it is nearly eight hundred years old. As proof, he points out that the *han*'s name includes the word *kiliseli*, which means that it belonged to a church and not a mosque. I had indeed previously heard that, in close proximity to the mosques, other related structures were built, such as bazaars, shops, and caravansaries, and that the revenue they generated paid for the maintenance of the religious edifice. This was, for example, the case of Bolu's *han*. Was this also done for Christian churches, such as the one at Gerede? Try as I might, I can find no confirmation of this hypothesis. And the idea isn't entirely convincing, either. Numerous churches survived the Ottoman conquest, being abandoned only after the Kemalist revolution and the departure of the last Greek Christians. Nevertheless, it's not so common to find vestiges of caravansaries in their vicinity.

On the morning of May 27, as I leave the city, I feel rather merry. My feet have almost completely healed, and, nicely bundled, they're no longer painful. It's cloudy out, the air clear and cool. The road, leading straight ahead, undulates slightly as it passes alongside the mountain. Down below, appearing ridiculously small, villages composed of houses with red-tile roofs look as though they're held down in the landscape by their white minarets, thin as pins. Clouds roll across the sky, sending their shadows scampering up the slopes of Köroğlu (*kuh-rohl'-oo*), a mountain spire about fifty kilometers away, topping out at 2,100 meters (6,890 feet) and still capped by winter snows. At an intersection, a police car is keeping watch. One of the officers gets out, comes over to me, and, since he speaks English, strikes up a conversation. He leads me back to his vehicle and offers me a Coca-Cola. I observe once again that the officers of the "*polis*," whose job is to regulate traffic, are not nearly as agressive as the *jandarmas*, who are more interested in fighting terrorism, or the "*askers*," the military police, who are typically arrogant and think that by acting that way, they might be able prove just how indispensable they are.

From time to time, a few raindrops fall, cooling the air even more, and this chilly temperature is ideal for walking. One more self-examination reassures me that my muscles have adjusted to the harsh routine I've imposed on them for thirteen days now. My pack feels light. My resting pulse has dropped to sixty beats a minute and never exceeds eighty-five, even when walking along. One of the privileges I now share with top-level athletes is that I recover almost instantaneously, so I can keep moving nearly nonstop without needing to take breaks. At sixty-one, despite all my fears on the *Samsun*, I've regained my physical youth. My first battle, that of getting my body to adjust to the challenge I've set for myself, seems to have been won. I feel a kind of exhilaration emanating from every cell in my body. In this breathtaking landscape, I feel as though I were flying. I've finally entered the walker's nirvana.

Just like last year on the Spanish Meseta, on the way to Compostela, I'm rubbing elbows with the divine. For that to happen, at least for me, three conditions have to come together. First, I must be completely alone. This is the first and most important requirement if I want to sail up to the clouds. Too secretive, too distrustful, and willfully remote, the gods do not open their door to tour groups. But it takes more than just being alone to gain admission into Olympus. You must also choose the right place. Sitting by yourself in your room in a city really isn't ideal. To draw nearer the altar, seek vastness. I'm a lover of mountains, but I can imagine that for some privileged souls, the sea provides a similar sense of the infinite. When nothing but the horizon blocks your view, or your eyes are drawn upward to mountain peaks touching the sky, nirvana is close at hand. But that's still not enough. The final condition, just as essential, is that body and mind must be in perfect harmony. As you're walking, when the muscles, acclimatized and seemingly lubricated through daily exercise, reach an ideal temperature—that is, when your skin is perspiring lightly—and when well-oiled joints deal effortlessly with the ups and downs of the trail, then a mysterious alchemy transforms the body, allowing it to levitate. Spirit, pure spirit, hovers along over the heath, the steppe, or the mountain peaks. Grain of sand in a sea of sand, invisible in the vastness, weightless as the flight of the butterfly:

all of a sudden, the walls of our familiar prison fall away. And the doors of heaven are opened. On these roads that he himself once traveled, I have often thought about Saint Paul and his vision of a great light on the road to Damascus. How, if he had been on horseback (which religious imagery sometimes assumes, without any proof) or riding atop a cart, the face of Christendom might have been quite different.

The traveler's bliss doesn't last forever. How long? It's hard to keep track of it. It comes to an end because some strong emotion sets the heart aflutter, disrupting the soul; or because a stone along the path throws off the subtle equilibrium; or when a farmer, leaning on his hoe, suddenly stops what he's doing and calls out you in a loud voice, waving his arms.

Come lunchtime, I eat a tasty *tas kebab* in a *lokanta*. It's twice the usual price. But what else can I do? Prices are never labeled in this country. They're calculated at the checkout or at the door, on a case-by-case basis. Today, the owner decided that, since I'm a tourist, I could cough up a little extra.

Five kilometers down the road, a strapping fellow comes out of another *lokanta*, shouting: *"Gel, çay!"*

He's the owner. He drags me almost forcibly into his restaurant. I agree to a cup of tea. But he motions to his help, and they bring me an assortment of *meze*, which, ordinarily, would be a real treat: there's nothing I love more than that profusion of flavors that can either be eaten together, or savored at the taster's whim. He insists that it's all free. I try to say no, but in vain. I just gorged myself on the kebab served up by the cook next door, but he really wants me to honor his offering, and I don't know how to tell him that I've *already* eaten. So as not to disappoint him, I have a few nibbles.

Once I'm back on the road with every intention of getting some exercise to help me digest, a minibus stops alongside me and offers me a ride. I thank him, but no: I'd rather walk.

"But for you, it's free," the driver assures me.

"Para yok, para yok! (no money, no money!)," the passengers all shout, thinking I don't understand.

I have to come up with clever ruses and muster a fighter's energy just to earn the right to walk. Others' thoughtfulness can, at times, be truly exhausting.

I plan to stop in the village of Dereköy (*deh'-reh-kuh*), nestled in a valley, a little over thirty-five kilometers from my starting point. I spot the village perched atop a kind of natural terrace overlooking a generous valley. At an intersection below, the road veers north toward the Black Sea, while State Road 100 continues heading east. From my bluff, I see Ismetpaşa, a small train station that I had spotted on the map. It is 5:00 p.m. I feel good. Common sense tells me to stop here. But who knows what evil demon it is that manages to convince me to keep going: to hell with caution, I decide to push on to Ismetpaşa, heading down over the grasslands.

I somewhat overestimated my strength. In no time at all, as I'm barreling down the slope, my wounds come back to life, and the station, like an oasis, seems to keep moving away the closer I come. When I finally reach my destination, I'm very tired. The houses are small, dirty, and run-down. The station, slightly back from the road, is the town's only solidly built, well-maintained structure. I decide to stop in a teahouse run by Mustafa, a sixty-five-year-old retiree. I tell him—or rather, I stammer my way through something intended to be a short summary of my journey—and I mention that I plan to stop here this evening. He's incredibly untalkative, goes into an adjoining closet to get four eggs, which he drops into a teapot to cook them. We eat them with salt and bread, in silence.

I hardly know what to think. Should I continue on? Look for another place to stay? Still mute, after serving me a cup of tea, my host gets up and goes out, leaving me alone. A refrigerated display case that has been out of order for a long time and four or five dirty tables are the only furniture in this "tearoom." Spread out on one of the tables are playing cards and a game of *stira*, a local version of dominoes. There's sand all over the simple cement floor to help absorb moisture. The walls have never been painted. The storeroom where Mustafa went to get eggs is separated from the room by a partition made of loose boards, such that I can see a mattress lying on the floor, no doubt the owner's own bed.

When Mustafa comes back, he's accompanied by a kind, honest-looking man in his forties. Cengiz (*djen'-geez*, with a hard '*g*') works for the railroad, operating a crane used to maintain the tracks. He informs me that I'm going to spend the night at his house. Cengiz lives in a railcar stationed on a siding line. A short distance from his house, kids are grilling fish they netted in a nearby pond, and they share a generous portion with us. My host, before preparing the evening meal, spends a long time adjusting the satellite dish moored atop the railcar in an attempt to pull in a French channel for me to enjoy. He finally picks up a program in my native tongue. Pleased at his accomplishment, he bursts into a loud laugh. Cengiz has teeth so white they could be used to represent perfect dental hygiene for an advertising agency. A notable exception, for the vast majority of people I meet display, over and over again, an array of decayed and broken teeth. The program that he found gives . . . the stock market report. So as not to ruin it for him, I act as though I'm thrilled but am a little overwhelmed listening to the latest quotes of CAC 40 companies.

Two teachers from the nearby school, notified by the children, climb up into the railcar to chat. One of them speaks French about as well as I speak Turkish, but it's already very late to be having a conversation, and we're in tight quarters made stifling by a red-hot stove. They explain how the Turkish school system functions. Several times throughout the night, trains make their way into and out of the little station without disturbing my host's sleep, accustomed as he is to being rocked to sleep by the heavy pounding of their diesel motors.

The sun barely over the horizon, I don't feel overly tired despite having trudged forty-seven kilometers the previous day. But today, I'll be sensible: I've decided to stick to a short stage, stopping this evening in Çerkeş (*cher'-kesh*), only twenty kilometers (12 miles) away.

CHAPTER V
KANGALS

Although my inclination is to head toward villages and side roads, this morning, out of concern for my recovering feet, I head for the highway. The weather is mild and wet, perfect for walking. Around noon, the sun, first somewhat shy, but then downright hot, sets me dreaming. My walkabout is finally just as I like it. After the first few kilometers, my body exults. I move forward effortlessly, free from gravity, pure spirit on the move. From time to time, the landscape's wild, flat beauty draws me back to reality. Views stretch as far as the eye can see. The grass is short and trees few; the sun meticulously paints the gentle slopes gold. By morning's end, as my skin starts to burn in the sun, I shade my scalp under a wide-brimmed canvas hat. And then nothing can disturb me. My body and feet, now content, are no longer a concern. My spirit glides over the plain alone. I dream on my feet, walking along.

For Michel Serres, passivity is "another form of the animal state."* In these daily exertions, this imperceptible but intense push to reach a yet-so-very-distant objective, this beneficial perspiration, I soar to the sky, I free myself from the chains of childhood, from fear, from conventional ways of thinking. I break the bonds society has bound me in, scorning armchairs and couches. I act, I think, I dream, I walk, and, therefore, I live. Although walking is conducive to reverie, thinking while walking is

---

* Michel Serres, *Variations sur le corps*, Paris: Le Pommier, 1999. Translation by Randolph Burks, in Serres, Michel, *Variations on the Body*, Minneapolis: Univocal Publishing, 2011, p. 23.

more unpredictable. The flight of an eagle, the path of a cloud, the flight of a hare, an odd crossroads, the heady fragrance of an unfamiliar flower, the call of a shepherd, or hills undulating off into the distance: whatever can be seen, smelled, and listened to frustrates the flow of thoughts. At any given moment, the walker is roused from meditation, distracted by a thousand tiny events, and forced to focus once again on the trail.

Walking is easier on the dreamer. Unlike thinking, reverie can be interrupted and then resumed without suffering much when the thread running through it breaks. Quite the opposite, in fact: the flight of the stork, the rustling of insects, the flamboyant purple of a flower or the unusual shape of a stone stumbled upon, all serve to stimulate the imagination. And it is not uncommon that, while walking thoughts wander off into the realm of the impossible. I often find myself having the ideal conversation with a friend or a woman I once loved. Everything falls into place, since, starting with my memory of them, I'm in charge of orchestrating questions and answers. And I'm not in the least bit ashamed to admit that, in this or that argument, I was in the wrong, since there is no one there to cast stones. Sometimes, when I reach the stopover, I send a note to the person involved, to whom it must come as a surprise to receive a card from half a world away given that we haven't seen each other in a long time.

Often, as I walk along, I commune with those who preceded me on these roads. John of Plano Carpini, for example, sent by the Pope in 1245. He was in such a hurry to reach the court of the Great Khan that he used Mongolian relays, precursors of the famous American Pony Express. The rider would change steeds up to seven times a day. Upon spotting a relay, he rang a bell. A new steed was saddled up, ready to run. The rider would leap from the tired horse, mount the perky new one, and continue on, flat out. It's thanks to these riders that the Mongolian emperors were continuously kept informed of what was going on at the opposite end of their empire, which stretched from the China Sea to the borders of Western Europe.

And then there is the shadow of another traveler, Guillaume de Rubrouck, messenger of Saint Louis, who occasionally ventured out onto the steppe. Long before Marco Polo, he gave an account of far-off Tartary, whose name alone struck fear in the hearts of the West's fiercest fighters. But through an injustice the explanation for which History has kept secret, only the name of Marco Polo went on to become famous.

What has changed in these landscapes since these illustrious travelers journeyed past them? The road is now blacktopped, telegraph poles have been erected? I have only to move a few hundred meters away from the bitumen, and the scenery is changeless. These fields, hills, mountains, croplands, houses, and peasant farmers are unchanged. These herdsmen, watching over their lambs and waving when they see me, live no differently from how their ancestors did who, from time immemorial, watched on as solo travelers or long columns of caravans marched by. Saint Paul frequented these hills. It is said that, in the space of ten years, he traveled over thirty thousand kilometers (18,640 miles) throughout the region. Mostly on foot. Were the shepherds to whom he proclaimed the good news any different from these?

But preachers and caravanners were not alone on these roads. Fearsome armies, too, fought one another here, viciously and without warning. This is why the cities are mostly positioned defensively on hilltops. Villages are hidden in the landscape, nearly invisible, blending in with the scenery. The earth used to build houses, dug up from the ground, has kept its original gray and red hues. Only the roofs, once made of straw or heather, and now made of tiles, stand out vividly against the colorless mountain slopes.

Çerkeş, like most Turkish cities, sits a good distance back from the main highway. Before entering the city, I skirt a huge food processing plant specializing in meat exports. It's the chief employer in this large town of ten thousand inhabitants. Prosperity brought by the factory made it possible to construct, on the edge of the old city, garishly colored multifamily housing. In the streets in the center of town, the small traditional wood and adobe houses have been abandoned and are falling apart.

The hotel is comfortable, and the night would have been a good one if, at 5:00 in the morning, I hadn't been awakened by a charivari.

Within a very small perimeter, Çerkeş has twelve mosques and just as many imams. When it is time for prayer, each one tries to prove he has the best radiophonic voice to draw in the faithful, so they crank up their sound systems. No sooner has one begun to chant the first verses of the Qur'an than twelve other loudspeakers break in wailing, each one louder than the other, as if those who flubbed their song's first lines wanted to make up for it in decibels. Their song? What am I saying? No doubt that in former times, muezzins actually had to sing from atop their minarets. Today, however, it's no song, but a medley of screams, a mishmash of notes, an uproar, a tumult, a screaming contest. The sounds spilling from the top of one minaret clash with those of the minaret next door, and they bound back and forth until they all converge in my room. Allah, looking down from the heavens, must plug his ears. Both of us can hardly wait for the silence of prayer to follow.

Shortly after noon, the truck traffic increases. No longer able to bear it, thirsting for some peace and quiet, I leave the highway and veer south. I've spotted a shortcut on my map, parallel to the main road, that runs from village to village and heads cross-country. Too bad for my still-delicate feet, I'll be treading gravel roads once again. I stop in to see the first *bakkal* I come across and buy a few cookies and some juice for my lunch in a short while. There's not much variety there, it's true, but I intend to make up for it in town.

I have no difficulty finding my way. The main roadway, a few kilometers north, is easy to keep track of with its procession of trucks, the noise of which, considerably muffled after being carried by the breeze, reaches my ears every now and then. To my right, a massif constitutes a barrier that no roadway dares climb. I scan the terrain for a spa town indicated on my map. Nothing. At the spot where it's supposed to be, I find piles of stones. Ruins, no doubt. I love ruins. They get me dreaming. I can rebuild as I please the walls and columns damaged by the hands of time. I opt for a small detour to see them up close and to stop there for my light meal.

Off to the side, a flock of sheep is lying in the grass, digesting a meal. Neither herder nor dog in sight. It's as if they're guarding themselves.

Probably for a simple reason: they can be seen from a long distance away on this featureless plain. I move closer. The ruins are the collapsed walls of former houses. These jumbles of large stones still delineate the square shape of the dwellings and the alignment of streets. In one spot, four walls have been reassembled, and branches lay atop of them for use as a shelter. A small donkey with a packsaddle on its back is grazing among one pile of ruins. It's a charming scene. I set down my haversack, take out my camera, and approach the animal, which raises its head just long enough to check me over, looking neither friendly nor ill-natured, then goes back to what it was doing. I'm about fifteen meters (50 feet) away when I freeze, petrified. Out from the middle of the flock, two light-haired dogs have sprung to life and are charging toward me, barking. They're almost the same color as the sheep, which is why I missed them. They're enormous, and there is no mistaking them: Kangals!

These fearsome dogs are one of the prides of the Turks. It's illegal to sell them abroad. Powerful and aggressive, they're sheepherders trained to attack wild animals, such as wolves and bears. To keep these animals from biting them in the throat, they wear protective spiked steel collars. A Frenchman once told me he had been chased by a Kangal while driving his car. The beast had no trouble keeping up with him, his speedometer reading 70 km/h (43 mph). And now these monsters are running straight for me. I look around frantically. Where's the shepherd? In the branch-covered cabin? I call out, but there's no reply. I dash over to my backpack, calling out once again. My voice is high-pitched, choked by fear. I have my camera in my right hand. Without letting it go, I grab my walking stick with my left. There's no point fleeing, I cannot run 70 km/h. My only choice is to confront them. They're coming straight on, looking as big as the donkey I was about to photograph. My mouth is dry, and I feel as if my heart has stopped beating. I can almost feel their teeth ripping through the flesh of my bare arms and legs. I can't even get to my knife, diligently stowed away as it is deep in some pocket in my backpack. But even if I could, a knife the size of a single Kangal fang wouldn't be of much use to me now!

My friend Alexis briefed me at length about how to calm a dog. Aim the stick at him, without threatening him, so as to establish a distance and keep the animal at bay. He didn't say what to do if there were two of them. So I improvise, gauging just how different theory is from practice. I move so that the wall is to my back and brandish my stick in turns, first toward the one, then toward the other. I shout, *"couché"* (lie down). They clearly don't speak French. They get each other worked up and start foaming at the mouth. They're wearing those infamous iron collars spiked with shiny points, sharp as their fangs and nearly ten centimeters (4 inches) long. They fortunately remain next to each other, so I can fend off both attacks at once. The defensive-cane theory turns out to have worked. They belch and drool, lips drawn back revealing glaring fangs, but they maintain their distance.

I begin to have, if not a little serenity, at least a glimmer of hope, and it's then that I get a crazy idea. Since I have my camera right there in hand, why not snap a picture? That way, if they tear me to pieces, at least everyone will know what happened. While keeping a firm grip on my walking stick that I hold out level with their chops, I point the camera as best I can and press the button. The sun is in my eyes, and my camera is a modern, "smart" model, which refuses to take backlit photos. So off goes the flash. The dogs, a little startled, back off for a moment. They're still barking but are less determined. One of them falls silent, takes two steps back, lunges once again with a bark, then leaves. Emboldened, I take another shot, this time aiming a little more carefully, but without letting go of my cane, of course. Off goes another flash. They back off several meters.

I stand perfectly still. The last thing I want to do is to hamper their retreat. They're still agitated but move away. They head back to their flock, then lie down between me and the sheep, ready to protect them. All is calm. I take a deep breath and curse myself. What a fool! And yet I'd been warned: "Keep away from sheep, for Kangals are never very far." I owe my mistake to the fact that I'd come to believe, without anyone ever saying so, that these monsters were as black as hell. So, I scanned for black near the sheep. I had always seen sheepdogs remain with their masters, away from the flock. I therefore never imagined that the dogs would be sprawled out right in the middle of the very sheep that are supposed to fear them. As for their color, aside from their dark muzzle, they're almost as white as the sheep. Later on, in Kurdish regions, I'll spot other Kangals whose ears and tail have been cut so that wolves and bears can't easily grab onto them with their teeth. These two, though, the first of these beasts I've seen, have magnificent long tails that curl like a sideways question mark, and their ears are intact.

Danger has wandered off. I sit down on a stone in order to catch my breath. I ought to get going. But first, I'd still like to snap a photo of the little donkey. He misled me, too. With his packsaddle on, I thought that the shepherd was somewhere nearby. I slowly approach him. I'm about ten meters away from them when the two Kangals charge me once again. I stop dead in my tracks, half-terrified, half-amused.

"Okay, okay, I've got it. You're defending him, so I give up. After all, I'll get by without a photo of a dumb old Turkish ass."

Holding my stick out in their direction, I back up until I reach my gear, never taking my eyes off them, and I let them settle back down. Having stowed my camera, I harness my pack and turn my back to the ruins and the beasts. At that very instant, someone calls out to me: it's the shepherd. He had gone off mushroom hunting. The Kangals, contrary to my expectation, do not go over to greet their master. We chat. His name is Adem. Under his protection, I can finally take a picture of him beside the little donkey. I attempt a few close-ups of his fearsome sentries—from afar, thanks to my zoom lens. With Adem holding him by the collar, I carefully inch over to Karakaş, one of the monsters. A growl tells me that I'd best keep my distance. These huge guard dogs hold nothing sacred, not even their masters' orders.

The shepherd points me to a clear water spring bubbling up in the middle of the prairie. It's the hot spring. We share my cookies and drink from the spring, the virtues of which he no longer remembers. It's probably best for curing Kangals of their compulsion to attack tourists.

In the next village, and for the very first time since my journey began, a couple kids beg me for gifts. I give one of them the little pin I'm wearing on my vest, and to the other, the last of my cookies. The countryside is magnificent, but I nearly step on a redheaded snake slithering across the path. It would almost have made me happy. Once you've confronted Kangals, you're not about to wimp out in the face of such a small enemy, not even one that's poisonous and meaner than sin. I feel cheerful, happy to have survived one of the dangers that I'd been menaced with a hundred times as much back in France as here in Turkey. From now on, however terror-stricken I may be, I won't give in to panic should I ever run across them again.

In a small village, as I am walking along the river that traverses it, the sound of laughing women from behind a low wall catches my ear. There are seven or eight of them, seated in a circle in the shade of the wall. In the center is a large sheet piled high with a mountain of billowing sheep's wool. They converse while carding the wool by hand. I wave to them, and they respond cheerfully. Emboldened, I go over to them, although I'm a little uneasy, because, once again, "one should not talk to women, especially in the absence of men" was what I'd been told. There's not a single man in the group. Two young girls in sweats step out of the house next door. Schoolgirls in their early teens, they are thrilled to put to use the various English words they've learned in class. The women are all wearing scarves over their hair and neck, and two of them, as I approach, rumple the cloth so as to also cover their mouth, a self-conscious gesture that I will see more and more often as I go east, where traditions are more deeply rooted. Several of them are in their forties. The youngest is the mother of the two little girls. She gets up, goes into the house, and comes back a few minutes later with a carafe of *ayran*, a refreshing beverage, and she offers me some with a smile. I linger and chat for a while. They tell me that when they have finished carding the wool, it will be used for a mattress. An atmosphere of simple happiness prevails here, and I am moved. The women show themselves to be no less curious than men: "*Memleket?* (Nationality?) *Nerede? Nereye? . . .*," the usual questions. I happily answer them. The encounter with Kangals lets me strangely feel more relaxed than I would usually be. "*Je suis Zen*" (I'm at peace), as my kids would say. I grow bolder yet and photograph them for a series of portraits, to which they agree, laughing.

"Where are the men?"

"Farther on, they're busy working on the village square."

So that's where I head, guided by the two young girls, delighted to have the foreigner all to themselves for a little while. In the time it takes to cover five hundred meters to where the men are, they bombard me with questions.

The men are hard at work. Pickaxes, shovels, and trowels in hand, they're building a waterhole for their animals next to a small communal building with a terra-cotta tile roof. The older villagers are seated in the shade of the oaks bordering the square, solemnly commenting on the work's progress, leaning on their canes or their backs against a tree trunk. A universal scene, familiar on every continent: the council of Elders, the wise men conversing in the shade of the largest tree on the village square. All just as cheerful as the women. And, of course, just as curious. Once again, I have to answer the same questions. The patriarchs are curious, too. A young man shouts to one man in the group, who is a little deaf:

"He has come from Istanbul on foot and is going to Erzurum!"

The old man points his cane to my calves, in disbelief, then utters a word that I will come to hear over and over again later on: "*Maşallah!*" (*mah'-shah-lah*).

The expression is used to convey surprise or admiration. It has its origins in the ceremony at which young Turks are circumcised, between eight and ten years old, and which marks their entry into manhood. They wear white clothes and parade about, followed by friends. Later, seated on their bed, they welcome visitors and receive gifts following their circumcision, which is conducted in public. During the procedure, they have to prove their bravery by neither screaming nor shedding a tear. The outfit they wear includes a silk belt embroidered with a word their friends repeat over and over again: "Maşallah," or literally, "See the marvel that God has desired." I'm pleased that my calves are one of the "marvels that God has desired." But it's not His work alone. I did my share as well, kilometer by kilometer, building their muscles!

One of the men hails another, "İsmail!" and then points to me. The man in question comes over to me and says:

"You're hungry."

It's not a question, but an affirmation. It's true that my frugal snack with Adem is long gone. İsmail Arslan asks me to grab my pack and follow him home, across from waterhole square. No sooner do we sit down than his wife places in front of us some cheese *börek* and tomato pilaf as if prepared expecting I would come. İsmail takes from his pocket a small leather bag from which he proudly pulls a copper stamp. He explains that he is the *muhtar*. The *muhtar*—in France, we would say the *le maire* (the mayor)—is elected along with four assistants to manage the town. The copper stamp, the unmistakable sign of his vested powers, serves to authenticate the official acts of his creation.

The meal is delicious, the *tandir* bread is fresh and has a wonderful aroma.

"Are you the baker?" I ask.

He smiles proudly.

"Yes, it's me . . ." He hesitates for an instant, then adds, ". . . my wife, actually."

She's dutifully seated on a sofa, silent and listening.

"And the yogurt, do you make that, too?"

"Yes, I . . . well . . . yes, she does."

When I get up to leave, I shake the *muhtar*'s hand appreciatively, then reach out to shake the hand of his wife, thanks to whom I have these tasty dishes. Arms dangling, she throws me a confused look. I've made a social blunder. I withdraw my extended hand. I'll try to keep this in mind: Turkish women can sometimes be spoken to but must never be touched.

This is the first time I've come across so much collective good humor in a village since my journey began. The memory of it will remain with me as a rural idyll of happiness. It has reminded me that the Silk Road I seek to follow is not that of trucks, but that of men and, given my experience in this village, of women, as well.

Nevertheless, I have to head back toward the highway, since the leaf of my map that I had in my pocket must have fallen out while I explained things with the Kangals, and, without it, I have no other choice but to return to the main road.

I don't like these busy thoroughfares, it's true, as for me, they are completely lacking in charm. Functional, practical, while they don't make a complete mess of nature, neither do they let it be; these are *neutral states* that, for me, will never inspire the slightest reverie or thought.

But since life has more than one trick up its sleeve, it's here, on this dreary highway lined with inexpressive poplar trees, that I have a most astonishing encounter. Visualize, at a junction of roads that seem to head nowhere, an old man sitting cross-legged, rooted to the spot not far from passing trucks. Set out in front of him is a basket of six eggs. The man is blind, and yet he has exceptionally bright, although inexpressive, blue-green eyes. He launches into a speech, and, as usual, I don't understand a thing, except that he wants to sell me his goods. I wouldn't know where to put them in my pack! I buy them from him but don't take them. He feels awkward and for a few steps tries to follow me to get me to take his treasure but finally gives up. The vision of this old man with angel eyes still haunts me today. No doubt because the marvelous holds our attention best. After all, what kind of a prankster god managed to concoct such a perfectly improbable scene on some lost Anatolian highway: an old man looking skyward, holding out eggs as if offering them up—where were they laid?—to a man who has walked from Paris!

A little farther along, a large man wearing a wool cap, with a striking white beard on a face leathered by the sun, is conversing with the donkey on which he is riding. The animal is already heavily burdened with long, thick branches. The scrawny donkey, barely visible under the limbs and the rider, is climbing a steep trail taking quick, deliberate steps and twitching its big ears, as if it didn't want to miss a word being said. A respectful distance back and taking small steps, his wife follows them, a slight woman, hunching her shoulders. The scene beckons me, I can't say why. Perhaps because it epitomizes a bygone era, like a picture book containing little dreamy shepherds, reapers painted by Brueghel, a mother seated in the grass who smiles at her little girl lying nearby; in short, a picture book in which nature is *present* and alive, whereby humankind's relationship with nature is one of equals, a relationship that is physical, a relationship of love. The picture book of a world in which old injustices still survived so tinted by time that we'd grown accustomed to them or artfully worked around them, and that we even came to consider as part of the landscape's virtues.

Here and there, in the villages, manure has been laid to dry in the spring sun. Cut into squares and stored until the following winter, it will serve as fuel in these desolate lands.

I head through Kurşunlu, and then Ilgaz the following day. In and of itself, walking no longer requires that I think about it. Like anyone in good shape, fit walkers are an ungrateful lot, hardly giving their body a thought.

The landscape has changed. I'm now back under an elevation of 1,000 meters, and the forest covers the slopes once more. I was more partial to the steppe with its endless horizons. In downtown Ilgaz, two old-fashioned pieces of equipment are on display that, in a few more years, will be bona fide antiquities: two driving carts and two ard plows. Here I have proof that in prioritizing the use of sturdy camels to transport goods, the peoples of Asia simply gave up trying to improve the cart. These particular vehicles, which must have been built fifty years ago, are so rustic that back home they'd look like something from the late Middle Ages: solid wheels, wicker bodywork, and no springs to dampen the impacts; they are neither sturdy nor lightweight. The wooden axles are still lubricated with beef tallow. Not a single piece of metal was used in their construction.

Starting in Ilgaz, I try to overnight in cities. It is simply easier to take care of my feet—yes, them again—in a hotel. Moving from city to city, without venturing into the villages, also lets me to cover ground more quickly. Paradoxically, slowpoke though I am—the same man who refuses to get into a truck, let alone a tractor—I'm in a bit of a hurry . . . and it's the Iranians' fault. Since to cross Turkey on foot I require at least eight to nine weeks, the Iranian Consulate in Paris made an exception and gave me a visa valid for two and a half months, instead of the usual two. But given the woes I've already experienced, I'm afraid of being delayed by another episode of poor health. In that case, I would run the risk of reaching the border after July 29, and my visa would have expired. An unthinkable scenario: it can take anywhere from two to four weeks to obtain a new entrance permit. Ideally, I ought to leave Turkey around July 14. Today is May 31. So I have a month and a half to cover from one thousand two hundred to one thousand three hundred kilometers (750 to 810 miles). That's doable, provided my guardian angel takes good care of me and I get ten days ahead of the walking schedule I set for myself. These complicated calculations keep me busy and tire me out at the same time: must the sweet and free folly of following the mythical Silk Road become so constraining and a source of such stress?

The distance I hike each day keeping as close as possible to the old caravan trail is determined entirely by the Silk Road's geography. To get to Kurşunlu, I walked thirty-three kilometers, and to reach Ilgaz, thirty-six kilometers. These are not arbitrary distances. Caravans traveled between thirty and forty kilometers a day; that is, nine to ten hours at the slow pace of a fully loaded camel. Yesterday's stopover cities were therefore spaced a one day's journey by camel apart, before motor vehicles shortened distances. Ever since a traveler can cover from five hundred to a thousand kilometers in one day (310 to 620 miles), the infrastructure intended for caravans is no longer needed. So the deserted caravansaries, now useless, have been allowed to fall . . . into ruin. The phenomenon is not limited to Turkey. In Europe, in France, starting in the early twentieth century, big cities experienced steady growth to the detriment of smaller communities. And in the villages where hotels have disappeared for lack of guests, town planners have built, thanks to the rebirth of rural tourism, guesthouses offering those who love to walk shelter at reasonable distances, a one-day journey on foot.

Hot weather has arrived. In the valley of the winding Devrez River, marshes were transformed into rice patties some thirty years ago. From the road overlooking the plain, the small, geometrically arranged squares of water are like mirrors, and above them glide storks and herons. There are great numbers of them throughout the region. Peasant farmers armed with shovels perform a tightrope act on the embankments around each parcel. In order to maintain the water level in each square, they've developed a clever grid of small drainage channels. The women, up to their knees in water, their broad dresses floating around them, are either planting fresh rice seedlings or pulling weeds. On the road, I catch sight of a young woman striding majestically toward me: she's leading a horse fitted with a packsaddle to which two huge wicker baskets have been hitched. The scene has a classic, even royal gracefulness about it. As I prepare to take her picture, she throws me a black smile: her mouth, completely toothless, is like the dark abyss of Hell.

The stretch from Ilgaz to Tosya is rough. It promises to be hot and long, if I'm to believe my map, which tells me it's a distance of thirty-eight kilometers. Overhead, a buzzard is lazily flapping its wide wings in the still air, looking for an updraft to glide on. I get what it's going through!

In a service station where I buy a bottle of fruit juice, a local farmer stops his tractor and rushes over to me pointing at my pack. "What is this motor on your back?" he asks. The Turks love machinery and know nothing about walking.

The road seems long, and I suddenly realize why. The distance shown on my map between two cities is the distance separating two crossroads, heading, for example, to Ilgaz or Tosya. But the centers of these two cities are themselves several kilometers from the main road. All in all, I'll have walked forty-six kilometers to reach Tosya. The last few are the toughest. It is a long, steep, straight climb to the top of the hill where the city is perched. One, two, then three kilometers go by, and I still don't see the city center. I'm thirsty. I filled my two-liter water jug twice today and bought several cans of coke and fruit juice. In all, more than six liters to fight dehydration—despite the salt pills I dutifully ingest. I'm crushed beneath my gear. If I find a comfortable hotel, I'll stay the day in Tosya to get some rest. But is there, in Tosya, a comfortable hotel?

Most often, in the smaller cities, there's only one hotel. So the choice is easy. I ask questions that I would never think to ask in France: Is there a shower? If so, does it have hot water? Even if the reply is yes, you still have to check. On one occasion, a hotel manager described a cold-water tap over an antique washstand at the end of a hallway as a "shower." And even when there is hot water, it's not always available. At seven in the morning, it may be boiling, at eight tepid, at nine it's cold, and in the evening, just as you check in, it's ice cold. Most often, rooms are shared, and so there's no key in the door. This is problematic: since each object stowed in my bag is absolutely indispensable, I can't risk having something stolen.

All climbs finally end. In Tosya, the first signs are a series of concrete buildings with dirt courtyards that have been raked and oiled and are heaped high with scrap metal. A common sight at the entrance to midsized towns: a hundred machine shops or auto repair garages for tinkering with cars, motorcycles, and agricultural machinery. As I crest the hill, I'm rewarded for all the effort. Off in the distance, Tosya's mountain is still covered in snow. The city, shaped like a cirque, backs up against a rocky cliff that protects it from the north wind. At this time of day, a blood-colored sun colors the walls of the city's little white houses with purple roofs, terraced like the steps of an ancient theater all the way into the center of the cirque where I am standing. Stage left: small grapevines enclosed by low walls provide a touch of green to the landscape. Stage right: a barren valley, long and narrow, sinks, beyond where the eye can see, into the heart of the Earth. It's magical. A harmonious balance between nature and manmade structures. This is the prettiest town I've seen since Istanbul.

The hotel—whew!—is comfortable. The pen pauses before scrawling the rate: regular or tourist? The tourist rate it is. But I could care less. The soles of my shoes are digging into my feet. My hips are bleeding, stinging from sweat and the friction of my hip belt. I unwind by taking a long shower, and the water is nearly hot. Then I tend to my wounds and stretch out for a half hour on the bed, allowing my strength to return little by little. The lamb bulgur I'm served gives me the rest of my energy back, and I scurry off in search of a cybercafé like a young bride to meet her betrothed for the first time. Unfortunately, for the fifteen computers, there's but one line. What's more, the lack of telephone infrastructure in the city means you can't always get a dial tone. But given how ready I am to overcome all the hassles that "civilization" has brought us, the God of communications grants me a connection for three seconds. Enough to find out that I have four messages. To hear them, I'll have to try again tomorrow. I turn in early. At 7:00 a.m., I'm awake, but so tired that I jump back to bed at eight and don't resurface till noon. I've slept for one full turn of the dial. That hasn't happened to me in thirty years.

In the afternoon, I set out to gather information on Tosya and the Silk Road. Jean-Baptiste Tavernier—yes, him again—states in his memoirs that he saw in this city "a beautiful mosque and one of the most attractive caravansaries." Tosya (the word means "three waters"), originally called Docea and then Zoaka during the Byzantine Empire, was invaded twelve times in twenty centuries. Incidentally, a conference is being held in the city to commemorate the seven hundredth anniversary of the Ottoman invasion of Anatolia. A retired professor, author of several historical studies on the city, tells me that a local tribe, the Lidyalı,* invented currency and minted the first coins. South of the city, but too far for me to make a detour, is the small village of Boğazkale (*boh-ah'-zkuh-luh*), the former city of Hattusa, the capital of the Hittite Empire.

Kürşat Konca (*kur-shaht' kon-djah*), a mechanical engineering student whose English is quite good, offers to be my guide. The beautiful shrine described by Tavernier still exists. Although called "the new mosque," it was constructed in the sixteenth century by a student of the famous Turkish architect, Mimar Sinan. It is he who, among other things, built the Süleymaniye Mosque in Istanbul. The imam proudly shows us around the edifice, which has undergone considerable maintenance and consolidation work, especially after a fire in 1913 as well as several earthquakes, the last in 1946. The temple can hold seven hundred of the faithful, a thousand on feast days. It boasts two curiosities. The first is a small column, flanking a window and neither cemented nor load-bearing, that can be made to rotate in place by hand. The legend goes that as long as it continues to turn, the mosque

---

* TN: The Lydians.

will be protected. The other oddity is a clock, whose walnut wood-work was recently restored and which recites its tick-tock litany next to the *mihrab*, the niche indicating the direction of Mecca. The imam doesn't know how old it is. No date has been found, either on the original frame or on the movement. The dial bears a name in its upper part—either that of the manufacturer or of the merchant: "*Makoulian*." Beneath the spindle of the clock's hands is written in French, in beau-tiful, ornate letters: "À Constantinople." It appears, therefore, to have been constructed before the city was renamed Istanbul, in the early fifteenth century. This is borne out by the fact that the reference is in Latin letters and not in Arabic characters. This is not surprising: in Constantinople, craftsmen working on clocks or other mechanisms in the Greek tradition were highly respected. I look over the piece care-fully: the "nails" indicating the hours differ as a function of whether the top of the symbol is turned toward the outside, or the inside, of the dial. It is, indeed, extremely fine workmanship.

On the other hand, and despite how hard I look, I find no sign of "one of the most attractive caravansaries" described by Tavernier. It has undoubtedly gone the way of the Ottoman houses, which, here as else-where, are crumbling for lack of repair. Still, I learn that, an hour and a half from Tosya in the village of Safranbolu, there is a kind of open-air museum, toured by a great many Turks because of its very beautiful tra-ditional houses. Proof that the country is indeed capable of celebrating its rich past. Why does everything take so long and happen so chaotically? This infuriates me, since—as if you didn't already know—I have a par-ticular interest in the preservation of caravansaries.

As the afternoon draws to an end, Kürşat and I go to the hammam where, once again, I see just how modest the Turks are. It's a bit of a surprise, as I'm used to locker rooms in the West where, in communal showers, nudity is the rule. The Turkish bath shower ceremonial takes place in very prescribed manner. We undress in a small room, then, cov-ered in a pareu-like towel from waist to toe, we enter a first superheated chamber, and then a second, which is like a steam room. The walls and benches are made of white marble. We splash ourselves, while chatting away, using a small dish, scooping up water from any of several different basins, also made of marble. After a half hour, a masseur drowns me in a deluge of soap, using a horsehair glove. In the changing room, lying on bunks and drinking a carafe of *ayran*, we continue gabbing away after an employee has bundled us up in thick terrycloth towels from head to foot. The caravanners, who, like me, took a good sweat bath out on the road, must have gone to the hammam: not a single caravansary that I visit throughout my journey has a washroom.

The city has one unique feature: almost all the vehicles are motorcycles equipped with sidecars. They're used for everything: to transport people and cargo, and, by and large, their owners manage small vineyards. They're all, of course, equipped with horns, and their drivers overuse them. A few young show-offs amuse themselves by driving about with the third wheel—that of the sidecar—in the air. Lightheartedness floats in the city air tonight, a noisy, generous cheerfulness.

In the evening, my guide's mother invites me for dinner. The family leads a European lifestyle. Neither the mother, a retired teacher, nor Kürşat's sister wear headscarves. Seated at table—and not on the ground, as in villages—we eat delicious *meze*: profuse, diverse, and colorful, in a word, royal. Emel, a slender teenager, is obviously thrilled to meet a Westerner, and his curiosity knows no bounds. Our discussion focuses primarily on the economic and political situation. Could the trial of the PKK's leader, Öcalan, be the first sign that the situation of the Kurds will be resolved? The Turkish economic crisis and double-digit inflation can be explained to a large extent by the considerable sums needed to maintain one of the world's largest armies. It's a well-known vicious circle: the soldiers earn double pay, owing to the conflict with the Kurds. So, quite naturally, they side, along with others of course, with the powerful and determined war party. Ruinous inflation is turning the poorest of the poor into street dwellers. And although the military's reputation remains positive, the prospect of having to do two years of service is no longer the source of any real pride among young intellectuals.

This dinner party revitalizes me: the limited exchanges that I've had in the villages, although they were often warm, did nothing to quench my thirst for connections and communication. Here, we have real conversation, all four of us, in a comfortable atmosphere of trust, and it's as though we all have something to gain from it. When it's time for farewells, Emel gives me a kiss. It's the only opportunity that I'll have during my entire journey to brush my stubbly beard against a woman's cheek.

As I leave the city very early in the morning in the direction of the large valley I saw at my arrival, I travel through the concrete-clad districts of the lower city that, fortunately, I hadn't seen two days prior. And so, for a time anyway, I was able to believe that I'd arrived at heaven's door. After four hours on foot, I finally locate what it would be a stretch to call a grocery. I buy a few cookies, which I nibble on farther down the road on an embankment. Meanwhile, a herd of cows grazing on grass in the shadow of a high cliff intrigues me; the animals seem to simply vanish, one after another. Too bad if it means a slight detour, I want to get to the bottom of this and figure out how the mountain can swallow up batches of cattle. Well, it is quite simple: there's an opening in the cliff such that, once their bellies are full, they can go digest their meal in the cool air of a troglodytic stable: their very own Ali Baba's cave.

The valley narrows as it climbs to the top of a mountain pass. Along the roadside at the summit sits a human torso. That of a legless old man who lives here, ten kilometers from the nearest occupied house. Beside him, a teakettle, black from soot, is purring away over a few sparse coals. He sleeps under the stars in a nearby thicket into which he drags himself at nightfall. A few good souls bring him water and food from time to time. Truckers toss him coins nonstop. I give him a note worth 250,000 liras, which he presses against his chest, and he launches into a long speech. I think he says something about Allah repaying me a hundredfold. A sum that, alas, still won't be very much. I'd rather He take better care of these beings who have so little. The image of the old man with his eyes turned skyward comes back to me: it would be fitting for the two of them to be able to keep each other company.

On the other side of the pass, I discover another plain of rice paddies, shining with the light of a thousand suns reflected in the water. Surrounding these perfectly aligned, flat parcels, rise up, in confrontational chaos, the Kös Dağı (*kuhs-dah'*) Mountains, still covered in snow. On the foothills of this massif, green soils supply an inexhaustible source of clay, which explains why so many brickyards lie along the road I'm traveling.

In late afternoon, I arrive in the village of Hacıhamza (*ha-djuh-ham'-zuh*), which was an important stopover along the Silk Road. The village is laid out in an unusual, interesting way. Unlike other places, there was no distinct caravansary in the village or anywhere nearby. Here, the caravansary was the village itself. It's still enclosed with walls made of a mix of earth and stone. It's a small, square fortress, about one hundred meters (328 feet) on each side. The houses built inside are supported by the perimeter wall. Each one has a balcony-like structure jutting out in corbelled construction, thus forming a tower for observation and defense. The village portal has disappeared. Inside, I find an immense, partially collapsed stable, about twenty meters (66 feet) across. The part that's still standing, a large brick archway of surprising finesse, is a good thirty meters (100 feet) long.

I strike up a conversation with a few of the faithful as they exit the mosque in the company of the imam. My presence is a source of concern to them: who can put me up? Once again, I feel like a hot potato. The imam suddenly spots someone and beckons to him. A small man comes over and plops himself down next to me on the bench where I've taken a seat. For a moment, Behçet (*beh'-chet*) says nothing, but then he turns to me and asks, in a thin, trembling voice:

"*Do you speak English?*"

Behçet Kumral is dressed in a plaid suit, artfully blending almost every possible shade of green. His gray mustache is thin; he is short in stature, frail, and his whole being seems like a fragile speck of dust in the universe. Piercing, black metal eyes bespeak a bright mind. As for many Turks, a two- or three-day-old beard gives him a slightly neglected appearance, despite an impeccable suit and shirt. Behçet is a retired farmer. A year ago, upon hearing that an Englishman was planning a visit, the friend of some friends, the seventy-seven-year-old decided to learn the language of Shakespeare. In the end, the Englishman never came, but this little man kept right on studying. We chat. My friend appears to savor the admiration he arouses in those around us, for, in the entire village, only he can speak a foreign language. A half hour or so later, he invites me to follow him, leading me up the main street with shuffling steps, stopping to pick up a few pieces of fruit for dinner.

Behçet never went to school; he learned to read all on his own, deciphering sentences in old newspapers. He's a passionate book lover. He has a personal library, something I had yet not seen in any village household since leaving Istanbul. His favorite story: *Don Quixote de la Mancha*. I'm honored when my little friend shows me his books, one by one, especially those by French authors, translated into Turkish, for which he has a particular reverence: Voltaire, Descartes, Rousseau, Malebranche . . .

"Have you read Malebranche?"

I admit that no, I have not. We find some common ground while discussing Bernardin de Saint-Pierre. My little friend also has two encyclopedias in his collection, and finally he confesses that, although he has been studying English, he has almost never had the opportunity to use it, and so he asks me to speak slowly. He has some trouble handling abstract vocabulary, pausing to think a long while before articulating his thoughts. He's elated, and his joy speaks volumes. He wants to do everything he can for me, thrilled as he is to have a guest from abroad in his home.

"Should we walk a bit while we wait for dinner? If that is your wish, of course . . ."

A little embarrassed, I judiciously reply that, if that is what he would like to do, then I would be very happy to accompany him, but that I have just traveled thirty-eight kilometers, so . . .

"You know, if you want to stay—a day, two days, a week—my house is yours."

The door opens, revealing a group of four high-spirited, mischievous-looking kids. These are my host's grandchildren, whose parents occupy the upper floors. It's clear there's a strong bond between these little ones and their grandfather. It strikes me that normally only boys are allowed to approach strangers like myself. Here, however, the two little girls and two little boys are treated as equals. The man who owns books has no interest in ostracizing women. Later on, back home in France, with thanks for having sent him their photograph, I receive a letter from Behçet written in a marvelous, grandiose style, and ending in the words: "*My grandchildren kiss your hands.*"

Although in every other village my presence occasions a parade of inquiring eyes, here in Behçet's home, I am finally incognito, as it seems that no one would dare bother this patriarch. Early the next morning, I jot down a short thank you note for him, leaving a few small gifts for his grandkids, and I open the door as quietly as possible so as to slip away . . . "à l'anglaise."* But then out he pops from the kitchen. He had been waiting for me. Breakfast is ready, he tells me, there's no way he is going to let me leave on an empty stomach. Just like last night, he hardly touches anything but watches me eat with such delight that I'm not the least bit bashful about feasting on everything that his wife has prepared. He accompanies me all the way to the main road. His wife, from the balcony, bids me farewell, waving her arms in the air. What a refreshing thought that, here and there throughout the world, there are still human beings as so fundamentally unique as this little man.

It rained overnight. The clouds rush toward the mountain peaks, which they soon swallow up. The Kızılırmak River churns its muddy waters and slams into the rocky massif, which it then hugs making a westward turn before heading due north, where, at last, it spills into the Black Sea. Motionless amid these moving elements, the rice paddies are visited by herons, which move across them taking cautious steps.

Yesterday, at my stopover point, one of my Achilles tendons started to bother me. It didn't go away overnight; rather, this morning, both my tendons are reminding me that they exist. Did I not get enough rest? Fail to drink enough water? Were my bootlaces too loose? At noon, I take a

---

* TN: *Partir à l'anglaise* = literally, "to leave like the English do," meaning "to take French leave," "to slip away unnoticed."

nap, stretching and massaging my painful ligaments, and I drink much more than I feel like consuming.

I should be able to reach Osmancık without too much difficulty. The road is magnificent. I move from one plain to another through narrow ravines where, so as to widen the road for trucks, they dynamited the rock and sliced into the mountain. Here now is another plain, with rice and cereal crops as far as the eye can see. And over there, in a half circle, a high chain of tawny mountains. Washed by the rain overnight, the air is so clear that the mountains appear near. Yet I'd have to hike for an entire day if I wanted to reach them.

At Osmancık, after forty-six kilometers, I look, in vain, for the "two most comfortable caravansaries" described by my trusty Tavernier. The old, fifteen-arch bridge he visited four centuries ago is still there, closed to traffic. But to spruce it up a bit, it has been coated with cement from top to bottom. I feel for the poor old stones, which must be terribly bored in their dreary sarcophagus of gray. The Turks love cement. On the *Samsun*, a retiree even said to me: "I buy stock in cement companies, as they keep going up." His stock is not all that goes up: so does the concrete.

The city is of no interest whatsoever. Neither of two hotels offers showers or hot water, and so it's hard to choose, as the rooms in one are just like the rooms in the other: unbelievably filthy, noisy, cramped, and so ugly that I suddenly feel depressed. Commanding a view of the city is an enormous crag, at the top which a fortress is about to lose the very last stones of its very last wall. Cement couldn't climb that high. Fatigue starts to get the best me. I am well aware that it's important to fight back against these waves of melancholy that often grip the solitary foreigner, and I take heart by reciting the Arab proverb: *"Esteem for those who travel, disdain for those who stay at home."*

CHAPTER VI
VENI, VIDI . . .

Between Osmancık (*os-mahn'-djuk*) and Gümüşhacıköy (*gu-mu-shah'-djuh-kuh*), the route heads into an imposing defile—or steep-sided narrow pass—a real danger zone. The confined roadway, near a roaring, turbulent river, slips between two smooth, sheer granite cliffs. Since the mountain stream must have once regularly flooded the roadway, a tunnel was dug just for it. The climb is steep. At the base, my altimeter reads 450 meters (1,480 feet); it will register 1,000 meters (3,280 feet) when I finally step out on the plateau.

Halfway up, the sweat pouring from my body by the liter, a car stops. The young driver offers to give me a ride. After I decline his invitation, he pulls off the road a little farther on, cuts the engine, and walks back to me with a bottle of cologne. It's a custom here. In restaurants, diners are offered a splash as they get up to leave, rubbing their hands and sometimes their face with it. I'm not big on perfume, and so I refuse. Not a bit discouraged, Kamil Zeyrek returns to his car, and this time he offers me an armful of promotional giveaways: pens, calendars, maps . . . I tell him that my pack is already too heavy . . . He expresses such disappointment that I wind up accepting a pen and a map. I'll offer them to one of my hosts. Seated in the shade of a broad stand of beech trees, we chat. Kamil, a traveling salesman, is passionate about walking and trekking and wants to know every last detail with respect to my hiking technique, what's in my bag, how good my boots are, my sleeping gear.

"Watch out for terrorists around Tokat. Don't walk too early in the morning or late in the evening," he tells me, before heading off to meet with his clients.

The view from the top looks out onto emerald green glens. In front of them is a plateau, about ten kilometers wide, where, thanks to a nearby dam, farmers employ large-scale irrigation. I stop in a roadside bistro where I gulp a glass of fruit juice and dry my sweat. From here on out, I have a bird's eye view of the Merzifon plain, several hundred meters below. This vast flatland, bulging here and there with several gentle hills and some sort of leaning sugarloaf formation, is atremble in the blistering heat and extends out all the way to the horizon.

In Gümüşhacıköy, the one and only hotel affords a minimum level of comfort. Once again, there's no shower. And the toilets down the hall are perfectly disgusting.

Across from the hotel stands the *Mehmet Paşa* Caravansary. Or at least what remains of it, as its exterior walls have been destroyed. All that has survived are a few ground-level cells on each side of a central alleyway. Their attractive geometry was spoiled when a line of streetlamps was erected, an attempt at modernization. At each end, an arched doorway constructed of alternating white-and-black stones would have been delightful . . . had they not committed architectural abomination by erecting a cement clock tower atop one of them. The edifice was four hundred and seventy years old, a venerable old age, when it was disfigured by this off-white monstrosity, less than fifty years ago. To accomplish this massacre, the gateway arch was broken and then crowned with a support structure of gray cement. The inoperative clock is spewing long trails of rust down the fake stones etched in the concrete.

In the shadow of the clock tower, in the small square next door where a wheat market is held, the great hammam, as old as the caravansary, suffers somewhat from being right nearby but has thankfully managed so far to have dodged the mania for cement. The same for a mausoleum, which is more interesting for the fervor it generates than for its originality of its architecture, another of the city's curiosities.

In early morning, while I was putting away a *çorba* (*chor'-ba*) (soup) in a small restaurant on the square before hitting the road, the owner calls over to me.

"In France, are you ruled by republican oligarchy, like we are?"

I've barely had time to understand what he said when the other patrons enthusiastically join in on the discussion. Some of them want me to comment. Eager to leave, I steer clear of a political discussion that my microscopic Turkish vocabulary would have made ludicrous anyway.

As I'm closing in on Merzifon, a police car stops, and the driver asks me to hop in.

"I want to converse with you, I need to practice my English."

At least he stated things clearly.

I manage to convince him to meet up with me in town so that we might chat in a more relaxed environment over tea. The first house upon entering Merzifon is a mosque, which, interestingly, is in the process of being demolished. One of the workers comes over to me and questions me in French: he wants to know where I'm from and where I'm going: in short, always the same questions.

Setin Yusuf worked for seventeen years in France, most of the time undocumented. He lived in a neighborhood of Paris I know very well, Rue Myrha in the Goutte d'Or district, on the east side of the eighteenth arrondissement. On vacation there two years ago, he suffered a severe heart attack. He can no longer work, has no medical insurance and no pension. Setin has time on his hands and makes himself useful by preparing tea for his retired friends as they tear down the shrine in order to build a bigger one. Originally designed for one hundred and fifty people, the mosque is too small now that the neighborhood has grown, so it has to make way for an edifice that can accommodate at least five hundred worshippers. The men who are here, all retired construction workers, take great pleasure in this undertaking, as it allows them to express their faith while putting their know-how to good use.

Setin pointed me to a hotel that is a somewhat short on comfort. But probably since he was promised a baksheesh, the very reasonable room rate I was initially quoted is adjusted upward. Two hours later, the price we agreed upon to wash my shorts and two pairs of socks has also doubled. Unwilling to be taken for a sucker, I relocate to a more comfortable establishment . . . only to forget a travel wallet that I always carry on my person and that holds a thousand dollars, my reserve funds in case of an emergency. The next morning, when I realize that I forgot it, I sheepishly head back to see the manager, who, without a word, hands me my bag with everything in it, his eyes filled with reproach.

In Merzifon, not far from the mosque, a once-beautiful stone caravansary is now in shambles. In keeping with a common practice, the revenue it generated served to maintain the religious building. The mosque is in excellent condition, while the caravanners' inn is in ruins. Both were constructed in 1666. One enters through a paved courtyard—an area of about twenty square meters (215 square feet)—through a monumental portal, the only opening to the outside. Two fountains provided water, one for the animals, the other for the men. Around the shaded courtyard were situated a dozen or so large rooms equipped with bunk beds. The storerooms and stables can be reached by a ramp a half-story high, above which still exist six corbelled rooms, for use by the stable boys. On the second floor, a circular gallery provides access to forty or so individual rooms. Each dwelling is equipped with a fireplace. Unfortunately, the roof is failing, and the entire building looks like it will soon collapse.

Across from the entrance to the caravansary is another ancient monument, a covered market called a *bedesten*, and it, too, is in very poor condition. It's a vast space comprising nine domes. Despite several attempts, I'm unable to get past the padlocked oak doors covered in rusty iron sheets designed to keep people out.

The following day, I decide to put the highway behind me, along with its many trucks and loud noise. My feet have finally fully triumphed over my hiking boots. The day off in Tosya reinvigorated me. I can therefore go wandering off once more into meadows, orchards, and hazelnut-tree Edens, which are so abundant in this region. I head down a small road that skirts the Ortaova military aviation camp for a long while, spiked with miradors in which the figures of heavily armed soldiers can be seen moving about.

A young boy, about twelve, rides past me on his bike. Intrigued by the unusual appearance of this strange pedestrian, he does an acrobatic U-turn, greets me, and then subjects me to an impressive interrogation. When I've satisfied his curiosity, he gives me his verdict: "Your performance," he says, "isn't bad . . . for an old man." I like his candor, and I continue by his side until we reach his village. Out on the village square, twenty buyers or so are huddled around a van packed with fruits and vegetables. They desert the merchant and form around us a kind of a silent guard of honor, simmering as they are with unasked questions. Workmen on the roof of a mosque under construction stop what they are doing and shout:

"*Gel, çay!*"

As he begins to realize the effect that my presence is having and wanting to get the most out of it, the kid, whose name is Ender Saka, yells back in a voice loud enough to be heard by the men on the roof:

"He is sixty-one and has walked all the way from Istanbul."

Then, satisfied with the results and like an actor who wants to keep the suspense building, he pedals back over to me. A swarm of kids swoops in, but Ender has my best interest in mind and turns out to be a first-rate guard. He allows them to follow us for one kilometer, then finally chases them away. He has thus preserved all his inside information. He once again fires several volleys of questions at me and then abandons me after informing me that I'll find a village and a restaurant three kilometers on.

There is neither a village nor a restaurant. After walking for two full hours, on the shores of a man-made lake, some country folk getting ready to eat invite me to partake in their meal. The sun is beating down hard and there isn't even the tiniest grove in sight, so we eat in the shade of the tractor's trailer. My hosts are the descendants of Azerbaijanis who came to the region in 1914. They'd like me to stay for supper and to spend the night, but their village is too far off my route. Their daughter, Fatime, has never had her picture taken, and so she begs me to take her portrait.

I take a snapshot of their twins as well, a boy and a girl, black as pitch, filthy, snotty-nosed and endlessly babbling.

The earthen berm holding back the lake dominates the plain. From here, I see five villages and can identify three of them on my map. I have no trouble finding my bearings, and so I head off cross-country. In Sahigili, the *muhtar*, Mustafa Müjde, offers to put me up for the night. It's a pleasant evening. Every one of the small village's able-bodied residents comes parading out to see the curious traveler. Two young people who speak English fairly well serve as interpreters. In the morning, they're nowhere to be found, and the master of the house and of the village, convinced that I don't speak a word of Turkish, avoids speaking to me. The situation makes us both uncomfortable, and I head off posthaste.

My next stop is in the big city of Amasya. The small road leading there snakes its way through a valley among profuse and luxuriant orchards. Turkey, and this very region in particular, is considered the birthplace of the cherry tree (*kiraz*). The harvest is in full swing, and so clusters of women are perched on scaffolds, carefully filling wicker baskets. Only men address me, encouraging me to eat as many as I want. I gorge myself on the sweet, fresh, and pulpy cherries, as well as on this friendly encounter, sweet and rich, earthy. Of course, it's a diet that does nothing to help the case of diarrhea I've been suffering from over the past two days, and I have to set my gear down in a panic several times behind the shrubs between the orchards and the road.

Around noon, a cold rain beats down on the region. For the last five kilometers leading into the city, the road resembles a highway. Zooming past, the trucks spray clouds of ice-cold water that thrash me, and so, when I finally catch sight of the first dwellings, I'm soaked and chilled, with a belly full of liquefied cherries. My ordeal is still not over: the suburbs seem to go on forever. Amasya is set in a small, narrow valley, and I have to walk more than three kilometers to reach downtown. Exhausted and frozen to the bone, I hop into bed at 7:00 in the first hotel I stumble upon, foregoing dinner, and I get a long night of dreamless sleep.

By early morning, the hot sun is back. Amasya, rich in history, is also an attractive city, where the reflections of Ottoman houses, which for once have been preserved, shimmer in the river. Squeezed into a kind of canyon, overlooking the city is a fort that was built, I'm told, by Mithridates. The kings of Pontus who, in the second century BCE, reigned over almost all of Anatolia made this their capital. Founded by the Hittites, conquered by Alexander the Great and then by the Romans and the Mongols of Tamerlane, under the Ottomans the city became a stronghold from which they launched all their attacks on the Persians. Traditionally, the Sultan's heir came to Amasya in order to put his education into practice and learn to govern.

My hotel faces the steep wall towering over the city center. Cave-tombs were carved in the rock for the kings of Pontus. I have every intention of taking a day off to rest here and use the time to gather information on the Silk Road. But it's a daunting task. As in every Turkish city I've visited where they in fact have a tourist office, it's extremely bare-bones and entirely incapable of providing even the most basic information. Two young people, neither one proficient in a foreign language, hand out leaflets. The same disappointment at the museum, whose director, Ahmet Yüdje, a trained archeologist, is thrilled about the recent discovery of a Roman road. But the trading history of the caravanners is a mystery he has never tried to unravel, no more than anyone else has. He refers me to a local celebrity, Ali Kamil Yaltchin, who, he claims, can shed light on the question and who also speaks English. I hurry over to the *Ilk Pansiyon* (Boarding House N° 1) the man manages. But he's away on a trip. The house he renovated is exquisite. I rent a room and move out of my dive hotel forthwith.

It's an Ottoman house dating from the early part of the last century. Of earth and wood construction, it has three stories with the first floor partially underground. A small paved courtyard, shaded by two trees, a walnut and a willow, is perfect for a siesta or aimless palaver. On display there are some ancient agricultural and household tools, part of the owner's collection. An outdoor kitchen is used for grilling meats, so odors don't spread throughout the house. On the second floor are the kitchen and service quarters. The third floor is accessed through a porch with a double stairway, sheltered beneath a canopy supported by columns, and opens out onto two large reception rooms. Abundant windows protected with wrought-iron grilles flood them with light. The top floor is divided into three bedrooms, one of which is adorned with a coffered ceiling decorated with stylized, pastel-colored abstract animal motifs. Ali Kamil installed bathrooms in the closets originally used to store bed linens during the day. I decide not to stay in the house itself, but in a small bedroom—a veritable refuge—whose entrance is hidden in a shady corner of the courtyard.

The Turks, originally a nomadic people, live in their houses as if they were in tents. Almost always, a single room is used for welcoming guests, for eating, and for sleeping: this is the original tent. The floor here is always covered with rugs, even in the most modest homes. Among more well-off Turks, the rugs also climb up walls and onto bunks. Floor pillows that were part of tent living are still ubiquitous, but increasingly the couch is becoming the one obligatory piece of furniture in Turkish houses. Indeed, by its transformable nature, it's suitable for both conversation and sleeping. As for meals, people still eat seated on the floor, the various dishes on a large platter set directly on the ground.

I also wander about for some time outside the "Sultan Beyazit II" Mosque, the city's largest Muslim temple. The edifice, as elsewhere in Turkey, plays more than just a religious role. It's also a center of community life. In the wee hours of the morning, after their ablutions in the attractive fountain near the entrance, the faithful go to prayer. Afterward, they may opt for tea in the neighboring parlor, or go for stroll in the shady gardens. Students have at their disposal a very handsome adjoining library, said to be full of rare books. I discover a work written by a Frenchman, Albert Gabriel, in 1934. In it, he provides abundant descriptions of Turkish monuments in Anatolia, but, unfortunately for me, this architect, who held an important position in Istanbul early in the century, says everything, absolutely everything about Turkish mosques, mausoleums, and fountains but shows no interest whatsoever in structures designed for merchants, the very ones, as I've already said, with which I've become so enthralled. Perhaps, as they were too commonplace at the time, they didn't stand out as particularly original, and so from an architectural point of view, no one thought them to be of any interest. I'm nevertheless very disappointed, once again, to have failed to find some trace of caravan buildings.

But I do spot, however, on an old photo of the city taken in 1928 from high atop the cliffs overlooking it, two enormous structures. They're the caravansaries where travelers were housed. So, for two thousand years, Amasya occupied a strategic position on caravan routes going east. It was also a staging post for traders journeying overland from the Black Sea toward Syria. Today, one of the two *hans* is gone. The other is in ruins. In the several cells on the ground floor that haven't collapsed, artisans have set up shops where they work with wood, iron, and copper. The domes of a large *bedesten* next door, whose second floor has been destroyed, still provide cover for bustling business activity below. On June 12, 1919, Atatürk, who at the time was still known only as Mustafa Kemal, gathered in Amasya a large contingent of his friends and laid the foundations for the soon-to-be-established Turkish Republic. Amasya, ever loyal, commemorates the event with a festival that people speak to me at great length about, telling me how disappointed they are that I'm not planning to stay three more days to be here for it. For today is June 9, and it's simply unfathomable to people that I would have come here for any reason other than the festival. But the soles of my feet are burning: I have to get walking. I often wonder about this phenomenon. What impels me to keep going? What unstoppable force, despite being barely awake, drives me out onto the road? My difficulty isn't walking but stopping, for I've achieved that special state of physical plenitude: as soon as most of the fatigue is gone—and that happens very quickly given my conditioning over the past few weeks—I long to get walking, to keep on walking.

It has been observed, among pilgrims in particular, that once an average of thirty kilometers a day has been reached, physical conditioning neutralizes our sensations of the body. In almost all religions, the pilgrimage ritual seeks as its main objective to elevate the soul by putting the physical body through hard work: the feet touch the ground, but the mind is nearer to God. This explains the intellectual side of walking, which laypeople fail to grasp. Those who've never experienced such an adventure themselves most often think that walking is suffering. That might be the case for those who, out of masochism or religiosity, inflict tortures on themselves, walking on their knees or barefoot on stones. But for distances less than thirty kilometers a day, walking is pure joy, a wonderful drug.

Solitary walking forces us to confront ourselves, freeing us from the limitations of the body as well as those of our usual environment that restrict us to conventional, acceptable, and prepackaged ways of thinking. After a very long walk, pilgrims almost always believe that they've been transformed. This is because they encounter a part of themselves on the road that they would no doubt never have discovered without such a long face-to-face experience. This is also why greater emphasis should be placed on solitary walking, which of course doesn't preclude happily meeting up with friends during stopovers. The advantage that a Silk Road pilgrim or caravanner has over me lies therein. In the evening, with other walkers, whether they all share their same beliefs, fatigues, and discoveries or not, they can exchange and compare sensations, their moments of awe, and submit to scrutiny the ideas they've developed throughout the day.

On the morning of June 9, having risen early, I eat a piping hot and delicious *çorba*—the staple of my meals—near the *Ilk Pansiyon*, when five minibuses full of soldiers in camouflage fatigues, armed with heavy rifles and machine guns and wearing bullet-proof vests, drive up and park out in front of the restaurant. An armored vehicle pulls up to join them. They were on patrol all night long on roads in the surrounding area. Kamil mentioned "terrorists" to me around Tokat. I'm not there yet, but the army's activities prove that, here too, security should not be taken for granted.

At 7:30, just as I am leaving the last houses behind me, two schoolboys, perhaps twelve years old, come up to me asking the usual questions, this time in English. They want me to talk about my travels in front of their classmates, who as it so happens are going to start the day in English class. I hesitate for a moment, as I like to take advantage of the cool hours of the morning for walking and today's destination is over thirty-five kilometers away. But they're persuasive, so I go along with the idea: I always have a hard time saying no to children. Flanked by the two youngsters—rather proud of having snagged such a prize—I head through the front entrance. The children are all in uniform. Everyone's wearing a blue blazer: white shirt and gray pants for the boys, white blouse and pleated gray skirt for the girls, who, in addition, are wearing a blue-gray chador. Forewarned by one scamp who is scampering on ahead, the teachers are ready and waiting for me in their lounge. We drink tea, of course, and then my guides take over once again and lead me to their classroom and their teacher.

A tiny woman, Öznur Özkan stands no taller than her pupils. But she must be one heck of a language teacher, because the children's level of English is excellent. In ten minutes, I've explained my undertaking. They listen enthusiastically and then bombard me with questions about my route, motivations, family, and about Paris. I answer everything, but they still want to know my favorite animal and the Turkish singer I like best. When the tide of questions finally ebbs, at least forty-five minutes have gone by. As for me, I tell them how surprised I am by their chadors. Öznur—who is not wearing one—explains that this is a religious middle school. In the public system, all distinctive religious symbols are forbidden. A particularly inquisitive and enthusiastic young girl, the only one in her class not wearing a chador, asks her teacher if she can accompany me to the school gate. After the souvenir photo, permission is granted, and only two pupils stay behind in the classroom. All the others rush to follow me out, thrilled to escape their regular lessons for a few minutes. I depart with an escort of even more circling and chirping children than when I traversed the vast schoolyard on my way in. All the children give me their names. As I head out the gate, they still don't give up but run along the park overlooking the road. Then they just stand there, waving and wishing me a good journey at the top of their lungs, until a turn in the road finally takes me out of view.

I traverse a village whose main street is called "the Silk Road" and a little farther on a hamlet named "the Silk Village." At least I know I'm on the right road. But those are the only signs. On a mountainside overlooking the road, the slogan *"ne mutlu Türküm diyene"* has been scrawled with large white stones, which I translate as "the greatest happiness is Turkey." Some inhabitants have painted this slogan on their houses. Expressions of national pride like this will crop up again and again. Other slogans, drawn with white stones, sing the praises of the region, the army, or the *jandarmas*. Speaking of which, the army is omnipresent in these parts.

I spot two soldiers positioned along the roadside next to a mounted machine gun; farther on, a small group of soldiers are stopping cars and trucks. They're taken aback to see a someone on foot. They make a few jokes about me but leave me alone, wishing me happy trails.

I give up on the main highway and head for the back roads. In two days' time, I will reach the city of Zile. This evening, if I get that far, I'll spend the night in a village whose name on my map has attracted my eye: Kervansaray.

The weather is hot and stormy. At noon, I stop in the hamlet of Yıldız (*yeel'-duhz*). I buy a few reserves from the *bakkal* and sit down in the neighboring teahouse. The customers are dying to ask questions, but none dare. A poorly-shaved, gaunt man with sunbaked skin comes in and seems to make an impression on everyone. Mustafa Asil glances around the room, spots my bag, and then, quite naturally, comes over and sits at my table. It's what the others were all waiting for. They grab their chairs and form a circle around us. While I answer their questions, they bring me more cups of tea than I can drink. Mustafa, with small, bright eyes like a shrew, writes his name in my notebook, and then another name on a blank page, then tells me why.

"If you make it to Kervansaray this evening, stay at this man's house; he's my friend, Göz Bektaş (*guhz behk-tash*). Tell him I sent you, you'll receive a warm welcome."

Like the children this morning, the curious step out onto the teahouse terrasse to watch me leave, waving good-bye until I disappear around the first bend in the road. The climb promises to be long and hard. I'm currently at an elevation of 450 meters. Kervansaray, fifteen kilometers distant, is at 1,200 meters (a difference of 2,460 feet). The storm that was threatening finally erupts. A young lad catches up to me, out of breath. He wants a cigarette. I haven't got one. But I'm surprised that he would run so hard just to have a smoke. He tells me to wait and points to a man with a gun over his shoulder at a switchback in the road below, struggling to catch up with us. Since the boy doesn't seem hostile, I decide to wait. The armed man, while walking, has taken the rifle from his shoulder and is now balancing it over his right forearm, barrel downward, the stock wedged up against his body. Friend or foe? The kid, sitting on the roadway and still trying to catch his breath, is not in the least bit threatening, or even nervous. While the other fellow approaches, I tell him where I'm from and where I'm going. When the man with the rifle finally reaches us, he breathes from his stomach, making his little potbelly jiggle. The boy repeats in Turkish what I just told him.

"A tourist?" the chubby one asks.

I answer with a nod. They both look at me calmly, then without a word head back down the hill. I'll never know if the kid ran so quickly just for a cigarette, or in order to warn me about an ambush. What was going through their minds? It's a mystery.

The village of Kervansaray sits on a barren, undulating peneplain. Out of the crater of a marble quarry come huge, flatbed trucks on which enormous blocks seem to balance perilously, no doubt only by the grace of Allah's blessing. The downpour came and went but in combination with the altitude has helped to cool the air. Stables and houses alternate, humble structures of earth and wood. Mud-caked children play in muddy streets. I barely escape the contents of a bucket of dirty water, hurled out onto the street through an open door. As I approach, daily life comes to a halt, the men and children stop to watch me, older women cover their nose and mouth with their headscarf. Isn't this the same reflex Western women have when they cover their face with their hand to express discomfort, confusion, or embarrassment?

Göz Bektaş's house is the very last one. He's a huge man, his oversize face dashed with a large mustache. Upon hearing the name of his friend

Mustafa, he immediately throws open his door for me. My host's given name is not *Göz* (eye), which is a sobriquet, but Demirci (day-meer'-djee). His nickname means that he has a determined and cunning glance. He's not a rich man: he has four cows and fifteen hectares of stingy land. But he knows how to share. He belongs to the Muslim sect called the Alevis (Shiite). Aside from one old, thin man, wrinkly as an apple, my arrival at Göz's house, fails to attract the usual procession. The village lacks the collective warmth that so charmed me all the way to Amasya. I noticed the silent suspicion of the man with the gun, and the same thing again when I asked several passersby for directions. Is it the ruggedness of mountain living? The presence of these armed men, both soldiers and civilians, encountered over the course of the morning reveals a state of undeclared war. Are there combat zones nearby? I ask but receive no reply.

One of Göz's sons works in interior decorating in Istanbul in the winter and spends summers here to help out on the farm. He's perhaps the reason why the house, as rustic as they come, is nevertheless quite neat and tidy.

"How many children do you have, Göz?"

"Four."

"I've seen two girls and your son; is the fourth a boy or a girl?"

"No, I have four sons and five daughters."

Girls don't count. A fact that doesn't spare them from hard labor. Two of them are crouched in front of the fireplace, stoking a few embers as they help their mother prepare the meal. Before long, Sati, the youngest, sets some sort of high tripod in front of us and places a large platter on top of it, followed by the food. Cracked wheat, tomatoes, onions, and yogurt are served with traditional flat bread, warmed in the hearth. Göz serves the tea, which he draws from a samovar. At the end of the meal, Sati, holding a jug of water, plants herself in front of her father and holds out a wash basin and a towel. Without getting up from his seat, her father washes his hands and mouth. He invites me to do the same. I refuse, as in my eyes this forced servility is humiliating to the young girl and I'm reluctant to have gentle Sati serve me in such a manner. I'll wash up on my own . . . if I can find a fountain, that is.

I don't find one and head out after dark on a risky expedition to the toilet, out behind the house. I finally manage to grope my way to the wooden outhouse perched atop a few wet and slimy steps. The roof must have blown off in a storm, so I can contemplate the stars, my buttocks poised over the manure pit.

I sleep in a bedroom opposite the sitting room where Göz first welcomed me; it also serves as his bedroom. The house, just like all others in the village, has five rooms: the kitchen is in the middle, and the four other rooms are at the corners. The central room, heated by the fireplace, is where the cooking takes place and is also used to stow various agricultural implements. The four other rooms, all rather cramped, have rough lumber floors covered with linoleum, and two of them have rugs. Everyone is constantly removing their shoes as they go from the kitchen, with its bare dirt floor, into the side rooms. There is a minimal amount of furniture. The bed is a bunk with nailed slats on which a mattress has been set. A very narrow board has been attached to two of the walls about two meters up. It's the clothes rack. It's spiked with nails: these are the coat hangers. Carefully folded away in a corner is a pile of blankets that no doubt come in handy during the four months of winter, since the fireplace is the only source of heat.

Like their houses, everyone in Kervansaray wears identical clothing. The women, beneath sweaters, some bright-colored, wear long dresses made of heavy, off-white material that drapes to the ground. They wear headscarves. I've noticed that the older women cover their mouth and nose in front of me only. Göz and the old man who paid us a visit, like all the men in the village, wear a cotton or wool vest over their shirt. The son is in a shirt without a vest. Although in cities it's commonplace for men to wear a tie—Turks are not very fond of the casual "French look"— here, shirts are worn open-necked. A low rubber shoe, like a snow boot worn barefoot, is the rule. Last, all the men wear caps. I'm definitely not sporting the local look.

Göz knows a few things about the Silk Road. Caravans heading south to Sivas by way of Zile used to pass this way so as to avoid the *paşa*'s heavy-handed tax collector in Tokat. He doesn't know, however, where the caravansary was that gave its name to the village. It's clear, however, that the distance from Amasya to Kervansaray, after the thirty-six kilometers I traveled today, would represent a demanding stage for caravans—demanding because of the 800-meter (2,625-foot) change in elevation.

At dawn, Göz walks with me to the edge of the village. The next town, Yaylayolu, was formerly called Bacul (*bah'-djool*). The houses, based on a design like that of farmhouses in the Alps, are built atop the stable, such that in the winter the herd does the job of a furnace. The village was inhabited by Greek Christians for half a millennium. They left around 1550, according to what an old man from the village tells me. But is information like that of any real use to me? And what is its source? How many details were changed, how many were lost until finally, when telling his village's story, he would come to sum up the life there with this bit of information? And what went on during the second half of the millennium? Does the man have a clue?

Bacul-Yaylayolu has probably changed little since, in 47 BCE, Pharnaces's troops traveled through the village on their way to battle. In a courtyard, I take a photo and chat with two women who are weaving a kind of long *kilim* with a loom that must have been from around forty-seven years before Jesus Christ, too. The rug, which must be at least twenty meters in length, is attached to a stake at one end of the courtyard. On the other end, a woman seated on the ground is pulling on the heddle so as to keep the threads tight. In the middle, the piece is suspended from a rudimentary tripod consisting of three long poles. The weaver is crouched down, sliding the shuttle to the right and to the left on the loom itself: two simple pieces of wood.

I photograph two other women as well, superbly hieratic holding their large, four-handled platter. I had already seen this kind of object—carried by two men and covered with victuals—in a painting, *The Peasant Wedding* by Brueghel the Elder. The women have piled onto this stretcher of sorts an impressive stack of large galettes. It's the entire family's bread for the week, which they've been cooking in the oven since dawn. Everything, in this place, seems immutable.

An hour later, I'm sitting on my rump in the grass on the undulating plain between erstwhile Bacul to the north and the village of Yünlü to the south. My altimeter reads 1,335 meters (4,380 feet). It's here that, on a day like today perhaps, warm and gray, a famous battle took place. A half century BCE, Pharnaces, king of Pontus, set his mind on reconquering the territory—encompassing Armenia, Cappadocia, and Galatia—over which his ancestors formerly reigned. He declared war on the Romans, who occupied a part of the territory to which he laid claim and launched his campaign. Caesar, residing at the time in Egypt, was ordered by the Senate to go with his army to bring this impudent upstart back to heel. It is here, on this mossy stretch of land before me, that the two men battled it out.

Looking out at the empty landscape, my back propped up against my bag, I daydream and let my imagination go. Pharnaces, who traveled the very route that I walked yesterday on my way from Amasya, his capital, took up position to my left. Caesar camped in the village of Yünlü and arrived from the south, from my right. The sun peers out over the horizon. Over there, to the east, the form of Mount Kocababa (great papa) emerges from the mist. The undulations in the terrain thereabouts allow the rivals to conceal their reserve troops. A mountain breeze shivers its way across the low grasses. The order is given. The Roman legion begins to advance in tight formation. And then Pharnaces unveils the terrifying weapon he invented hidden behind a fold in the terrain: carts with wheels fitted with scythes. The results are dreadful. The small, scrawny, and high-strung horses, like those grazing here near me now, lashed by their charioteers, charge into the ranks of the foot soldiers, carving furrows that flow with blood. For five hours, the battle is merciless. The men are exhausted. And then Roman Knights triumph. And Caesar, writing to the Senate, has his men engrave on a tablet the shortest and most famous battle report in the history of warfare. On this field where so many of his men died, he simply dictates: "*Veni, vidi, vici.*"

These rolling hills, having witnessed the flash of naked swords and heard the cries of men casting themselves into the jaws of death, the moans of the wounded, the snarl of arrows and the crack of whips, have, for the past two thousand years, known calm. Today, the silence is broken only by the sound of the wind rushing over the steppe and the trill of larks climbing high into the sky. I sit dreaming for a long time before picking up my bag and getting back underway. As for the cunning idea of fitting scythes on the wheels of carts: it has a great career ahead of it in Hollywood B movies.

Yünlü, the other village to witness the battle, is located off the main road to Zile, on the hillside. You get there by leaving the paved road and onto a dirt one. I happen upon two old men out for a walk. Once I've satisfied their curiosity, they inquire, staring at my bag: "In any case, you must be well armed. Rifle or handgun?" The question strikes me as absurd, so I answer with a loud laugh. But to them, it's no laughing matter.

Down a side street I come across Hüseyin. As much as I'd have preferred to avoid him, there was no way: he's seated on the ground, his head in the shade of the wall of his house and his dirty bare feet out in the sun, blocking the road. With a sharp adze like the one Ahmed the carpenter had, he's carving very strange pitchforks, shaped like tridents with prongs that curve inward. They're unlike any I've ever seen. They have three large opposed fingers: below, the index and the middle finger, slightly curving upward, and facing them, the thumb, curving downward. In order to engineer such shapes, Hüseyin guided how the shrubs grew in the hedges bordering his field for three years, then he clamped them and let them dry to get the right shape. Once the points are fully sharpened, all he'll have to do is attach a handle.

Hüseyin joyfully calls out to me, taking a break from his work. I take a picture, as I'm fascinated by antique agricultural tools. And these particular tools have been made in the same way from time immemorial. Hüseyin invites me to lunch. I'm hoping to reach Zile early, and so I decline his invitation, but he won't have it: in a friendly but firm manner, he grabs me by the arm and drags me—then pushes me—into his house. In no time at all, I've set down my pack, having been led *manu militari* into the reception room. There's no resisting Hüseyin's cordial hospitality. It envelops you, it warms you up, and any reluctance you may have melts away. He wants to know everything. From the kitchen, the women listen in, taking turns coming back to the sitting room to glean bits of information and then reporting back to the others. There exists, in this house, an air of simple happiness, delightful images we can sift back through whenever the world fills us with despair.

My host suddenly asks me to get up from the bench chest I'm seated on, lifts the top, and from a cage takes out a partridge that he has domesticated and is raising in his house. It parades about the room, coming over to steal a few leftovers from our plates. Hüseyin is happy to host a foreigner, and his joy is contagious. He touches my arm. He pats me on the shoulder. He seems to want to connect. If he let himself go, he would take me in his arms, hug me, and give me a kiss on the cheek. He's a generous, caring man. A brother. A kind spirit. And when I pack up my gear, he insists on walking with me for some distance.

The rocky road descends abruptly, full of ruts from passing storms, it's rough and so steep that only those on foot can travel it. Our feet roll over the loose stones, skidding on the dry earth. Five hundred meters farther down meanders a mountain stream. The road to Zile follows it slavishly. Hüseyin walks next to me, taking my arm in his, as though fearing I might fall or leave him behind. It feels awkward to be in such close contact, but I've often seen Turks holding one another this way. And I'm moved by his show of affection. This man's friendship is tactile. We reach a kind of outcrop with a view of the rest of the path leading to the main road. I continue the descent alone, but, for a quarter-hour, each time I turn around and look up, I see Hüseyin, looking very small atop his rocky perch, waving his arms to bid me farewell.

All warmed up inside by this very spontaneous and freely offered friendship, I rejoin the main road, which, sloping gently, leads me all the way to Zile. In the narrow valley, two men high up in a cherry tree invite me to join them in their feast. I gorge myself on the fruit. In Yaylayolu, 500 meters (1,600 feet) higher up, the cherries were still green.

Zile has managed to preserve its beautiful Ottoman houses. From atop the ramparts of the citadel that overlook the city, looking out to the east in the direction I'll be headed tomorrow, I count six villages scattered over a broad cultivated plain. In town, I fail to find an internet café. But, after a lengthy search, some young people I ask lead me to the house of a photographer, Ihsan, also a computer enthusiast. He lets me use his computer. In my inbox I find, among other things, an invitation to Rémi and Rabia's wedding, to be held on August 6. They've speeded things up, since back in Istanbul, Rabia told me it was on their mind but that nothing had been planned. Well, on August 6, I'll probably be somewhere between Tabriz and Tehran. So, in my reply, I simply send them my best wishes. While I was reading my mail, Ihsan called one of his friends, Haydar Cuhadan, a correspondent in Zile for the daily paper *Milliyet*.* He interviews me for an article and films me for the regional television station. This is a role reversal: after a life spent asking the questions, for the first time, I'm the one answering them.

The following morning, as I head out on the road, Emre catches up to me on his bike. He's twenty years old with the face of an angel. He's unemployed but will soon be leaving for seasonal work in a seaside resort on the southern coast. For ten kilometers or so, he dreams aloud about his future life, and he's optimistic about it. In fact, this summer, he hopes to win over a rich Englishwoman and marry her. He'll then be able to make his dream come true: to live on the green Isle of Albion with no need to work. I congratulate him on getting such an early start on a successful career as a gigolo. Miffed, he turns his bike around and deserts me. At noon, there's not a single restaurant in sight. I ask a gas station attendant who confirms that I won't find anything for another fifteen kilometers or so. He has nothing for sale, neither juice nor cookies. I'm about to get going again when he calls out to me.

"But I have my lunch. Come on, we'll share it."

---

* TN: Published in Istanbul.

CHAPTER VII
ONE THOUSAND KILOMETERS

With hundreds of eyes staring at me, the appropriately named "Main Street of Pazar" feels endless. My arrival coincides with the exodus from the mosque after Friday prayer. The city is teeming with men who just attended the service. The sidewalks are overflowing, so I opt to walk in the middle of the street. No one greets me, no one says anything. People fall silent at my approach. Patrons in teahouses and shops step outside to stare at me. I've walked thirty-five kilometers in the heat. My shorts and T-shirt are soaked, as is my blue canvas hat, on which the sweat has traced white stripes. A man on his cart stops his horse to have a better look at the Ostrogoth who just arrived. I feel like a Martian with antennae and a flashing nose.

The expression on the faces looking me over is neither stern nor inquisitive; it's mostly one of stupefaction. With several variations on the theme. Young people elbow one another and laugh. Adult men try to wear an expressionless mask. Older people throw me an unabashed look of disapproval. I recall something that took place in Amasya. I was touring the city in shorts when a storm blew in. I put on my large rain poncho and got into a bus. While seated next to an old man wearing the cap of a pious Muslim, a section of my poncho slipped, revealing my knee. My neighbor, with an imperative gesture, lifted my poncho back up to cover up the patch of skin he didn't want to see.

As I slowly make my way up the oh-so-very long and dusty Street of Pazar, I come to a decision that I'd been putting off for several days, and that is to no longer go out in public in shorts. Yes, the heat will be harder to bear. But since I intimately share in the daily life of the people I meet or with whom I stay, it's important for me to respect their convictions. The fact that I'm here surprises them, I can't change that. But if the sight of my legs shocks them, then I have to do something about it. In any case, it's good preparation. For I'll soon be in Iran, where it will no longer be an option. No matter how hot it gets, I'll have to walk with my arms and legs covered or risk being arrested by the formidable "*komiteh*"—the police officers in charge of enforcing Islamic law.

Pazar is where I come across a municipal hotel for the first time. It's inexpensive, clean, and has a perfectly functional shower, and with hot water, to boot. A triple stroke of luck. Spruced up, wearing clean clothes, I hurry off to visit the Seljuk caravansary at the edge of the city. The massive, square-shaped structure is made of large blocks of red granite. From the outside, the high wall is smooth, without windows or doors, and is flanked at each corner by an octagonal tower. The entrance is extraordinary. A very tall first door rises to a classical arch, topped by a keystone. But immediately behind it, a second door, although not as tall, is striking because the Roman arch above it is made of finely-carved stones with chiseled edges. It has no true keystone. The stones are a perfect fit down to the millimeter, following a broken line pattern. I tilt my head to the right and to the left, trying to figure out what design these zigzags might correspond to, but it doesn't resemble a thing. Then I get the idea of looking at the blocks upside down. So I turn my back to the structure, lean forward, and glance up between my legs. Each design very clearly stands out as the profile of a man's face. I count fourteen profiles perfectly aligned in a circular arc. That's as far along in my examination as I get when I notice a man watching me, astonished at my posture. I straighten back up and smile at him, but he takes to his heels, convinced that the tourist he happened upon has lost his mind.

The decaying interior gives an idea of the structure's strength. Massive pillars of large, beautifully carved stones support gargantuan Romanesque arcs. In spite of one thousand years of stormy weather, the structure, overtaken by weeds, still stands. And with a little preservation work at the top of the walls, it could easily survive another thousand years. But will someone see to it?

In the evening, having gotten to know several teachers who are delighted to practice their English and invite me to dinner, I'm surprised how proud locals are of their caravansary while nevertheless letting it go to ruin. The only response I get from my interlocutors, philosophers themselves, is a shrug of their shoulders. *Inşallah.*

Along the road the next morning, a hunched-over old man is gathering grass, stuffing it into a large jute bag. He has a small goatee and blue eyes so clear that against his weathered face, they seem to be illuminated from within. We chat and walk for a while; him with his large bag cutting into his shoulder and me with my satchel heavy on my back. A pickup truck, piloted like a racecar by some young dandy, screeches to a stop to offer us a ride in the back. The grass man, surprisingly limber for his age, hops into the bed after tossing his bag in first. The show-off driver is displeased when I don't follow suit, and, to show how annoyed he is, he takes off again gunning his engine and angrily spewing exhaust fumes in my face.

Around noon, I'm reluctantly back on the highway, but there's no other way to get to Tokat. A group of peasants hails me, inviting me to partake in their meal. They're seated in the corner of a huge tomato field, under a roof of branches set atop high poles protecting them from the sun. In the ditch, they've dug a hearth and covered it with a stovetop fit with a long pipe that keeps them from being smoked out. It's a joyful group, and they are delighted to have a tourist join them, an unusual event in their monotonous existence. There are four men, about ten women, and a child. "Work is hard," one of the women tells me, "but tomatoes pay well." Each person's meal consists of a piece of flatbread served with a tomato and onion. It's all washed down, of course, with tea drawn from the samovar now humming away on the makeshift stove. The women eat separately from the men, and they all sit on cleverly designed beanbag chairs made of plastic bags filled with oat husks.

One of the youths suddenly asks if he can travel with me to Paris. I don't know what to say. But he insists. He asks me to give him ten minutes, enough time for him to run home to grab the two shirts he owns. No one seems to want to reason with him. He begins stretching, convinced that it's as easy as that. How will I convince him that stringent regulations exist among countries? Has this wide-eyed teen ever even heard of administrative red tape?

"You want to emigrate? Okay then. Do you have a passport?"

"No."

"That's the first step. It'll take a few weeks, and I can't wait."

Surprisingly, he immediately admits this major setback to what he'd like to do, and his dream of exile disappears as quickly as it appeared. Everyone witnessed the episode, they each had something to say, either pro or con, but now that the boy's fervor has waned, they all return to their tomatoes, and I get back on the road to Tokat.

In the seventeenth century, under the Ottoman Empire, this city, which today has a population of nearly one hundred thousand, was Christian. Jean-Baptiste Tavernier—in whose footsteps I'm faithfully following—tells me that Tokat once had no fewer than twelve churches, four convents (two for women only), and that it prided itself on the presence of an archbishop. There was also a Jewish settlement. There are still some Jews in the city, but not a single Christian. One Jew, Nuri Amca (*ahm'-djah*), to whom I was referred since he's an amateur historian, knows the road's history well. But unfortunately, I won't be able to meet up with him during my two-day stay.

The city's vast, renovated caravansary is not nearly as majestic nor as large as the one in Pazar. It comprises several dozen small bedroom-cells, each with its own hearth, which gives the roof an unusual appearance, bestrewn as it is with sixty-some chimneys. Merchants and artisans, working with copper here since time immemorial, occupy the tiny rooms now converted into shops. The courtyard is vast, partially paved and planted with thorn trees providing shade for the tables of the inescapable teahouse. This isn't a particularly old caravansary, but the enormous central heating radiators that can be seen everywhere, the aluminum frames on the windows looking out over the courtyard, and the green sheet metal roof with which it has been afflicted fail to blend in as period additions.

Tokat, which was subjected to fourteen different occupying powers over its two thousand-five-hundred-year history, has one peculiar attribute: the city's soil has risen five meters (17 feet) since the thirteenth century, the result of earthquakes that shook layers of sediment down from the surrounding hills. To such an extent that the subsurface no doubt contains a trove of hidden treasures. I visit the *gök medrese* (*guhk mehdreh'-seh*) (the blue Qur'anic school, *gök* meaning both "blue" and "sky"). It has been converted into a museum and was constructed on one level. As for all the ancient monuments in the lower part of the city, you have to go down a flight of steps to visit it. Some of the beautiful blue ceramics that once adorned the facade and gave the building its name are still visible. Inside, one of the vestiges of the city's Christian past is a surprising wax figurine of Saint Christine, martyred at the hands of the Romans.

The city, which was the sixth largest in Turkey under the Sultanate of Seljuk, came to an abrupt halt once it was captured by the Mongols of Tamerlane. Under the Ottoman Empire, it later regained some of its importance, thanks to its privileged position as an important hub along the Silk Routes. I also visit, on my day off, the very beautiful Ottoman-era private mansion *Latifoğlu konağı* (*lah-tee-foh'-loo koh-nah'*), which is open to the public.

I wander for most of the day around the western district, which overlooks the city. In the narrow, winding streets where I wander, the houses lean in at such a sharp angle that there's hardly any sky. With tiny shops, mosques, and perhaps a derelict *bedesten*, the district has retained the feel of Ottoman culture that has been erased almost everywhere else. Here, concrete has not replaced the wood houses. Huddled together as though in numbers they might better fend off the bulldozers, they are sources of inspiration, like old-fashioned poetry, and you tell yourself that this must be a place of rebellious, fraternal, and stubborn spirits. Houses, too, have souls. It's hardly surprising, then, that it's here, on a small square in the shadow of a collapsing mosque, that I bond with three elders who've fulfilled their life's dream of making their pilgrimage to Mecca and who display long white beards as if they were flags. I stay with them a good while and time stands still: I am happy.

I also befriend three young men who launched their own computer business. They work day and night. They began with a computer one of their fathers bought. Today, at twenty years old, one of them is the company CEO, while at the same time fulfilling his military service. His brother, who is only fourteen and still attends school, and his other nineteen-year-old associate are equally motivated and enterprising. The company operates out of both floors of a building. Business equipment, computer courses, sales and repair, internet café, software programming: they do it all. In speaking with me, they're eager to show a Westerner that they're tech-savvy and interested in new technologies and modernity from the West. I reassure them: in France, I don't know many people as young as they are with as much business sense and who show themselves to be so ambitious and professional. My words are music to their ears.

Finally, I decide to make a sacrificial offering to my taste buds, having eaten for the sole purpose of maintaining my strength ever since leaving Istanbul. I've heard that at the *Husuk Restaurant*, they serve a mouth-watering dish, *Tokat kebab*, available nowhere else. It consists of two kebabs cooked in an oven rather than over coals, and that completely changes the flavor. The first skewer has chunks of lamb, potatoes, and eggplant, and on the other—for the cooking time is different—there are tomatoes and hot peppers. The dish is served with a head of garlic that has been grilled and crushed. It's such a wonderful delicacy that I'm back again the following day.

The way back to the hotel is swarming with uniformed men carrying machine guns who are checking every shop, every corner, every car. At the bottom of a terrace stairway, six stern-faced soldiers stand guard, each holding an assault rifle across his chest, finger on the trigger. Music spills out from beyond the top of the stairs. I want to inquire, but a soldier yells at me to keep moving. The grunt seems sufficiently edgy that I comply. In a nearby ice cream shop, the manager explains: the army's having fun and the officers are throwing a party. They worry about "terrorists" crashing their party. Terrorists . . . Should I translate that as "the Kurds"? In any case, I'm clearly entering a danger zone.

When I leave Tokat, I feel strangely depressed. After considerable reflection, I come up with several reasons. Fatigue is number one. For two weeks now, I've been traveling long stages, some too long: one was forty-seven kilometers, two were forty-six. Telling myself to slow down hasn't done any good, it isn't so simple. To get from one city to the next, there is often no alternative. And I have good reason for wanting to stay in cities. Stopping in villages, I can't wash up, relax, and sleep as well as I can in hotels. Upon leaving Tokat, I'll be starting a ten-day walk without a single city along the way, which means ten days without a balanced diet, ten evenings of watching entire villages parade by, ten days of having to rise at dawn at the same time as my hosts, and, above all, ten days without a shower, having to stew in my own sweat. These are unavoidable difficulties. The hardest part is taking the first step. Add to that the facts that for some time now every village is just like the last, that flatlands are followed by more flatlands, that the excitement of discovery has clearly worn off, that even Kangals no longer scare me. It will come as no surprise then that, having lowered my guard and with my enthusiasm at half-staff, there's a little less spring in my step right now.

As I leave Tokat, a police officer, directing traffic by wiggling his arms around like worms, literally lunges at me, bawling me out at the top of his lungs.

"Where are you going? Where are you going? Where are you going?"

When he thinks he hears "Erzurum," he thinks I'm messing with him: he starts yelling even louder, jostling me before rummaging through my pack. I dread to think how he might have reacted if I'd told him the truth: "Tehran." His partner intervenes and, praise be to Allah, gets him to calm down. The valiant fellow apologizes on his partner's behalf: "My buddy's a little jumpy." From which I learn nothing, and, in any case, it doesn't help to cure my blues.

Fortunately, a little farther down the road, I crack a smile when I

stumble upon a scene that is, to say the least, nonsensical. It's the middle
of nowhere; the straight, monotonous road seems to completely ignore
its surroundings. There, beneath a half-finished wooden hut, two men
sit cross-legged in front of two mounds of watermelons, waiting for customers. It's hard to imagine a more unlikely spot to conduct business,
but the two men seem confident, completely relaxed. They jabber away
smoking cigarettes. Since I offer to take their picture, they give me some
cherries. To my question "Do you have a lot of customers?" they answer,
"No," and smile disarmingly, and such undaunted optimism in the face
of life is all I need to cheer me up. It's an image I need to bear in mind
and think back upon whenever the world's annoying side tries to take
away my peace of mind.

Later on, out in front of a school building, as is the case every Monday
in all Turkish schools, the principal is waving a baton, leading his school-
children in patriotic songs, and the scene brings to mind a memory: in my
hometown in the country, I'm six years old, and we're singing *Maréchal
nous voilà* in the "big school" where I just started, but that I will have
to leave a few weeks later because of the war. Children the world over
display the same fervor singing at the top of their lungs songs of which,
by and large, they have no understanding: a great show of confidence
and unquestioning obedience: this is how we turn children into young
combatants.

At the Kızıliniş Pass, I attack the climb, which will hoist me to an
elevation of 1,150 meters (3,800 feet). Tokat's broad plains, planted with
tomatoes and poplars, gives way to a rugged mountain road, carved
through the rock itself. Wild mimosa trees release their sweet smell,
much to the delight of bees swarming upon them by the thousands in a
buzzing banquet. Vast stretches of fertile land, planted with grain, undu-
late off to the horizon. Here and there, an oak tree rises from the landscape, casting a shadow on a steaming samovar, the promise to all who
work in the sun, both women and men, that there will soon be time to
rest and sip some tasty tea. At noon, a restaurant provides me with a
meal—a trout fished from a large pond—and a restful pause; I take the
time to savor them both.

As I enter the small village of Çiftlik (*cheeft'-leek*), I'm approached by two rascals who seem to come from nowhere. They don't beat around the bush: one of them wants my watch, the other wants money and crudely shoves his hand in my pocket to help himself. I break free. Are they going to assault me in broad daylight? Three or four peasants working in a nearby field come over to find out more about this traveler who has wandered into their village, looking like a packmule. After a few pleasantries exchanged with the farmers, I make a discreet getaway, glancing back two or three times to make sure the two rogues aren't following me. What a fool I am. I'd been warned to watch out for thieves. My watch, with its large face and chronometer-like appearance, is a source of temptation. I tuck it away, deep in a pocket, and I'll only take it out from now on when I need information: the elevation, the barometric pressure, the direction I'm traveling, and, of course, the time of day.

As I'm leaving the village, an imam is waiting for the bus with his wife, who's rocking a baby in her arms. He seems on edge and asks me if I'm afraid. In the gas station nearby where he buys me a cup of tea, he brings the subject up once again: really, I can tell him, he'd totally understand—aren't I afraid? For, after all, he exclaims, "there are terrorists," and he mimics a bad guy aiming his gun at me. These folks are all acting so nervous, they're gonna wind up giving me a nasty case of the jitters! And it won't take much. Solo travelers never leave home without a little fear tucked away in their baggage. It silently slips out in the silence of the forest or the night and is near at hand, first and foremost, in every encounter. To walk alone, pack on your back, is to open yourself up to danger and to the Other. You cannot flee as you would on a bicycle or take refuge as you would in a car. Up to this point, apprehensiveness remained bottled up, a source of shame, in my pack. Each day, each encounter, was a celebration. But here I am now facing insidious, creeping fear.

To be honest, I have mixed feelings about terrorists. My professional curiosity makes me want to meet them. I could question them on their politics and methods, even write a report—though commissioned by no one. Of course, I'm fully aware of the fact that they could hold me hostage, and that's one of the reasons why I introduce myself as a former schoolteacher rather than a journalist. At the same time, I sometimes fear random acts of violence, a sniper who aims, shoots, and flees or a gang of slapdash terrorists who have no time to deal with an uninvited guest. Another fear cropped up only a little while ago when I met those two bandits at the entrance to the village: the fear of being robbed, and there's no ruling out the use of force. I quickly sweep aside this most recent worry: being robbed would have serious consequences for me—losing time, for example—but it wouldn't be catastrophic.

For a week now, there's no denying it, there are growing signs that I should be worried. Not a day goes by without someone asking whether I'm armed, or who mimics terrorists aiming a gun at me or running a blade under my throat. The man toting a rifle in Kervansaray and the two thugs who wanted my watch are both warning signs. I remember the advice given me by the traveling salesman who wanted to weigh me down with giveaways: "Watch out around Tokat." Collective psychosis or real danger? I want to remain calm and keep things in perspective rather than simply give in to some vague sense of fear. But I nevertheless draw the following conclusion: from now on, I'll only seek hospitality from the *muhtar* in charge of each village. This political leader can provide undeniable protection.

Ten minutes after having said good-bye to the imam, I find the ruins of Çiftlik's caravansary. I also locate two villages, Tahtoba and Ibibse, which do not appear on any of my maps. The fact that there are caravan stopovers here is no coincidence. To avoid the *paşa* of Tokat's tax collectors, caravans headed due south of Amasya by way of Zile in the direction of Sivas and sought room, board, and safety in these small inns, which had relatively limited capacity but were close to one another. Another village, also named "Karvansaray," figures on the map, not far from here. A little farther along, thirty-two kilometers now from Tokat, I photograph the ruins of a small *han*. A precious photo: the last stones of the stable's vaulted doorway have at last fallen into the brambles and nettles.

I say good-bye to the main road to Sivas. For the next ten days, I won't see any pavement. I veer east toward Kızık, the first leg of a push into the deep countryside that will take me to Suşehri. On the dirt road headed in that direction, two or three tractors offer to take me on board. In accordance with rural hierarchy, the men are riding on the tractor itself, while the women ride behind them, on the trailer. I decline all these invitations. Another tractor comes my way and stops just in front of me. A hefty young loudmouth seated on the mudguard jumps off yelling: "Papers, passport, police, police!"

He's clearly no policeman, and I'm not impressed.

When I question his identity, he takes from his wallet a piece of paper bearing his photograph, indisputable proof that he's no policeman. This is a country where a cop would never bother to prove who he is. The document he shows me, which I can't make heads or tails of, doesn't bear the word "polis" or "jandarma," which are the only two words related to the police that I know. He rants and raves all the more, but seeing his document has no effect on me, and I hold my ground:

"I only present my papers to the police or to the *muhtar*. I'm going to seek hospitality from the *muhtar* of Kızık."

He simmers down, gets back on his tractor, and leaves. It goes without saying that my passport is extremely important to me and I have no intention of showing it to just any old joker. I have no other form of ID: to lose it would be calamitous.

I'm given a very warm welcome by Mustafa Güsköy, the mayor of Kızık. And, as usual, I have to satisfy the appetite of all the village's able-bodied inhabitants who parade by for three hours. In the evening, among the curious, I spot my "policeman," looking rather sheepish. He tells me that in reality he is the *bekçi* (game-warden). I was the wrong kind of game . . .

Mustafa tells me that Kızık has a caravansary that someone will show me the way to tomorrow morning. This route, he explains in a scholarly tone, was not along the Silk Road, but rather on the "Road of Osman, Imperator." He can tell me no more. There were three Turkish sultans who went by the name of "Osman." He has no idea which one of them goes by the name of "Imperator," nor does he know the exact route taken by that particular road. It's likely something he heard here or there and that he's restating without any further knowledge. Incidentally, the next morning, when I mention that I'd like to see the caravansary he told me about, no one knows where exactly it is.

I hit the road under a cool sun that feels more like spring. A dam being built near the village made it necessary to reroute the roads, and my map is useless. I manage to find the one I want, and, very abruptly, it heads uphill. With my altimeter reading 1,300 meters (4,265 feet), a car passes me up on the dirt road and comes to a stop one hundred meters farther on. Two fellows get out, position themselves next to the car, and wait for me. As I approach, I immediately put up my guard: their faces are grave and tense, even hostile. The taller one, who also seems the most malevolent, has one hand in his pocket. I have no doubt he's clasping a pistol or a knife. I do my best to smile despite my apprehension, and, advancing with hand outstretched, I introduce myself: I am French and visiting Turkey. There's a dramatic change in their attitude. The shorter one tells me that he is the *muhtar* of Kargıncık, two kilometers distant, and that his name is Nihaze. The other fellow removes his hand from his pocket and holds it out to clasp mine. Fear—which, on both sides, had raised its ugly head—suddenly scurries back into its lair.

They offer to give me a ride to the village. I refuse, but at the first houses a half-hour later, Nihaze is waiting for me beside the road. He takes me to his house for tea. While the women get it ready, he tells me he has six children: five boys, all of whom are in France, near the city of Dreux. Instead of a simple tea service, the women have prepared a veritable meal. A delicious eggplant-and-onion dish that I devour. Nihaze takes only a few small bites. He tells me that he raises bees and sells the honey. It's his main source of income. He's the only mountain dweller I've encountered so far who keeps bees. A lot of honey is produced here, but it's still the monopoly of beekeepers who come from the Black Sea coast in summertime.

Nihaze walks with me to the edge of his village. The mountains rise before us, almost straight up. He points to a path: this is the "route suitable for vehicle traffic" shown on my map. Before long, it fades beneath the grasses, then disappears altogether, such that I have to follow my compass through the pastures. The landscape is so majestic, and my walk through the thick grass so pleasant, that I climb with glee, unmindful for the time being of any possible misadventures.

After an hour-long workout, soaked in sweat, I reach a kind of small platform—its surface area is probably no larger than that of my little house in Normandy. My altimeter reads 1,700 meters (5,580 feet). The view is breathtaking. I set down my pack and lie on my stomach in the grass. One of my childhood pleasures comes back to me all of a sudden: the sense of being embraced by the Earth itself, like a protective mother. Before me, the immense Tokat plain stretches to the north, and the city is visible, nearly forty kilometers away. To the south, the Sahırsivis tepe, culminating at 2,100 meters (6,890 feet), blocks the view somewhat, but I have 340 degrees of fabulous scenery. I carefully examine the lower hills that rise in terraces both to the east and to the west. My T-shirt is soaked. I take it off and head over to a kind of trough built by shepherds. A spring there is gently burbling. I splash some of the water onto my face and then my chest. Finally, after checking not just once, but twice, that there's nobody around, I take off my clothes and plunge into the improvised bathtub. The water is ice-cold. It's a brutal shock, but once I'm numb, I manage to let go. There was no opportunity to wash up yesterday or this morning. The bath is pure bliss, especially since I must be in the highest bathtub anywhere in Turkey, and knowing I'm free to enjoy, even for a moment, being so near the Gods.

Still, I avoid overdoing this invigorating, icy bath, lest the Gods take offense. I scrub myself down, dry myself off, and, to warm myself back up, I run through the soft grass down the other side of the pass, shamelessly crushing pretty bellflowers with my big boots. In the valley where I finally come to land, I notice that the houses have given up tile roofs in favor of sheet metal. At Çırçır (chur-chur), the collapsed minaret is being rebuilt. A village elder, Osman Chahine, tells me he has a brother who left for France twenty years ago and never once sent news. Does he think I know him?

The *muhtar* who takes me in, Talat Tekine, is *kafka* (Caucasian), as is the entire population here. He tells me that their ancestors arrived in

1874. There isn't a single Turk in the entire village, and the inhabitants only speak Caucasian. But no one knows how to write in that language, since only Turkish is taught in school. The two other Caucasian villages that I later go through give me the same impression: there is a strong and self-sufficient sense of community, like little Anatolian kolkhozes.

People are mentioning terrorists again. And although I take these warnings seriously, I can't help but notice with a little amusement that the "terrorists" are always other people. At Tokat, where I'd been fore-warned that they were everywhere, people said that there weren't any. The imam at Çiftlik said they were somewhere around Kızık. In Kızık, they said I'd find them in the vicinity of Altınoluk and Çırçır. Now that I'm there, they tell me that they're mostly near Tokat. We've come full circle. Still, it's a warning not to be taken lightly. Garrisoned in this backwater village is a detachment of *jandarmas*, tasked with fighting terrorism, and their presence here is certainly no coincidence.

My host, in his fifties and going gray at the temples, is strapped into an impeccable three-piece suit. He resides in a newly built home. But there's nothing new about it. It's based on the very same model as all the older homes, both in terms of layout and the materials used to build it. As in the old houses, there's no special bathroom, just a washbasin next to the toilet. The furniture exudes a certain degree of comfort and aesthetics. The most striking example is in the opposition between a single chromo print on a wall and a bountiful bouquet of plastic flowers on a table. I sleep in the living room, on a mattress laid on the ground. Talat's daughter, who just brought me a pillow for the night, has a stunningly beautiful face. When her father tells me her name, she says something to me, probably, "welcome to our home," but I'm so taken by this vision of beauty that I mutter some endless compliment that begins in Turkish and ends in French. In brief, she sends my heart aflutter, and I show it.

In this little village, just like in the village yesterday, the welcome isn't as warm as it was during the first days of my journey. As good Muslims, my hosts take me in and satisfy their curiosity, but that's where it ends.

In the morning, Talat accompanies me out onto the road. He's one of the rare peasants I've met who knows how to read a map, and he shows me clearly the path I should follow: "At the first intersection, go right, then at the intersection after a bridge go left." He gives my hand a squeeze then heads home, never looking back. Thanks to him, I'm once again on friendly terms with forks in the road.

This morning, June 16, regardless of all that, nothing can undermine my optimism. The sun, for its part, is celebrating with me. For deep inside, I'm celebrating: according to my punctilious calculations, having checked and rechecked my addition of kilometers traveled since leaving Istanbul, today I'll be crossing the one-thousand-kilometer mark. I reckon that *the event* will take place around 11:00 a.m. It has been one month and two days since I left the Turkey's largest city. Back then, I was afraid I wouldn't be able to adhere to the agreement I'd made with myself. Even though I'm not quite halfway through, I'm satisfied with the pace I've kept, since I've walked thirty-five kilometers a day. If I take into account the days off, my average is still thirty kilometers a day since May 14. I've overcome infected feet, I've survived Kangals, and I've made some progress, albeit modest, in learning Turkish. I'm also in very good physical condition, and the stages—thirty-five kilometers on the day before yesterday, and thirty kilometers yesterday, including a mountain climb—leave me feeling fresh as a daisy the next morning. The despair I felt upon leaving Tokat is already long gone and forgotten. Forgotten, too, my resolution to walk with my head in the clouds and nothing on my mind, paying no attention to reference points, benefits, and balance sheets. Wisdom, 'tis well known, is found at the end of the journey.

The first village I have to traverse is called Akören. As I approach, I see a man step out of the first house. He spots me, goes back inside, and comes promptly back out with what, from a distance, looks like a stick. As I pass him by—he's in a squatting position, ready to jump me—I notice that the stick is a rifle. The man looks at me with hostile, stern eyes. Panic paralyzes me, and, for a moment, I'm afraid that my knees might give out. Despite the fear gripping me, I muster the courage to hail him with a sonorous and affable "hello," but unfazed and stubborn, he says nothing. I continue on at a pace that's as neutral and light as possible, as if my inexistence might ward off the volley of lead the scoundrel intended for my backside.

A little farther along, on the village square, two old men who had seen me coming look away as I draw near. The young whippersnapper washing up at the fountain points the road to the next village when I ask him about it, without even turning around. Once again, I'm stricken with fear. A diffuse sense of fear that makes my heart beat faster. I've heard about "terrorists" for a long time; perhaps now I'm in their midst? The day before yesterday, Mustafa, Kızık's mayor, told me, "There are some in Altınoluk." That's one of my next destinations. The three men, like the man wielding a "stick" a short while ago, are uneasy. They're not hostile; they're simply paralyzed by fear. It's not the same fear that seized me when I saw the rifle and that, in a flash, drained me of my energy. No, the fear they feel is permanent, it's something they live with. It dictates their every move. I also noticed that not one of the few vehicles that passed me on the road, cars or tractors, stopped to offer a ride. Fear trumps curiosity. And workers in the fields no longer wave to invite me over for tea, as they often did before Tokat. I've entered the land of fear.

The man driving three young calves out of a pasture has a friendly face. He has a slight build, a dark complexion, a short mustache, and a three-day-old beard. He chuckles and says, raising his hand in friendship:

"And just where are *you* headed?"

He smiles and so do I.

I string together, in Turkish, something that I intend to mean:

"To Erzurum. Don't tell me it's far, I know that. I've come from Istanbul on foot, and that's even farther, right?"

My vocabulary and grammar didn't betray me: he bursts out laughing. He's exuberant, he pokes at me as if we were two partners in crime and drags me into his house. The calves go back in their stable, which occupies the ground floor. Fazıl Önel, which is his name, protects me as I head up the stairs to the second floor, because lurking just under the steps is a Kangal as big as one of the calves, ready to swallow both me and my bag in two gulps. The first question I ask, of course, is whether there are any terrorists in the area. Again, he laughs. He has a hearty laugh and an open, trustworthy face.

I will indeed encounter terrorists, he tells me, if I continue heading east. In his opinion, there are three Shiite villages where I really ought not wander, and he advises me to make a detour around them. I draw a circle around the three names on my map, a precaution that, no sooner having done it, I regret. Yes, the names of these little villages are impossible, and I mix them all up. But if I'm stopped, I'll look pretty slick with these rebel areas underlined and gear that everyone thinks mistakes for a portable arsenal!

I had indeed planned to go through one of them, Ovatabök. Fazil's daughter, a pretty fifteen-year-old brunette, gestures desperately to her father. She clearly wants to talk to him. He gets me settled out on the patio, then goes to see her. He comes back laughing harder than before: "She's afraid *you* are a terrorist!"

One Turk thought that I had a motor hidden in my bag. Does his daughter think it conceals a bazooka?

The girl and her sister prepare the tea. In the meantime, Fazil and I chat, along with Ali, an elderly neighbor who bears the title of "*haj*" ever since he made his pilgrimage to Mecca. This evening, I'm planning on seeking hospitality in a village that has the same name as he does, "Alihacı" (*ah-lee-hah'-djuh*) (Ali the Haj). The prestige of those who, in olden days, went on foot or by horse all the way to Mecca was such that the entire village shared in it. And the inhabitants sometimes even renamed their town with the name of their hero.

Fazil tells me that he has seven children: four boys and three girls. The boys aren't here, they're all in college.

"And the girls, they're not in college?"

He has trouble understanding my question.

"But the girls work on the farm!"

"And they've never gone to school?"

"Yes of course, but only the usual studies, age seven to eleven."

When, before leaving them, I take a snapshot of Fazil and Ali, the teen girls run off to hide in the house, as though the devil himself had appeared to them.

The weather's spectacular. The sun's playing hide-and-seek in a fluffy sky, and the air's cool, ideal for walking. I'm in my element. A light breeze sweeps over the grasses, I feel free, relieved, full of joy. Three kilometers after having said good-bye to Fazil, I stop. The road is a wide track of hard-packed dirt and white gravel that gently undulates from one hill to the next. In the distance, I can see how it winds its way over the prairie, disappearing for a while, and then reappearing; it lingers a little to the left, and then, like a prankster, it vanishes once again behind a green hedge. I soak up this peaceful scene. The road is bordered by flowering pastures and plowed fields. The mountain range I crossed yesterday appears less formidable, perhaps because, at the moment, it's bathed in blue light.

My appetite for new landscapes is inexhaustible. I'm like an unfaithful lover: each new beauty draws me in, effacing the one before. Hardly have I had my fill of one dreamlike vision, when the next one—and that one alone—grabs my attention. For me, happiness is always hiding, just past the next plain, behind that rocky outcrop; it's hiding in a fold in the terrain, around the bend of a river, at the far end of this narrow pass. Driven by a desire to hold it in my hands, I lose all sense of time.

When I take my watch from my pocket, it's 11:30 a.m. I look around to be sure that I'm alone. I take a running start, laughing like a madman on this deserted road, and, as far as the weight of my pack will allow, I take a giant leap.

I just crossed over the one-thousand-kilometer mark.

CHAPTER VIII
JANDARMAS . . .

Shortly before noon, some peasants invite me to join them for their snack, and then to hop on their tractor for a ride back to their village, two kilometers away. I accept the galettes, tomatoes, and onions, but I want to walk. The patriarch appoints his youngest brother, Yusuf, to keep me company and show me the way. When we get to the first houses, a stout man with a distrustful look on his face is waiting for me next to my host. He says that he's the village *muhtar* and wants to see my passport. The document appears to do the job as the man relaxes, and in no time the joking begins. My host family is exultant; the neighbors parade by. In the room where people greet me, the mattresses are stowed, raised to lean against the walls next to piles of neatly folded blankets. At night, this must be a large dormitory. But I have no desire to test it out. I'd rather get to Kuzören, on the other side of the hill, overlooking a field of grain, busy with farmworkers. The red, clayey soil is as hard as concrete. The first drops of rain turn it into glue that sticks to your shoes. Behind me, Mount Yıldız (2,550 meters/8,370 feet) has its nose in the clouds. From a vantage point on the hill, looking east, I can make out the peaks that I won't get to for two more days.

The temperature is up. My walking stick sinks into the hot tar, and around 4:00 p.m., my jug is empty. I knock on the door of a solitary house, a short distance from a village, to ask for water. The man answering the door invites me into a room where three of his partners are busy at work, bent over computer screens. I'm flabbergasted by such modernity so deep in the countryside. I learn that these natives are land surveyors, and that they're working on the country's first land registry. It's a long-term, complex, and monumental task, requiring careful attention to detail. Until recently, property rights were transmitted orally, which often resulted in arguments between neighbors and made it all but impossible to set up and administer a system of property tax. They explain that in Turkey, when a man dies, his wife inherits one quarter of his belongings and his children receive three-fourths. They are taken aback when I tell them that French Napoleonic code gives everything to the children and nothing to the wife. As I head back out, my thirst quenched, they weigh me down with a good pound of cookies.

Two kilometers farther on, a tractor stops, and its passengers invite me to hop on board. There are three of them, all in their thirties. When I turn them down, they head off, and—in the now-classic scenario—they stop two hundred meters on. The driver, a sturdy, bearded fellow, remains seated on the vehicle; the other two get down and pretend to be washing their hands at a spring. They're clearly waiting for me, and, in fact, as soon as I'm near, they come over to me. A small fellow in a light-blue suit, greedily sucking on his cigarette, is all smiles with his questions, showing off all thirty-two of his yellowy teeth. While he asks me the usual questions, I lose track of the other one, who has come over to stand off to my right. Suddenly, I realize that he has ever so gently zipped open one of the pockets of my pack and that he's in the process of removing my camera. I pounce on him, rip it from his hands with a booming "No!" and take off running, camera in hand. With the weight I'm carrying, I have a hard time running quickly. I'm in the middle of the countryside, far from civilization, at their mercy. Maybe it would have been wiser for me to head in the other direction, toward the village . . . The two men have climbed back aboard the tractor, and it quickly catches up to me. It forces me onto the left side of the road. It's impossible to get away, since the road follows a cliff. To my left, a ravine opens below me, two or three meters deep. If I jump, I may very well break a leg. There's no escape route to my right, either: vertical as a wall, it's the mountainside.

The tractor has caught up to me. The man who tried to take my camera, seated on the mudguard, leans over and grabs my backpack, trying to pull it off. He can't do it, since the hip belt holds it to me securely. But he throws me off balance, and the tractor's large tire brushes up against me. The driver steers even farther toward the ravine. This time, I can't go any farther without falling headlong into the abyss. The tractor stops. The man on the mudguard is still holding my bag. I'm trapped.

Then, out of nowhere, a car pulls up from behind us. The man lets me go. I straddle the tractor's front wheel and make a run for it. It's too late, unfortunately, to stop the car that has already zoomed past. I'm out of breath because of the sprint I pulled off a little while ago. I can hear the tractor starting back up behind me. They're going to try again, and this time . . . But to my great surprise, they drive right past me. I quickly see why: a short distance away, at the foot of a small hill, is a beekeeper encampment. All I'd have to do is call out, and they'd hear me. The tractor heads off and disappears. Phew! I'm saved.

I sit down on the side of the road. I can barely feel my legs. The bastards! They almost had me. From day one, I've kept a careful eye on my gear. I never leave it in my hotel room unless the key's in my pocket. Otherwise, it's always within reach. At any moment, I might need one of the small objects it's carrying: ointments and remedies, my miraculous Swiss knife, my water jug, and above all, my maps, books, notebook, and scratchpads. The only object thieves would be interested in is the camera, but it would be a fool's prize: it's a very new model, one not yet for sale in Turkey, and a special process is required to develop the film.

Once my heart rate is back to normal, I head off again, but not without waving to the beekeepers, to whom I owe a great deal of thanks that I'm still in one piece. Unaware of the role they played, they wave back but keep right on working. They've come from the Black Sea coast to make their full year's salary in just three months. So, just like their bees, they're relentlessly busy.

I head up the small hill at the foot of which sits their camp. I reach the summit, and, just ahead, in a curve in the road, I see a shadow, that of a man or animal, hiding from me. More cautious now, I come to a halt. An opportune hillock to my left should serve as a mirador. I climb to the top, making sure that the "shadow" cannot see me. Then I rediscover the moves and tricks I used as a child, when we pretended we were Indians hiding from the enemy. And the enemy is really there, ready to ambush me. One of the three cowboys has his eye on the road, the other two are smoking. They've hidden the tractor behind a rock.

I don't want a war—especially since I'm not up to the challenge—and so I choose to head back and have a chat with my beekeepers. I don't really understand what they're doing, relentlessly nailing little wood trellises that miraculously seem to fit into the hives, but what I do understand is that I'm a bother to them. They of course offer me tea. I tell them about my journey, wanting to stall and, above all, to avoid being alone. After a half-hour, the situation gets complicated. There are long spells of silence. Should I tell them about my three bandits? I'm not sure. Around us, the bees are swooping by, and I find myself absorbed in idle contemplation, as if the study of apian species were my favorite way to relax. In fact, it's getting late and the youngest one, who must think that I—the old man next to him—am friendly but slow-witted, shows me his watch and tells me what I'll translate here as: "If you want to be in Alihacı this evening, you'd better get moving. In an hour, it'll be dark, and it isn't smart to walk alone around here after sunset."

Or before, for that matter, judging by the attempted robbery a short while ago. So I give in and blow the whistle on the three shady fellows waiting for me around the bend. The boy is a valiant soul: he suggests either that I share in their meal and sleep here tonight—under the stars, he advises me, since their tent is rather small—or he'll drive me to the village. I opt for the second alternative because that way, even if they call off the siege, at least I'll have my three attackers behind me.

Climbing into Mustafa's van, I'm furious with myself. In Istanbul, I vowed that I would walk from the former Turkish capital all the way to the former Chinese capital, without skipping a single kilometer. And now here I am, being driven like grandpa in a minivan. Sure, my safety is at stake here, and if I'm robbed, it could well be the end of the journey. But nevertheless: although I'm choosing the better of two bad options, my self-esteem takes a major hit.

It hasn't been long since my assailants broke camp, and we pass them not far from the spot where they tried to jump me. I can't hold back a *bras d'honneur* as we go by. The stocky one with the beard laughs; at least he's a good sport.

In the village of Alihacı, Mustafa calls a young boy over and tells him to take me to the *muhtar*; then, in a hurry, he heads off again after having refused the money I handed him to pay for gas. The *muhtar*'s not there: I'm told that he's away on a trip. His daughter, who promptly looks me over unceremoniously, asks the boy about me. "*Misafir*," he replies. She frowns. Clearly, she does not like taking in transients, as they must mean more work for her. I take off my pack and decide to calmly wait to see how things turn out. Experience has taught me that it's usually a matter of patience; it takes time for news to spread throughout the village. So we wait, the silent kid and I, in the shade of a line of poplar trees. The air is slightly warm; farmworkers are silently returning from the fields, exhausted from a full day's work in the hot sun. Since the start of my journey, I never saw a village so glaringly poor. The houses, crammed one next to the other haphazardly, look the worse for wear. Over here, a roof in poor condition likely lets in water; over there, an inhabited house is partially caved in; leprous walls are everywhere. Dark-faced, shabbily dressed kids play on the dirt roads where a little stream has turned cow dung into mud, and it runs off as yellowish ooze. Slurry pits lie alongside the houses, and the stench of manure is heavy in the evening air.

Finally, the *muhtar*'s son arrives: he's a little man, thin as a rake, and his elusive eyes don't make me want to trust him. But he asks me to follow him, and I comply, noticing, however, that he doesn't head in the direction of his father's house. We traverse some of the village, and little by little the whispering crowd dwindles. In a nook that must serve as the village square, two men are waiting, the *muhtar*'s assistants—village councilors of sorts, if I am properly deciphering the introductions. My guide takes a key from his pocket and opens the door of a small construction that opens out onto the square. In the first room we come to, a tiny space with a cement floor, we take off our shoes and then go into another room, hardly any bigger, where the floor is covered with rugs. On the left, a large bunk with a few sorry pillows on it occupies most of one bare wall. That's where I take a seat.

With the exception of the girls who are systematically made to leave, men and boys pour into the entrance room. With a seating capacity of about ten, it soon holds thirty. There they are, rowdy, packed like sardines, all wanting to see the marvel—me—and to listen as the mayor's son clobbers me with questions. I'm seated at one end of the bunk seat, with my pack next to me. Several kids, with the help of a nasty-looking fellow, plant themselves right beside my gear, and, without delay, little hands are trying to open the zippers. I do what I can to stop them, explaining as best I can what's in it. At the room's only window, all the little girls who were not allowed to come in are elbowing one another trying to get a look at the stranger, but someone chases them away, like flies.

It's now 6:30 p.m. A resourceful-looking kid made some tea, and the little tulip-shaped cups are filled over and over with the lovely amber liquid. They let fly with the questions. No one in this village speaks a lick of English or German or heaven knows what. Dictionary in hand, I do my best to answer the avalanche of inquiries, wondering what kind of a certificate I might be entitled to if I pass this test. A place to stay tonight, perhaps? But, although I fail to grasp all the subtleties and quibbles of these impromptu sophists, I notice one word that everyone is interested in: *para*. Do I have money? How much? How do I make my money? What's my salary? Do I have a car? How much is it worth? Am I rich? How much will my ticket cost to fly back to France? And every time, the word *para* is accompanied by a gesture understood the world over: the thumb sliding over the index finger. Am I armed? According to them, I ought to be afraid. The word "terrorists" makes the rounds. Accompanied by a nasty smile, there it is again, that other universal gesture: the pointed index finger moving from left to right under the chin.

There are constant comings and goings. Generally, village elders reach out their hand and bid me welcome, then someone gets up to make room and they sit down. Someone tells them who I am, and inevitably they react by asking yet another question, always connected to money. Irritated, I finally ask:

"But is money all you are interested in?"

"It is because we are so poor, so very poor . . .," replies a man with a large mustache sprawled out at the back of the room, lighting one cigarette after another.

It is enough to have walked through the village or to have a good look at the people assembled here to believe it and know that these people lack absolutely everything. Even air is rare in this room, and if they continue to pile in and harass me, I'm going to die of suffocation. I make it clear that I'm tired, hoping they'll focus on something else . . . And since I'm starting to get grumpy, and the crowd has had enough entertainment, little by little, they all give up on me and begin talking among themselves. The tiny, overcrowded room erupts into a brouhaha. People start shouting to one another: someone asks a question, setting off a volley of thirty answers. Everyone has something to say and insists on saying it.

Not upset that they're leaving me alone, I lie low and busy myself with the day's notes. Two events—crossing over the one-thousand-kilometer mark and the attempted robbery—are still very much on my mind, and I don't want to forget any details. A good half-hour has gone by without me paying any attention to the conversations, when the *muhtar*'s son comes over, followed by two musclemen, looking just as unfriendly as he does.

They want to see my passport too, but I'm adamant:

"I will only show it to the *muhtar*, when he arrives."

The son doesn't insist. The able kid has already put away the teacups and the samovar and, in a few trips, has brought the victuals that it was the women's job, ousted from the room, to prepare. A meal is served on a large platter in the middle of the room. I'm invited to sit with the *muhtar*'s son and two elders. The scene evokes that of the king of beggars eating with his councilors at court. I've positioned myself so that I can keep an eye on my pack, hardly a pointless precaution given that everyone has a hankering for it. Never has a backpack been so coveted: groping hands caress it, lifting it up to see how heavy it is, greedy eyes leer at it. Then, all of a sudden, a burly fellow, whose voice I have not yet had the pleasure of hearing up to that point, plops himself down right in front of me. It would seem he's on an important mission. He must've been asked to speak on behalf of them all: he has been delegated to tell me that I've passed muster, and, ultimately, it has been decided that they like me just fine. Did I understand that correctly? Before going back to his seat, with everyone looking on in approval, he throws me a hint of a smile. Maybe I did get it right after all.

By now, it's dark out. I walked thirty kilometers today, from Çırçır to my friendly beekeepers, and the day's emotions have drained me. I'd like to be left alone so that I can rest. But where will I sleep? I still have no idea and am waiting for the *muhtar* to come to settle the question.

The man lying down, the mustache man who said they were poor, now comes forward and plants himself in front of me. Everyone stops talking. And, in total silence made all the more eerie by the earlier brouhaha, it's the start of a surreal interrogation, one that would I would find quite amusing if I didn't have the feeling that how I answer has a bearing on my safety. If I were to transcribe the main points of the exchange, it would go something like this:

"What's in your bag?"

"A first-aid kit, clothing, food, a sleeping bag, a notebook, a few books . . ."

"Do you have a map?"

"Yes, I have a map."

The man triumphantly turns to the crowd and repeats in a loud voice: "He has the map!"

The crowd responds in unison with a satisfied, "Ah!" Just what are they thinking? Sensing some kind of misunderstanding, I clarify: "I have a roadmap and a compass. What are you talking about?"

"You have the treasure map."

I'm dumbfounded.

"The treasure map?"

"The Silk Road treasure. We know that there is treasure hidden along the Silk Road."

The suggestion is so preposterous that I cannot keep from laughing. But I'm alone in this. Their faces are grave. They stare at me unsympathetically.

"Show us."

I take the roadmap from my pocket, or rather a piece of my map. To keep it in relatively good condition, I cut each fold out separately. I've often handed my map to peasants so that they could show me where I am. Each time, it was the same scenario: the sheet was handed from one person to another, everyone wanting to touch it. Up till now, no one ever took it for a treasure map! It's pretty clear that if I give it to him—when you're given a treasure map, you don't give it back—it will go around the room and finally disappear. In this completely unfamiliar territory, I cannot get by without my map, its imperfections notwithstanding. I ask the fellow to sit next to me, and I produce the leaf of paper as if concealing it beneath my cloak, trying to attract his attention by tracing with my finger the route I'm taking, pointing to the villages I'm traveling through. His hand, as if beyond his control, convulsively grabs at the document, trying to snatch it away. Each time he tries to take it, I pull it away, knowing full well that I'm only making things worse, giving substance to the idea that I really do have treasure to hide. After endless explanations, he returns to his seat, seemingly appeased. But as the evening wears on, I have the impression that what was not said, what was misunderstood, and what was implied are gaining ground.

Around 10:00 p.m., five people, whose attire gives the impression that they're part of the slightly less destitute class, enter the room. Silence once again settles over the assembly. The two women aren't wearing chadors. I'm introduced: they're the schoolteachers. They're from the area around İzmir. They're not interested in my travels—everyone has filled them in on that—but in . . . my profession. At least what I say I do. From the outset of my journey, as I said earlier, I've been introducing myself as a teacher. I'm therefore a colleague. I say, in a sincere voice, that it's a difficult profession, and then I shower them with questions so that they don't ask me any. One of the women can utter a few words of English but is unable to understand. We go back to speaking Turkish, which

means that I'm limited to very rudimentary discourse. They divulge that
they're not happy here. That life here is very difficult, and that it's hard to
practice their profession. They dream of returning to their hometowns,
but before they can do that, they have to serve for several years in this
remote burg.

When they leave, it's 10:30, and the woman who spoke the most with
me takes my hand saying, with great feeling and as though overcome
with pity for me:

"I wish you much luck, much luck."

Her statement reminds me of what Can, the banker back in Istanbul,
told me: "You will need a lot of luck."

Up till now, I can't complain, I've had my fair share of it. But her
merciful tone has me worried.

No sooner have the teachers closed the door behind them than the
muhtar's son steps forth once again, still followed by his two thugs, and
the ensuing interrogation might, once again, be transcribed as follows:

"I want to see your passport."

"Where is the *muhtar*?"

"He's not coming."

"Where am I going to sleep?"

"Here."

One of the two guard dogs insists:

"He is the *muhtar*'s son, it's the same thing. Show him your passport."

I can no longer stand my ground without the situation getting out
of hand. I agree to take out my passport, but only to the short, spindly
man. I don't want my passport to be handed around the room: I'd never
get it back.

So I ask him to sit down beside me. The onlookers are all there, circled
around me, shoving one another to get a better view. Without letting go,
I open my passport to the page that shows my identity so as to prove that
it really belongs to me, then to the page with the stamps from Turkish
immigration. Above our heads, thirty pairs of wide eyes peer down. The
mayor's son takes the booklet, thumbs through it for some time, wants
to know the meaning of all the other stamps—from Japan, China, the

United States, and Africa, in connection with my recent travels—and then stares at length at the Iranian visa that takes up an entire page. Breaking his promise, he hands it to someone next to him. That man riffles through it in turn. I'm as taut as a bow stretched with an arrow. It's now or never. At the moment when the man, having looked at it for a long time, is about to pass it on to a third thief, and with thirty other hands stretched out to grab it, I literally throw myself into the scuffle and snatch it as it flies past. I put it back in my pocket, which I carefully zip shut, while a hostile silence takes hold, laden with the frustration of thirty onlookers. I'm furious that they broke their promise and am ready for this inept charade to come to an end. In a loud voice, I declare that I'm tired and would like to get some rest. No one seems to hear. They've regained their seats, are lighting up cigarettes, and the deliberations start up again, plausibly fueled by wild speculation of which it's probably best I can't understand a thing.

I let another half-hour go by, and then, completely exhausted, I reiterate my demand. In further support, I open the door, awkwardly inviting my hosts to give me some privacy. A long silence settles over the room once again; no one budges. I implore the assembly a third time and sense that I'm beginning to lose all patience. Another silence, then one of the spectators—for this has indeed been quite the show—gets up and heads out the door. Two others follow him. I thank them, loudly wishing them "*iyi geceler (ee-gah'-djeh-lehr)* (good night)." A young student asks me on his way out:

"At what time are you leaving tomorrow?"

"7:00 a.m."

"I'll be there and will walk with you."

I appreciate his promise, and it gives me the assurance that I won't be alone as I walk through the infamous Shiite village Fazil told me about. When he leaves, a dozen more do the same. I continue to hold the door and cast a rather nasty glance at the remaining attendees. The *muhtar*'s son and the two thugs stay put. Fatigue is making me pushy. I've done everything I can to remain calm and I'm pleased with myself for that, but now, overwrought, I literally shove them out the door.

Behind them, I slide the iron latch. Now very cautious, I check around to be sure that it's the only entrance in to the place where I'm going to sleep. The middle lock has no latch, and I don't have the key. I block the door with my walking stick. There's no way to secure the small window, which can be held shut with two wooden pins pivoting on a nail at the top and bottom. One good strike of the elbow, and they'll give way. *Inşallah.*

From the faucet in the first room, I fill my water bottle for the next day, dropping in a few tablets to sterilize the water overnight. I quickly freshen up with some ice-cold water and jump into my sleeping bag. I try to sleep, but it isn't easy after the day's events. On top of it all, the entire village has gathered outside the house. The conversations are in keeping with all that has transpired: intense, vehement, their voices impassioned. People are shouting out to one another, laughing and screaming. As far as anyone in the village can recall, it must be that no one has ever seen a foreigner. I know how pathologically curious the Turks are, but the commotion is beyond belief. The *muhtar* never came. Is he really away, or has he refused to receive me, and if that's the case, then why?

I turn out the light. They'll soon calm down and go home. I finally relax and fall asleep. I must have been asleep only a few moments when I wake up. The hubbub has grown louder. Annoyed, without turning on the lamp, I go over to the small window and imperceptibly pull back the curtain. What I see makes my blood run cold. A man—one of the spectators a short while ago, as I noticed his unbelievable mustache—is clutching an army rifle, old breech-loading model. Standing still, as if at attention, his eyes are fixed on the door of the building I'm in, paying no attention to the commotion around him. The whole village is there. The little girls have even been allowed to slip in among the men. People are chattering away, making wild gesticulations in the faint light of a bare bulb hanging from the wall of a neighboring house.

Standing in my birthday suit, behind the window, I suddenly start to shiver. I'm tempted to hop in my sleeping bag, but then I think to myself that if they're going to kill me, I'd better at least look presentable. For what kind of respect would they have for an enemy dressed in nothing but his birthday suit? I pull my clothes on in the shadows. What am I waiting for? Are they going to break down the door? I'm cold. Fully dressed, I slip into my sleeping bag and pull a blanket over me. I'm shivering, from either the cold or the fear. I know it's childish, but I take my pocketknife out of my bag, a handsome *Laguiole* that my sister Hélène gave me, with my name engraved on the blade. I put it under my pillow, ready to defend myself, if it comes to that. But I'm under no illusions. Imagine the scene: on whom would you place your bets? One thing is now perfectly clear: the gods have abandoned me. What do these pitiable little people want from me? Are they planning to rob me? To kill me? Or both? What are they waiting for to break down the door? If they wanted to plunder me, or polish me off, why didn't they do so earlier? I obviously have no answers to these questions that I'm simply asking myself to pass the agonizing time. Minutes seem like hours. I'm dead tired. My watch reads half past midnight. Little by little, my fear begins to fade, giving way to exhaustion. I slowly begin to sink, and then fall headfirst, into a deep sleep. For how long? I haven't the slightest idea, when someone suddenly begins knocking on the window, jolting me out of bed. What, for heaven's sake, do they want from me? Exhausted, exasperated, I decide not to answer. Let them prepare their devilish deed; I'm not about to place my own head on the chopping block. They knock again, this time at the door, then once again on the windowpane. Someone yells something I don't understand. The chatter stops. This sudden silence has me worried. In stocking feet, I walk across the room and lift a corner of the curtain. A soldier in camouflage is standing at the door, pointing a machine gun. I can't hold back a gasp. The bastards! They've called the *jandarmas.*

While lacing up my boots, I tell myself that it's better that way anyway. I'll explain who I am, and everything will be resolved. Before opening the door that they're now knocking on harder than before, I force myself to relax and calmly stow my knife back in its pocket. Behind the soldier, there are two officers. The entire village is there, elbowing one another to get a better look. The show, apparently, still goes on. When I open the door, for ten seconds, it's so quiet you could hear the buzz of a mosquito.

The two officers size me up. The taller one addresses me in clear English. They want to talk to me, he says. I step back to let them in. The mob is, predictably, ready to follow suit and cram their way in, but I stand in their way. If they want to play Judas, fine, but I'm not about to actually reward them for their betrayal.

"Not them!"

With a wave of the hand, the officer orders them to get out. One of the armed men has come in with the soldiers. He goes over to stand at other end of the room, still pointing his rifle at me.

"Is that your bag?"

"Yes. What's the problem?"

"Your passport, please."

Outside, the crowd is muttering.

"Please follow us."

"Wait. I'm a tourist. I'm visiting your country. What have I done wrong? Are you arresting me?"

"Not at all. It's for your safety. Follow us."

"I'd like to know where we're going."

"Next door."

The officer bars me from taking my backpack. The soldier grabs it. Out on the small square, the group of men who, a short while ago, told me that they liked me is relishing the spectacle.

As I make my way through the vengeance-thirsty throng, I have the one small consolation of shouting back to them in a booming voice a phrase I know by heart: "Thank you for your hospitality!" At least I feel as though I'm leaving the place with my head held high.

In the street that crosses the village, I'm flanked by two soldiers, while a third carries my pack. The crowd is close on our heels. They don't want to miss the final act. For my part, in total amazement, I discover that there's a real spectacle in front of us. Every ten meters, soldiers in camouflage fatigues have taken up position on each side of the main road, a finger on the trigger, their weapons aimed at the houses and the shadowy side streets, keeping close watch on an invisible enemy. They're all wearing helmets and bulletproof vests. A vision of war. Above all, if you're out there in the shadows, you'd better be careful not to sneeze: you'd be instantly shot. It wouldn't take much to convince me that, in fact, there are snipers everywhere, their guns pointing at us. How many soldiers in all? They're everywhere, like statues, keeping an eye out for the slightest movement. I'm dumbfounded. Finally, humor gets the best of me. Is this all just for me? At the head of the pack following us, the man who was guarding my door is now brandishing his blunderbuss like a church candle. The expression on his face exhibits the humble gravity of a hero. Oh yes, the joker can boast of having scared the bejesus out of me. This is an historic moment for the village. It was almost one for me, too.

For my part, I'm feeling at once quite angry with these people who tricked me, having violated the conventions of hospitality, but also extremely relieved. After I am sure at the sight of the rifle-toting joker that my final hour was at hand, the army's presence is reassuring. We stop in front of a house with walls that overhang the street. Two troopers stand guard at the bottom of the steps. The two officers in fatigues, another soldier, and I head upstairs. I want to reclaim my gear. The officer instructs the soldier carrying it to come in. The landlord is one of the men who came to welcome me this afternoon, the old hypocrite. It's he who called the *jandarmas,* since he's the only one with a telephone in the village. Must be his way of welcoming tourists. I try to catch his eye, but he keeps looking away. In the presence of the officers, he kowtows, catering to their every whim. It's grotesque. At the request of one of the officers, the informant leaves the room after having offered the use of his telephone. The officer who speaks English asks me for my map. I hand it to him with a chuckle: is he looking for treasure, too?

The two officers lean over the piece of paper. If they look hard enough, they'll spot the little marks I scrawled to indicate the three Shiite villages Fazil told me about. They seem not to notice. They spend a long time on the phone. I'm too upset to try to catch what they're saying. In any case, I have no idea how I could hope to derail the process already underway. Let's wait and see: that's the sensible attitude I need to have. When he hangs up, the man has very specific orders.

"You'll have to follow us."

"Where?"

"To headquarters. For your safety."

"I am not in any danger."

I can't believe I had the gall to say that after just having the hell scared out of me. But I go on: "Where is your base? Is it far?"

"No."

"One kilometer, ten?"

"Three or four."

I try to object.

"No, I'm going to stay here. I want to leave early tomorrow morning."

The officer gives an order to the soldier, who hurries to open the door where the other two soldiers are standing. One of them takes me by the arm to lead me out. I flare up:

"I can walk on my own. If I'm under arrest, then put handcuffs on me."

The officer gives a new order to the soldier, and this time he leaves me alone. But it's clear that I am indeed under arrest.

The situation is already crazy enough as it is. I'm not about to play the hero and descend into the burlesque. And with soldiers, you just never know. Visions of *Midnight Express*—with dank dungeons and brutal wardens—flash before my eyes. I no longer know what to think. I decide to follow them without a struggle. After all, Part Two might be just as interesting as Part One. What's my best option? To be in the hands of these military men who see terrorists everywhere, or held by the villagers who fantasize about a "Silk Road treasure" and who could very well wind up slitting my throat just to steal my "treasure map"?

The throng that was expecting me to be shot as soon as I came out of the house watches on, sad to see me leave. The comments they're making follow us, but not the people. Two soldiers hold them back while I'm led, under constant guard, toward some cars parked a short distance away. When the soldiers regroup, I'm curious enough to count them. There are forty-six of them, in addition to the two officers who have a black, unmarked car at their disposal. I've never had so many people concerned for me. I feel like I'm headed for stardom. The soldiers split up into three minibuses and an all-terrain vehicle equipped with a machine gun. In one of the minibuses, my two guards sit next to me on the first bench seat. And the caravan of vehicles heads off into the night. I turn around to catch a final glimpse of my "hosts." The windshield is covered in dew, and all I can see is the surrounding night.

It isn't long before I realize that the officer lied to me. On deeply rutted roads—the path to stardom is no doubt just as impenetrable as are the ways of the Lord—we creep along. The drivers zigzag to avoid potholes. We travel five, then ten kilometers. I ask where we're going. The conscript to my right refuses to answer, the one to my left, who has a face like a farmer in Normandy, utters a single word: "Sivas."

So they're not taking me four, but at least forty or even fifty kilometers. During the ride, I don't know what to think. The officers don't seem hostile. Why, then, did they arrest me? Was I really in danger? In that case, two or three *jandarmas* could have warned me, protecting me if need be. Did the soldiers let themselves get worked up by the villagers, who perhaps told them I was a dangerous individual? What's going to happen when we're at the base? I've read several articles on the methods used by Turkey's army and the *jandarmas*, and what they said is far from reassuring. Several days before setting out on my journey, I read an article in *Reporters sans frontières* (*Reporters Without Borders*) describing how a Turkish journalist had been tortured by the police. I am not Turkish, nor am I—officially at least—a journalist. But will they care? What if they were to find out that I'm a journalist?

Like a scene from a movie, the evening I spent in that village plays over and over again in my mind. With hindsight, the villagers' behavior tonight becomes clear. If they refused to leave the house where I was holed up, remaining outside the door, it's because they wanted to be there to witness my arrest. And if the *muhtar*'s son came back to see my passport, it's because the military had asked for as much information as possible before moving in. So they all knew the *jandarmas* were coming. When I threw them out, I spoiled the dramatic turn of events they were hoping to see, imagining that my arrest would go something like this:

"The armed men break into the room, machine guns in hand; I resist, gunshots ring out." Or better yet: "A terrorist is killed, and the village is awarded a medal." As for the clown with his toy rifle standing in front of my door, he was a surrogate, the kind the army sometimes recruits in villages. With their old rifles, they're supposed to act as a kind of local militia, providing a measure of self-defense against the men of the PKK. They are, in a sense, their anti-Kurdish *Harkis.** He had taken up position fearing I might escape before the soldiers arrived. Thank goodness I didn't step out to pee: I'd have taken a bullet. That's how destinies can play out one way or the other.

It is at least three o'clock in the morning when we finally get inside the garrison, guarded like Fort Alamo, armored vehicles at the entrance and soldiers everywhere. Once again, one of my guardian angels grabs me by the arm. I freeze and refuse to budge. He understands and lets me go. I'm led to the English-speaking officer's desk. It's in a large room with walls adorned with portraits of Atatürk. The officer's name is inscribed on a plate on his desk: Gökgöz (blue eyes or blue sky). The name is everywhere: woven in two little rugs framed in miniature looms, on the walls. He is proud of his family name, and he must be glad that his grandfather chose that one when, after the fall of the sultanate, the Turks were enjoined to conform to the western tradition of a given name and surname. I notice, incidentally, that his eyes are not the least bit blue. Mendel's law is harsh, but it's the law.

He invites me to take a seat in front of his executive desk.

"Çay?"

"*Yes.*"

Trying to make the best out of a bad situation, I strive to keep my anger to myself, in spite of his big lie with respect to the distance between Alihacı and the base.

---

* TN: Mercenaries. The term refers to Algerian soldiers who fought with the French during Algeria's War of Independence.

"I'm going to have to search in your backpack. The villagers reported you as a terrorist. It's because of your pack."

"Have they never seen a backpack before?"

"I have to search it."

"I suppose I have no choice, but if you don't mind, I'd first like to call my consulate first, to let them know I've been arrested."

"Tomorrow morning."

"Then wait until tomorrow to rummage through my pack. What's the plan for right now?"

"We'll put you up for the night."

"So I'm under arrest…"

"No, you're our guest."

I chuckle. He's got some gall, this tall, somewhat portly fellow who speaks with a high-pitched voice while drawing out his words, and graceful gestures like those of a clergyman. A grunt standing at the office entrance goes over to my pack, opens it, and begins the task of emptying it out. As he takes objects out of it, he hands them over to the other soldier. The second soldier carefully examines them and then sets them on the ground. Without reading it, the soldier hands Blue-Eyes anything handwritten or with typed letters on it. Blue-Eyes then fastidiously combs through everything, holding some of pieces of paper over his desk lamp, trying to see through them. Book, maps, notebook, address book (for postcards), pocket logbook: nothing escapes his fanatical eye. As I'm naturally cautious, in recording events or thoughts related to them, I never wrote the name of Öcalan, or the initials of his party, the PKK. I invented my own system of code. This is obviously what he's looking for. Moreover, since I send my notes back to France each time I stay in a city, most of my narrative is already safely back in Paris. The documents that I'm taking into Iran and those I put in a separate location until needed (book, maps . . .) are also examined very carefully. I find this search extremely irritating. I feel like I'm being strip-searched. These objects that, as I said earlier, have no material value but are vital for my journey are now scattered all over the floor. Given how careful I've been since starting out to stow everything neatly away, it looks like one heck of a mess to me, and I show my displeasure by getting up from the seat where I've been confined since my arrival.

When, at long last, the bag is empty, the soldier and his superior walk around it purposefully and cautiously as though it were some malefic entity, finally feeling the stitching with their fingers. They pat it down: looking for what, for heaven's sake!? And then the officer tells his subordinate to put everything back. Whoa! There's no way I'm going to let them transform my neatly organized pack into a chaotic jumble. I myself set about putting each object back in a plastic bag, then each plastic bag in one of the compartments. Blue-Eyes, who has now completed his search, and the other snooping soldier watch on as I silently put everything away. I exact a little payback by going about the process as slowly as possible. While stowing my knife back in a pocket, I can't hold back a little provocation:

"Did you notice that I've got a weapon?"

Then, when I've finished:

"Well, are you satisfied? You've seen for yourselves that I'm not a terrorist. Are you going to take me back to Alihacı?"

"No. Tomorrow if you want. In any case, it's a dangerous place. Between now and then, I suggest getting some rest, and so will I. It's late."

"Couldn't you have searched my pack in Alihacı and left me there?"

"..."

"Would you be willing to take me to a hotel?"

"No. You are our guest. I'm going to . . ."

"But I don't want to be your guest!"

". . . Someone will take you to your room. We'll have to lock the door. I'm also going to keep your camera, since you're on military soil and it's forbidden to take photographs. I'll return it to you tomorrow morning."

"You're keeping me against my will and you're locking me up. Whether you say so or not, I'm under arrest."

"Let me say it again, you are our guest . . ."

He's about to get up, but then stops:

"Are you angry?"

I'm taken aback by his question. After having infuriated me, now he has the nerve to ask if I am angry! At least, that's what I think he said.

I don't hold back, and since he asked, after having tried so hard all the while to contain my exasperation, the dam finally breaks.

"You want to know if I am angry? You bet—I'm angry to have been pulled out of bed like a criminal even though I did nothing wrong. Yes, I'm angry that you lied to me, telling me that we were only going four kilometers, when in fact you've taken me fifty from the road I'm traveling. I'm angry that I'm not allowed to call my consulate, angry at the hypocrisy of pretending that I'm not under arrest when I evidently am, and am being held against my will, angry to be traveling in a country that claims to be a democracy, though the term *habeas corpus* apparently can't be translated into Turkish. I'm angry because, although I grant you the right to ask for my papers and tell me I'm risking my life by going into dangerous villages, I don't recognize your right to decide for me. I'm of lawful age and can make choices for myself. As a tourist, you can warn me, and even take measures to ensure my security. But you have no rights over me, provided I abide by your country's laws, and that's what I've done.

In the presence of the two stunned military men, one who understands and the other who doesn't, I let loose all the resentment that I've been holding back now for too long, I come close to yelling, purging the fear and anger I've endured since this morning. I conclude with a few general considerations, feeling that I'm at the top of my form:

". . . and you want to join the European Community? You might first want to take evening classes to review the Universal Declaration of the Rights of Man."

"But . . ."

I cut him off, as I'm not done:

"I'm a French tourist, on vacation in your country. I have rights, you owe me some consideration. The first step should have been to call the French Consulate. They would have told you who I am. But you're denying me this right. Stop wasting all your money on propaganda and claims that you're a vacationers' paradise."

The grunt, who doesn't speak a word of English and for whom this deluge of grievances must completely overwhelm, leaves in the middle of the storm. Blue-Eyes finally manages to get a word in edgewise:

"But all I wanted to know was whether you were *hungry*," and this time he clearly aspirates the *h*.

Blue-Eyes had in fact very politely asked if I was *hungry*, but he had pronounced it "are you *angry?*"!

I realize my mistake, but I'm glad to have spit out all my anger at him. In any case, there's no way to take back everything I said. I continue, now in a softer voice:

"No, I'm not hungry. But I am thirsty. A beer would be great, since I can't go into town to have one."

"I don't have beer. It's forbidden here. But I do have some whisky."

"Then let it be whisky!" He serves me a tall shot that I drink in small sips. It's my first taste of alcohol since leaving Istanbul. My anger subsides, fatigue sets back in.

Before handing me off to a soldier who's going to show me to my room, Blue-Eyes tells me, as if to apologize, that the people of Alihacı thought I was a terrorist and that it was his job to check the situation out. I agree that he had a right to do that, but not to bring me here.

Still in a bad mood, I refuse to lock my door. The soldier, who I don't want to be too hard on, has his orders. If I don't lock the door, he tells me, he'll be punished. So I lock the door, chuckling to myself at the absurdity of the situation. What are they afraid of? That one of their recruits might rob me, or maybe knock off the supposed "terrorist"?

It's all very exhausting, and most of it is beyond my powers of comprehension. Just like I find it hard to understand the lack of experience or perhaps naïveté of Blue-Eyes and his sidekick. If I had compromising documents, I surely wouldn't hide them in my backpack. I would have kept them with me. But the idea of patting me down never even occurred to them.

I fall asleep just as the loudspeakers of the mosques nearby start broadcasting the call to prayer. It's 5:00 a.m., and this is a June 16 that I will not soon forget. After putting one thousand kilometers behind me this morning, the attempted robbery at the hands of the three scoundrels on a tractor, and then my arrest in Alihacı, I've had enough excitement for one day.

I'd like to think that this was nothing but a string of bad luck and that, once my carefree attitude is restored, I'll continue serenely on my way. Just before I give in to my dreams, though, I'm no longer all so sure.

CHAPTER IX
CARAVANSARIES

It's 7:30 a.m. when my soldier-valet comes knocking on my door. I've slept very little, and, probably because of the fatigue, I'm still angry.

"First Lieutenant Gökgöz would like you to come to his office."

"Once I've had breakfast," I tell him in a haughty tone.

The grunt panics. Used to obeying Blue-Eyes's orders, he's caught off guard when I don't. He heads off to find out what he should do and comes back a short while later with a platter. I had fallen back asleep. I take my time eating. I wait out the clock, dragging my feet: 'tis the weapon of the weak. When I've finished, he picks up the platter and asks if I would be so kind as to get dressed and join him downstairs.

"I'll shower first."

Once again, he goes for instructions. While I wait, I observe what's going on the garrison grounds outside. A noncommisioned officer, motionless in the center of the training area, is demonstrating how sadistic he can be in trying to wear down a squad of young soldiers by putting them through firearms drills, running races, and push-ups. I smile as I recall the answer I was given by the young soldier seated next to me while they were driving me to Sivas. Having asked where I was from, I tried to explain walking to him, and the Silk Road. Something he said gave me pause, so I asked: "You know what the Silk Road is, don't you?" "Of course. It's the paved road." And I thought to myself that the commanding officers ought to teach them their history instead of making them run in circles like donkeys round their waterwheel.

Seeing that my soldier-valet hasn't come back, I go out into the hall-way, crowded with *jandarmas* biding their time, and head off in search of the shower room.

It's after 8:30 a.m. when I go into Blue-Eyes's office. He has been wait-ing for an hour. Across from him is seated a young ranking officer who speaks very good English. The lieutenant has no intention of repeating last night's pronunciation mistake: he has brought along an interpreter. We have a cup of tea. Then I decide to go then and there on the offensive.

"I got to thinking last night. You may be right, and I don't want to take any unnecessary risks. So I'm going to skip the two or three villages past Alihacı. So let me suggest that you take me back to the road I was on, but a little farther, to Yeniköy. But first, as we agreed last night, I want to place a call to my consulate."

"We'll see about that," Blue-Eyes replies, in a conciliatory tone. "But first, the commanding officer is going to decide . . ."

Before he has time to finish his sentence, I pounce.

"What? Decide? Decide what? I'm not a soldier, I'm not even Turkish. Your commander can decide what he wants for you, you're his subordi-nate. But for me, he has no say. And I insist on having my consulate on the phone before anything else, as you agreed last night. If I can't do that, I won't have anything to do with your commanding officer."

Blue-Eyes throws a weary and expressive glance at the young soldier who hasn't said a word. It means: "You see, you can't talk to this guy." Without a word, he gets up and leaves. Nearly an hour goes by before he comes back.

"We're going to hand you over to the Alien Police Service."

So Blue-Eyes and his commander have decided to get rid of me and to hand me off to someone else. A different soldier takes my pack and leads me to a chauffeur-driven car driven waiting in the courtyard. Ten min-utes later, we're on the premises of the *"polis."* I'm still angry. To Mustafa Kaçar (*ka-char'*), chief of the Alien Police Service, I repeat what I kept telling Blue-Eyes.

"I want to call my consulate."

"Of course," he says. "While we wait, would you like tea or coffee?"

"Since last night, I've taken it that I'm under arrest. With you, am I free to go where I please?"

"Of course. Furthermore, I don't understand why no one informed me. I'm the one in charge of everything regarding foreigners, so the *jandarmas* should have called me right away last night."

The man is calm, pleasant, and expresses himself in excellent English. In addressing his subordinates, his manner is such that they're clearly happy to do whatever he asks. Our conversation reflects the man's concern for me; it's both courteous and intelligent. Mustafa tells me he's originally from the Dardanelles region.

At the French Consulate in Ankara, a man and a woman take turns speaking with me over the phone. It would be an exaggeration to say they're ready to rush to the aid of their fellow countrymen. This is what stands out from their explanations: there are danger zones; I managed to go poking around one; the *jandarmas* do whatever they please; there's no point in arguing with them. Consequently, they have no intention of filing a complaint on my behalf with respect to the way I was arrested or how I was searched. If I wish to continue my hike, I should expect to be stopped again, arrested, and even put under surveillance—for a day, a week or even two—if that's what the *jandarmas* want to do. Clearly, for them, my trek across Turkey is little more than a source of potential hassles. They want a fax of the first few pages of my passport, since the consulate in Istanbul didn't forward them my file.

While they're sending the photocopy to Ankara, Mustafa and I pick up where we left off. He's a pleasant, cultured man, keenly interested in world affairs. Unlike most Turks I've met, the reason he speaks such excellent English isn't simply part of his culture, but the mark of the great interest he has in all things foreign. He is also well aware, having traveled a great deal, of the deplorable image that Turkey has among Western democracies. When his assistant comes back to tell us that that the fax has been sent and hands back my passport, Mustafa wants to know what my immediate plans are.

"Since I'm here, I'll tour Sivas, which was a very important stopover city along the Silk Road. And tomorrow morning, since First Lieutenant

Gökgöz offered as much, I'll ask him to have someone drive me back to my original route." Mustafa reaffirms that the mountainous region I'm heading into is very dangerous. The *jandarmas* are continuously patrolling the area. PKK militants lie in wait, fire a few shots in the late afternoon, and then vanish into the countryside, which they know like the back of their hand. He suggests I avoid the zone beyond Alihacı, places a call to reserve a room for me in a hotel downtown, negotiates the rate, discounting it by half, and drives me there in his own car. Before leaving, he gives me his personal phone number and urges me to call him should I run into any difficulties in the Sivas district.

The night was short and turbulent. I can't help but think, before giving in to a restorative nap, that I've met two men, Blue-Eyes and Mustafa Kaçar, who represent rather well the two faces of modern Turkey. Mehmet Gökgöz is the direct descendent of days when "Turk" was synonymous with "soldier." This was in the Asian tradition of warfare and regalian law. He's one of many who represent an army that, in reality, rules the country never doubting its impunity, resorting to the use of force and sometimes even a coup d'état when things are not headed in a direction that it considers consistent with its views. Mustafa Kaçar, on the other hand, is opening the way for the many college students I've met, or the young middle schoolers in Amasya, whose openness to the world and hunger for foreign languages and travel stand as proof of their generation's special fascination for Europe and America.

Central Sivas holds several beautiful architectural treasures from the Seljuk period, mosques and Qur'anic schools having survived earthquakes, multiple invasions, and—more devastating than even the worst acts of barbarism—the pouring of cement. Visit, photos: I'm a bit of a tourist for the day. But my mind is elsewhere. I can't get last night's adventures off my mind: have calamitous times finally come?

Crossing over the one-thousand-kilometer mark, the attempted robbery, and the intervention of the army are events that capture perfectly the dangers caravans faced for over two thousand years. Sitting on the second floor of Sivas's caravansary, now converted into a *salon de thé*, I muse on the following five plagues that traders and camel drivers so

feared: ill health, injuries, natural disasters, thieves, and war. The Silk
Road is strewn with tombs. Death hung over the mountains and deserts,
striking without warning. Is it any wonder that, when the Polo brothers
and young Marco returned after having been gone for twenty-five years,
they had been presumed dead and their estate divvied up?

It's by way of the Silk Road that the plague arrived in Europe, spread-
ing death in stopover towns along the way. Yesterday, I completed the
one thousandth kilometer, it's true, but who's to say whether I'll make it
to the two thousandth? Aside from my sore feet, I haven't had any health
issues thus far. I'm fit as a fiddle. But there's still a long way to go. And
the conditions in which I'm traveling, sometimes in blatant disregard of
basic nutritional or bodily hygiene, by no means guarantee that I'll arrive
in Tehran well rested and raring to go.

Theft was a constant threat on the Silk routes. My adventure yesterday proves that it still is. Gangs would lie in wait for the caravans at
narrow passages, ambushing the merchants, steeling their bundles and
animals, taking the gold and sometimes the travelers' lives. The silk,
spices, and precious merchandise that paraded by day in and day out
right before their eyes aroused envy in the sedentary populations. I too,
quite unwittingly, stir up those same desires. In poor villages like Alihacı,
I look like a wealthy man from a land of plenty. From that perspective,
perhaps it isn't just a stretch to think that my pack conceals stores of
treasure. No one actually did anything, though, until the tractor incident
on the road to Alihacı. Although my watch is now tucked away deep in
my pocket, it looked a lot like a portable computer, arousing envy. I've
already been asked several times if I wanted to exchange it for a cheap
bazaar timepiece. Two young men suggested I simply give it to them.

Bandits thought twice before attacking thousand-camel caravans, as
they were accompanied by a hundred men practically looking for a fight.
The lead caravanner also paid several armed men (usually Armenians)
to ensure the convoy's security. Inside the caravansaries—veritable for-
tresses—security was good. When there was a particularly serious threat,
the paşas lent escorts, consisting of dozens of lancers, to accompany the
travelers for a certain distance. Revenue from the Silk Road was the local

lords' chief source of income, so they had a vested interest in providing security; otherwise, the caravans would change routes: farewell, then, to all the taxes levied on those transporting precious bundles. Their concern for the merchants' peace of mind was so great that the authorities of the day invented insurance. If, despite all the precautions, a traveler were robbed, he would submit to the *paşa* a list of the stolen merchandise and would be reimbursed, either by the *paşa* himself or by the Sultan. Today, of course, gangs of highwaymen are a thing of the past in Turkey. But alone and unarmed, I'm an easy, tempting target. It wouldn't take fifty people to steal my "treasures."

Since ancient times, war has been a permanent way of life on the Silk routes. It's just as prevalent today, and the entire region of Central Asia is still in this day and age ravaged by local, violent conflicts. While I was preparing my journey, I had to bear this in mind in choosing my itinerary. I had the choice of several ancient routes. I would have liked to begin on the Mediterranean in the ancient city of Antioch and traverse Syria, Iraq, Iran, and then Afghanistan. They are magnificent countries; their peoples and lands are rich in history. But the dangers are all too apparent.

I couldn't take the route through the Steppes, either. The Turkish–Armenian border is closed. As for the Caucasus, the smoldering insurgency going on in Chechnya seemed as if it might flare up again at any moment . . . and it finally did. But the most unpleasant peril seemed to me to be the country's new unofficial national sport: the kidnapping of foreign tourists, with ransom notes posted in Grozny Square. No, I have no interest in heading over there just to set myself up as bait . . .

In the meantime, on the route that I did choose, I'm confronted with the Kurdistan Workers' Party's war against the State. My arrest yesterday suggests that things could heat up after Erzurum—on the edge of Turkish Kurdistan—especially since the trial of Öcalan that is taking place right now is making headlines in newspapers and on television, stirring people up.

In the face of all these dangers, how did the caravanners get their information? They were better off than I, as I can't understand what's being said in the media. As for the English- or French-language press, the route I'm traveling is off the tourist track, where it is blatantly ignored. Merchants of the past had everything available in one place: the caravansary. Offering all necessary services, it was also a veritable word-of-mouth news outlet, where guests exchanged whatever information they had on a daily basis. One merchant might say to another: "I'm coming from the East and you're coming from the West: tell me where you've seen epidemics, bandits, and wars, and I'll tell you what I know on my end."

In my journey, does the village of Alihacı mark the border between a zone that's not dangerous and another that is? In Çiftlik, two men tried, albeit halfheartedly, to take my watch and money. Yesterday, three men tried, more aggressively, to rob me. But the worst violence was that of the inhabitants of Alihacı, their collective madness, their greed (money, treasure . . .), and ignorance (wearing a backpack means I'm a terrorist). The army's intervention probably saved me from their madness. But I would rather have dealt with soldiers who were a little more diplomatic. Like Mustafa, for example.

On the morning of June 18, I ring Blue-Eyes back up and ask if, as promised, he would send someone to drive me back to the road where he picked me up. He sends a car and driver along with two soldiers armed with machine guns, with instructions to take me to Alihacı. I'm not so keen on that, and so I ask them to drive me to Yazıköy, thirty kilometers farther. The soldiers, who do things by the book, check with their commander. Blue-Eyes refuses. That's not his turf. I can take the bus: the army will even pay for my ticket.

He knows as well as I do that there's no bus to Yazıköy. To hell with him. The man lied to me every time he opened his mouth.

How am I going to get back on the route that I had mapped out? It would take me at least two days to hike there through a sector that is, beyond any doubt, dangerous. After pacing up and down the Sivas bus station for a while, I finally find a bus heading to Suşehri. One of the stops is Ekinözü, where I was planning to seek hospitality. I'll have the driver drop me off there. The bus also heads up the mountain road and over the famous pass at Karabayır. It was so steep that caravanners gave it the nickname of "*beguiendren*," which means, more or less, "where the lord must descend from his horse."*

Viewed from the bus, the landscape is superb. Along the road, a restaurant proudly proclaims "The Silk Road" in Turkish—which is normal—and in English—which is unexpected. To the north, tall peaks still covered in snow shine brightly in the sun. Instead of veering north toward Suşehri, the bus crosses an intersection and continues straight east. I scurry over to the driver. He tells me that a new road has opened that's more direct and in good condition, and so the bus no longer travels the old route, which is too difficult and dangerous. Farewell Karabayır pass, farewell Ekinözü. This new setback means that I'll miss a total of three stages between Alihacı and Suşehri. But in the end, are these places I should be sorry to miss? Mustafa Kaçar warned me I would have been endlessly bothered by army checkpoints, or worse, I might have been target practice for PKK sharpshooters. There are certainly times when I need to be careful. And I'm more careful now especially since the intense fear I experienced on June 16—my "day of disaster"—has not entirely faded.

Above all, the vision of the man standing in front of the door to my room, gripping his rifle, still haunts me. In that moment, I thought they wanted to kill me. Rather strangely, however, although I'll admit that I was frightened, I didn't panic, nor was I really afraid of dying. In our hypersheltered societies, death draws near in clever disguise. We keep it secret, we bottle it up, we reject it. I've often thought about my death. There have even been times when I would have welcomed it. But I had never, in my experience as a man, seen it close up, face-to-face. And it's true, "neither the sun, nor death can be looked at steadily."† And then there it was, my death, dangling from the nervous index finger of an ignorant halfwit, scared stiff by my backpack!

---

* From Jean-Baptiste Tavernier's *Les six voyages de Jean-Baptiste Tavernier: qu'il a fait en Turquie, en Perse et aux Indes, Volume 1*, 1681, p. 13.
† François de La Rochefoucauld.

Since leaving Venice, I've often reflected on the risks I'm taking. Of course, I risk my life on this road. But no more, as I see it, than on the highway connecting Normandy with Paris, or than when walking across the Champs-Élysées, even keeping to crosswalks. But I'm not naive. When we choose to walk, we open ourselves up to relationships. Some are kind, and some are cruel. If I wanted to die in my bed, then I should've stayed home. But on that topic, I have strong views. Those who want to die in bed and never stray far from it are already dead.

At the point where we're about to head over a mountain pass at an altitude of 2,000 meters (6,560 feet), I ask the driver to let me off on the deserted road. Stunned, the passengers watch as I get off ten kilometers as the crow flies from the nearest inhabited village and twenty-five kilometers from Suşehri. The driver almost refused to leave me there. It's too dangerous, he said. So I explained that I wanted to walk to the nearest village, Aksu, by trail. Truth is, I'm itching to get back on my feet. The weather's far too nice to be sweating it out in this box on wheels. It moves too fast, and I want to contemplate this tormented landscape at my own speed. There is silence once more, broken only by the sound of my steps on the gravel and that of a truck, from time to time, roaring up the inclines of the new road. It follows the course of a rushing stream that, over several millennia, has cut through the mountain, leaving the rest of the job to bulldozers.

Vast carpets of crocuses quiver and buzz: upon closer look, I see millions of bees, industrious, obstinate, and gorging themselves on pollen. In some regions of Turkey, crocuses are still grown for the production of saffron. One kilogram of saffron requires harvesting one hundred thousand crocuses. Saffron was once used as a form of currency. In the small city of Safranbolu, near Tosya, known for its lovely Ottoman houses, two families still produce "true" saffron, cultivating the crocus satilus.

As I lose altitude, the air grows warmer. Clumps of trees between the stream and the road provide cool shelter from the sun. Under the branches of a poplar grove, I lunch on a bit of bread and cheese and take a short nap. Little by little, the stress of my "day of disaster" melts away. My sense of calm returns.

Later on, as I cheerfully get back out on the road, a car stops and asks if I'd like a ride. I merrily decline the offer: if people are once again stopping for hitchhikers, then fear is no longer a factor. Finally, to top it all off, an ambulance screeches to a halt, asking if I'd like to hop in.

"No thank you, not yet. Maybe later on . . ."

The driver and passenger laugh. They want to know all about me, so they park their vehicle and get me to tell them about my journey. Then they drive off, but not without first handing me a chocolate bar.

Suşehri was a busy staging point along the Silk Road. J.-B. Tavernier recounts that when he stopped for the night in the city, there were so many caravans that no one paid the tax. The caravanners just kept going, brushing the tax collectors aside, as they were very poorly organized and overwhelmed by so many travelers. Today, it's a small, provincial city of no touristic interest whatsoever. At the post office where I had told people they could write me, the employee tells me that there are indeed a few letters waiting for me. It's so unusual that the envelopes were placed in the vault. But unfortunately, his colleague went on vacation and took the key with him. In the hope that there's nothing urgent, I suggest he send the letters on to Erzurum, where I'll be in about ten days.

In the morning, when I leave the restaurant where I just had a hot, rich *çorba mercinek*, I bungle my second photo. The first one I botched was in Gerede. As I was walking down a side street, I saw, in a barber's window, a venerable old man with a no less venerable white beard, who, in a tide of foam, was having his head shaved. It was a truly comical sight: imagine the hawk-like profile of a swarthy-skinned man elongated all the more and capped, with great symmetry, by a foamy tuft, white as snow. If I were at all good at drawing, I'd do a quick vignette sketch for you. Unfortunately, there was no film in my camera. In Suşehri, the must-have shot is that of a tractor carrying a load of joyful, laughing passengers. It has young people sticking out all over it quite literally. They're clustered on the mudguards and on the hood, they're crammed onto the seat and hanging onto the tilling mechanisms. By the time I get my camera out, they've all jumped off. I count them: seventeen young

men, including the driver, perched on the machine. It's confirmation of
something I already knew: I'm no good as a photographer.

I leave Suşehri without regrets and am heading down toward the
artificial lake behind a dam at the edge of town when a man comes sprint-
ing up. The post office employee sent him to tell me that, if I'm willing
to wait until 4:00 p.m., he'll have figured out how to get his hands on
the key to the vault. I'm endlessly fascinated by the mysterious methods
for communicating used by peoples who have not made communication
itself the focus of their business. By what unfathomable means will the
vacationing man manage to deliver THE key, and, furthermore, by what
route has this stranger managed to catch up with me, though I'd already
left the city? Therein lie all the mysteries of the Orient.

But no, I'm not about to wait around. I have no desire to stick around
forever in this charmless city. I follow the lakefront for some ten kilometers. The air is hot, but my gait and salt intake must be right since I'm
barely perspiring. Should I stick with this rather heavily traveled road,
or head back out to wander through the villages? Naturally, so long as
I continue to avoid it, I'll continue to harbor deep down the fear that
took hold of me on June 16. And the longer I wait, the stronger its grip
will be.

So I dive right in and take the mountain road, which, south of the
reservoir, leads into the deep countryside. It's a steep climb. The scenery
changes. To the right, the earth is sandy and crumbly, green in color,
with vertiginous downslopes and, nearly directly below at the very bottom, a rushing stream whose rumble reaches my ears. On the other side,
earth of dark ocher, the color of rust. There's no vegetation other than a
few clumps of shrubbery at the stream's edge. Children are playing in the
water, and the sound of their laughter brings a human touch to this cold
and lunar landscape.

In the small village of Akşar (ak'-shar), I chat for a moment with two
men putting the finishing touches on a restaurant in preparation for its
grand opening, scheduled for the day after tomorrow. A third companion
is frying eggplant in a smoking pan of oil. He's stripped to the waist but
has a gun hooked on his belt. When I express my surprise, he tells me

that he's a cop and is cooking to help out his friends. After Akşar, the road vanishes, and I have to navigate by sticking to the path trodden by ranging herds. When I reach the top, I catch sight of Erence (*ay-rahn'-djeh*), the village where I'm going to spend the night. But before I get there and since my T-shirt is wet, I change clothes beside the mountain stream I wade across and seize the opportunity to rinse my shirt in the current and hang it on my pack to dry. Pinned to my back, one might easily mistake it for a white flag: a rather appropriate symbol in these regions.

Thus attired, I step foot into the yard belonging to the *muhtar* of Erence, Arif Çelik. The man is surprised, uncommunicative, even hostile. He asks for my passport, jumps on his phone, and calls the *jandarmas*. Standing in the middle of his yard, pack still on my back, I think to myself that the troubles are about to begin. The telephone rings, Arif indicates that it's for me. The *jandarmas* instruct me to proceed to their headquarters, eighteen kilometers away. I laugh out loud. Eighteen kilometers to show them my papers and as many for the return trip: that makes thirty-six kilometers. I've just traveled forty from Suşehri to here, and I have no intention of doing it all over again this evening. If they want to see my passport, let them come here.

I camp out in the middle of the yard, next to my belongings. Arif tends to his business. He's visibly disturbed by my presence and can't figure out what attitude he should adopt. But I do: I have to wait. I'm seriously starting to wonder whether I'll be spending another night at the base. The phone rings several times. The *jandarmas* insist. They want to speak to me again. I stand my ground and advise them to call Blue-Eyes or, even better, Mustafa Kaçar, if they want more information.

In the meantime, Arif has struck up a conversation. He's dumbfounded to learn that I walked all the way from Istanbul. In my notebook and on my maps, I show him the route I took. This settles him down, and we go on a tour of his small farm. I offer to take a picture of him on his tractor. In poor or remote areas, the tractor is such a vital piece of machinery that it's often decorated with brightly colored fabric or carpets. His is adorned with a drugget sporting geometric designs dyed in hues of gray and green, reminiscent of army camouflage. It turns out that we're exactly the same age. This strengthens our relationship. Now that he feels reassured, I believe he's trying to calm down the *jandarmas*, since the phone calls become less and less frequent, and then finally stop.

He invites me in for tea. Several of his friends come to join us, as well as the village's young imam, and we have a rather pleasant conversation. A little later, while I'm getting ready for bed, my host goes to get a chair and sits down in front of me. He watches on in silent fascination as I brush my teeth. His own teeth are in rather poor condition—one in two are missing—but I love to watch him laugh in a show of his piano keyboard. I find it fascinating that, when he closes his mouth, the upper teeth fit perfectly into the gaps on the bottom, and vice versa. And so, with his mouth closed, Arif looks as though he has all his teeth. My laughter must be infectious because, by the time to go to bed, we're the best of friends.

He invites me to sleep in his own room; he and his wife squeeze into another room along with the rest of the family. By 5:00 a.m., I begin to hear noises. It's Arif and his wife preparing breakfast so as not to hold me up, since I told them I wanted to leave early . . . without specifying that, for me, "early" means two hours later. Joined by the imam, just back from morning prayer, he walks with me for some distance. My heart is heavy when I take leave of this marvelously good man.

Once again, I've changed my itinerary. The *jandarmas* affair yesterday turned out okay, but I suspect it's going to happen again. I'm still too close to the turbulence zone to head out onto side roads. I need to get back on the highway. At 5:30 a.m., I cross back over the mountain stream and begin a long climb. When I reach the pass, at 1,800 meters (5,900 feet), Erence is no more than a tiny hamlet napping in the valley. On the other slope, the mountain's northern side is still cloaked in snow.

In the first village I go through, a kind old man uses a stick and draws in the sand the path I need to take. But then a rascal appears, mistrustful and combative, and puts me through a veritable police interrogation. I'm sure the *jandarmas* will soon have more news about me. Once again, people in the fields and along the road stop greeting me.

After a two-hour-long journey, I'm again overlooking Suşehri's artificial lake. This immense reservoir along with the geometry of the fields create such a grandiose spectacle that I have to sit down and take it all in. The mountains to the north are mirrored in the water, hemmed in by yellow fields of ripened wheat and black squares of plowed soil. Abandoning the winding road, I run downhill and straight on into the low grasses where herds of cows are grazing. Beside a spring where I fill my water jug, a young shepherd comes over to ask for money. What does he want to buy?

"Lots of cigarettes," he says.

On the paved road, I find myself once again barely five kilometers from the place where I left it yesterday. This was no useless detour—after all, aren't detours also ways of going straight to something else?—for it allowed me to meet Arif and to explore landscapes whose memory has remained with me ever since. I'm walking at a good pace, despite the heat. After a good *çorba* in a cool, dark *lokanta*, I take a short, one-hour nap in the grass. My plan is to stop in the little burg of Çataklı (*chah-tahk'-luh*) and seek hospitality there. At 6:30 p.m., I realize that I left Erence over thirteen hours earlier and am now out of water. Without a single village in sight. A truck driver offers me some warm, questionable water kept in a dirty plastic jug under his seat. I do what I know one should never do: I greedily gulp down a good liter. Five hundred meters farther, just my luck, I come across a small mosque and a cool water spring.

In Çataklı, a passerby assures me that the small city of Gölova, five kilometers off the highway, boasts a hotel. But a second passerby who has since arrived disagrees: he is certain that no such hotel exists. I am very tired, but the prospect—despite being merely hypothetical—of sleeping the whole night through and—who knows?—of taking a shower spurs me on. By the time I reach my destination, I've walked fifty-five kilometers over the course of the day, and I'm completely wiped out.

Osman Kurt, the town's mayor who is having tea out on a teahouse terrace, says that about a month ago, on a bus headed to Istanbul, he saw me walking along the road near Ismetpaşa. To now find, sitting next to him, the very same oddball that he was astonished to see from the bus makes him gush with emotion: his disbelief soon turns to excitement. This is no everyday occurrence, and he realizes that he's now at the center of a story whose narrative he already finds utterly delightful.

My informants were both right: there's no hotel, but there soon will be. The mayor proposes that I sleep there even though it isn't entirely finished. Constructed by the municipality, it won't be open until the end of the week. So I'm the hotel's very first guest, and Osman Kurt refuses to let me pay, insisting that I'm his guest, neither for dinner—he's the owner of the restaurant—nor for my room, which has been hastily furnished with a bed for me to use. The shower is not yet working, but my host has gone through a lot of trouble, so I'm not about to be difficult.

In the morning, I take a shortcut across the meadows to rejoin the highway. From atop the hills, I survey the artificial lake of Gölova, and the small natural lake adjacent to it. The countryside is beautiful. After walking for two hours, I stop under a flowering acacia tree besieged by insects. And there, I am like a bee too, but instead of pollen, I glean colors and scents, giving in to the sweetness of living. Then it's back to the main road. After a brief lunch, I settle into a secluded lane for a nap. A woman spots me. A few minutes later, two brawny loudmouths show up out of nowhere to make inquiries. Their wariness quickly fades, but they tell me time and again how careful I must be: there are plenty of terrorists in the area.

Yes, indeed. The only traffic I encounter in either direction is either armored vehicles packed with soldiers carrying assault rifles who shout loudly at me as they go by, or trucks full of camouflaged *jandarmas*. After Altköy, I enter a spectacular narrow gorge. Here, as I've seen several times before, the rushing stream, helped here and there by bulldozers, has carved a deep channel into the rock. The high walls on each side are stunning. The soldiers whose job it was to protect the caravans must have shuddered at the sight of such danger zones. In the middle of the valley, I see one of the armored vehicles hidden in a depression in the road. The machine gun is pointed higher up, which a soldier is scanning through a pair of binoculars. They call me over, offer me a cola, and question me about my journey and my age. "*Maşallah!*"

The Refahiye Hotel is one of the filthiest ever. There is no shower, just a sink whose original color disappeared long ago beneath the grime. When I turn the faucet on, ice-cold water spills out onto my feet on account of a missing basin plug. There's a puddle of urine in the water closet. The electricity is not working. I grope my way over and lie down on a grimy bed on which I'd unrolled my sleeping bag. On the floor below, the restaurant, open around the clock, is playing popular songs over a sound system cranked up to full blast. Out back, machine shops and body repair garages operate through much of the night. In bed before sundown—in spite of all the racket—I sleep well.

I wake up before five o'clock and wolf down a *çorba*, hoping that the kitchen is cleaner than the bathroom. *Inşallah!* In this steppe landscape, there's not a tree in sight. It's cool out. I don't feel the least bit tired, since yesterday's short walk allowed me to recover from the one the day before. Two hours into an uneventful journey, I take a break in a small roadside restaurant. Once again, my arrival has quite an effect on the people around, and I'm cross-questioned by an armada of truck drivers. When I tell them that I've come from Istanbul, they line up, one after another, and ceremoniously shake my hand, a gesture accompanied by a little bow of respect. The manager refuses to let me pay for my soup, and one truck driver insists on buying me a second bowl.

So, it's with maximum energy—and a full belly!—that I begin the climb up toward the narrow gorge and mountain pass at Sakaltutan that will take me from 1,600 to 2,200 meters (5,250 to 7,200 feet). Four kilometers from the summit, two jeeps jammed with soldiers come to a stop. An officer demands to see my passport in a voice devoid of diplomacy. I ask him if they happen to have any water, since my jug is empty and the climb has been extremely tough. He rebuffs my request: "There's some further on" he says, full of himself. It takes me nearly an hour to reach the summit and locate a source of water and a restaurant. I'm famished and happy at the chance to order some grilled meat, but here again I'm unable to pay, since the people at the next table over with whom I was conversing paid for my meal. As I have lunch, the crews of armored Toyota jeeps equipped with machine guns on turrets come to drink tea, while a minibus packed with soldiers patrols the road. In a few words, the atmosphere seems tense, suspicion reigns, danger cannot be far off.

On the other side of the pass, the towering, majestic landscape has colors like those of a naive painter's palette. Arid soils and chalky rocks, grays, browns, and reds and, here and there wherever a spring allows, the dark green of tiny grassy pastures for grazing sheep. Off in the distance glisten the everlasting snows atop Mount Keşiş Dağı. And there, down below, a grove of poplars at an intersection provides some shade, a rarity at this elevation. By 3:00 p.m., I've walked forty-five kilometers, but there's still no village in sight nor on the map. I'm moving along at a good pace. Soldiers regularly stop and ask for my papers, and jeeps on patrol pop up again and again. They've strongly advised me not to be out on the road after 5:00 p.m. I want nothing more than to stop, but where? At 5:30, I'm still eighteen kilometers from the next city, Erzincan (*ayr-zeen'-djan*). I've walked sixty-two kilometers and climbed over a mountain pass at 2,200 meters (7,220 feet).

This is now my new record since leaving Istanbul. My legs are heavy. The cliffs on each side of the road seem ominous. When a truck stops to pick me up, I finally cave. Irfan, the driver, stops five kilometers farther along in a roadside hotel-restaurant. Had I known it was so near, I wouldn't have gone back on my vow to never rely on a motor. The room is packed with soldiers waiting for nightfall to start their patrols. I have a cup of tea with Irfan. He tells me that he earns eighty million liras a month, but that his cigarette habit alone costs him eighteen million. How can he possibly provide for his four children and keep a roof over his head? He "gets by." His answer leaves me baffled.

The hotel is almost as filthy as the one in Refahiye (*reh-fah'-hee-yeh*), but it's better in that it offers hot showers—albeit for a price—in the basement. In the morning, I stop a truck headed in the opposite direction and pick up my hike at the spot where I met Irfan. I don't want to miss out on a single kilometer of my Silk Road journey. I know: scruples like this might seem like the compulsiveness of a madman, the bookkeeping of an old stickler. But that's how it is, and my conscience is now at peace, even though my feet rail against the eighteen kilometers standing between me and Erzincan, and that seem awfully long after the previous day's protracted stage.

The city projects an unusual image. In 1939, a devastating earthquake killed thirty-five thousand people, one-third of the entire population. Another, in 1992, caused six hundred more deaths. Nevertheless, and even though there is plenty of land, buildings were reconstructed to stand four stories tall. The city's inhabitants seem to be calmly awaiting the next quake. But developers are not the only culprits. Turks consider it tacky to live in a house, whereas apartment living is the ultimate in chic. Needless to say, not a single old stone has been left standing. The head of the tourist office has no information on the Silk Road, despite the fact that this was an important stopover city. But, he tells me, he'd be delighted if I were to invite him to see Paris.

The sun is blazing hot. On a shady bench in a public park, I watch women as they stroll lazily by. How do they manage in such extreme heat? How much clothing a woman wears depends on the sect her husband belongs to. A husband's religious rigor is revealed first and foremost by the quantity of fabric covering his wife—and second by the way he himself is clothed. The more tolerant men impose a simple chador. A long robe I can understand, but a cloak? In this heat? That's only for the first degree of religious fervor. Fundamentalism demands even more. Under the long, black canvas called the *çarşaf* (*char-shahf*"), some women reveal only their eyes and hands. I spot one woman in dark glasses, walking suavely along and shouldering beneath a dark-brown cotton garment all the mystery of the world. An even more radical sect requires women to go out of the house in a kind of coarse brown blanket through which they likely see only shadows along the way. Even their hands are hidden under wool gloves. The Western eye has to learn to rediscover the imaginative possibilities occasioned by what is *suggested*, far from the practice we've come to accept of *revealing everything*. May imagination once again regain its former prestige, and may we be guided by our dreams: such are the thoughts that come to my mind as I observe this dark, evocative figure.

Out in the city's main square, I'm drawn to a large gathering of police officers. A banner appears, which, obviously, I can't read. I inquire: why are these police officers demonstrating? My question is answered by looks of incomprehension and surprise, even laughter. Contrary to what I thought, the officers aren't there to demonstrate but to keep an eye on a gathering of factory workers demanding more pay: all that can be seen of them is their banner.

I feel extremely tired. So I rest up for much of the afternoon in the city's best hotel. After a very long night, it's 10:00 a.m. the next morning by the time I set out.

The army's presence seems to have increased. Over the course of three hours, I count about fifteen armored vehicles on patrol, each one equipped with a machine gun attached to the roof or the roll bar. Not a single one stops to ask for my papers. On this main thoroughfare, it must be that I look like a tourist and my presence here seems normal. The plains of Erzincan are fertile and planted with cereal crops and apricot trees, but—to my great regret!—the fruits are not quite ripe.

At noon, I'm "invited" to lunch by five men who work in farm irrigation. They tell me that they are Shiite, partisans of Ali, Muhammad's cousin and son-in-law. In this mostly nationalistic and conservative country, their views are more to the left, and they tell me, furthermore, how much they admire French socialists. The youngest one in the group is about to hand me a plate of bulgur when he freezes, as if some doubt suddenly occurred to him:

"Are you a democrat or a fascist?" he asks, point blank.

Those terms don't mean the same to them as they do to me. They launch into a drawn-out criticism of the Turkish regime, which they label as "fascist." The Turkish government is clearly not that, but I eventually realize that for the one using it, the term simply refers to anyone who espouses a different political viewpoint. As I'm a partisan of democracy and say so, the cracked wheat drops into my dish.

As evening approaches, I cross the Euphrates (*Firat Nehri*), which, along with the Tigris and the Nile, witnessed the birth of the most ancient civilizations. Lost in thought, I contemplate for a long time the water rushing over the stones. But I have to keep going, as night is not far off. My plan was to stop in a small village shown on my map: Taniyeri. I think I'm almost there when I stop in a gas station to buy a bottle of juice. The manager tells me that the village I seek no longer exists. And there is no other inhabitation for another fifteen kilometers.

So I prepare to bivouac on the parking lot beside the station. As I'm pulling my gear out to prepare my campsite, four armored jeeps, two operated by *jandarmas* and the other two by the army, pull into the station. Both groups question me for a long time on my itinerary. They are clearly impressed. As we drink tea, they tell me that they'll be out on patrol all night long. They never once set down their weapons. There are, they tell me, terrorists in the area. Judging by the density of policemen and soldiers since leaving Tokat, these must be tough times for terrorists.

As they are about to leave, one of them comes over to me and, pleased with himself, whispers in my ear:

"I know how you achieve such a high level of performance: you do drugs."

"What makes you think that?"

"My buddy saw you put amphetamine tablets in your water bottle."

I show him the pills in question, which I use to sterilize the water I drink, but it's no good, I can't change his mind. As he and his companions see it, everything now makes sense. My performance was "abnormal." But since I take drugs, everything is now once again "normal."

I have a hard time sleeping on a bench. The cold, the clouds of mosquitoes, the merry-go-round of trucks filling up with diesel fuel, and above all—above all—the music playing at full blast in the station to lure in god-knows-who while keeping the night watchman awake prevent me from getting any shut-eye. Just as I'm about to drift off, a storm blows in. I take refuge in the shop with the attendant.

Twenty-five years old, tall, and thin as a fence post, Metin works eighteen hours a day, three hundred sixty-five days a year, for he's trying to put some money away in order to get married. He chose January 1, 2000, despite the fact that that as a Muslim that date means nothing to him. He takes out his wallet and shows me photos of his fiancée, a plump little woman who looks a little feisty, as well as of his brothers, parents, and himself when he was a soldier whom I obviously can't recognize with his head shaved alongside twenty-five other shaved heads; credit cards, civilian and military ID cards, and various other documents. All of Metin's life is summed up here in pictures.

A loud noise on the road suddenly gets us to look up. I believe it to be some mythological creature. In a way, that's what it is, for it's a tracked tank that emerges from the night, sparkles for a few seconds beneath the station's spotlights, and then disappears heading east in a clatter of clanking steel.

CHAPTER X
WOMEN

From behind the sandbags, a helmet pokes out; then the barrel of a rifle glares at me with its black eye of polished steel. The soldier aiming at me yells something that needs no translation. It can only be: "Don't move!" In a calmer voice, he calls out. An officer comes over to me and barks at me to show him my passport. I'm about to hand it to him when a burst of laughter comes out of nowhere. It's a truck driver who, without stepping down from his cabin, shouts to the officer: "It's the tourist who has walked all the way from Istanbul!"

The officer looks at me with surprise, and then interest:

"Where are you going?"

"To the grocery."

"Do you have Turkish money?"

"Of course."

"Okay then."

I tuck my passport back into my pocket; he never even opened it. It's a decidedly wacky scene. But after all, it serves me right. Metin, the gas station attendant, when I left him early this morning, tried to dissuade me from leaving: "It's very dangerous to be out walking before 7:00 a.m., you have to wait until the army has cleared the road." But I had hardly slept, and my stomach was screaming for food. So I left, opting for a short distance today: twenty-six kilometers to the town of Sansa. Little by little, the wide valley has turned into a narrow gorge. Near a bridge straddling the river, I noticed a grocer's shop alongside a teahouse, and I really wanted to stop there.

But I hadn't seen the small blockhouse hidden in the ditch, from which sprang the soldier.

In the teahouse, people look me over with curiosity and not without a hint of suspicion. Despite several attempts on my part, no one wants to talk. There's a sense of discomfort, heavy and indefinable. I take my time eating and unwind. There's no reason to rush today.

About ten kilometers farther, as I head into the narrow pass, I face another military blockade. On the left is a tank with its gun pointed toward the top of the ribbon of roadway. On the right, an armored car covering the other side. The crews are at their posts. A soldier calls out at me, he orders me to approach and wait. Another goes into a small, half-collapsed structure and comes back out accompanied by a baby-faced junior officer. Tall and fat, he's like a sausage in his camouflage fatigues, giving him the look of a roast ready for the fire. He struggles up the slope separating the shelter from the road and asks for my papers.

"You can't get through this way," he tells me.

"Why? With all the soldiers around here, is there still a lack of security? Are there terrorists?"

"No."

"So if there are no terrorists, then I can keep walking in perfect safety."

"No."

Finding his answers to be overly curt, I protest, explaining my journey and how important it is to me. The soldier who went to get his supervisor comes to my aid:

"*Paşa* . . ."

He has no time to say any more. With a quick command, the officer shuts him up. I try to make sense of it all. *Paşa* means "leader" in Turkish. Are these then orders from the leader? But why, since, as the officer said himself, the zone isn't dangerous? I try to break free and continue on my way. I seize my pack, but before I can take four steps, on their commander's injunction, two soldiers stand in my way. One of them grabs my gear, and they drag me *manu militari*, quite literally, back to the officer who never budged. On his field telephone, he asks for instructions. Ten minutes later, he has his answer. I won't be allowed to travel through the gorge, at least not on foot.

They stop a truck. The soldier holds a briefing with the driver that must relate to me, since he points at me several times. The soldier hoists my pack up into the cabin, and then the officer turns to me, asking to see my map. He points to a village, Kargin, twenty kilometers from the spot where we're standing. My understanding of what he said to me must more or less be: "The driver has orders to drop you off in this village. Don't try to get out before then, or you'll be in serious trouble."

And he shows me his two joined wrists, podgy like those of a baby. It's up to me to grasp the meaning. And I do. So, with a heavy heart, I climb up into the cabin. I'm tired of these *jandarmas* who keep giving me unwanted rides. If this continues, I'll have crossed a third of Turkey in a bus or truck. I know I'm exaggerating, but at this point, I feel like thinking the worst.

The driver tells me that every week he travels from Ankara to Tabriz, in Iran. He offers to drive me all the way; he'll be there in just two days. No thank you, I'll get there, but on foot, stubborn as a mule perhaps, but more bent than ever on achieving my goal now that they're throwing obstacles in my way, trying to persuade me to give up.

Five kilometers past the blockade, I finally get what the word *"paşa"* meant. What they're so jealously guarding is the camp where their commander—the *paşa*—of antiterrorist forces is headquartered. It's located on a tiny plot between the road and the river. It's actually an encampment of collapsible tents and barracks enclosed by a barbed-wire fence. Twenty or so tanks are all perfectly lined up, the eye of their cannons looking straight at us. The *paşa* wants to get a good night's sleep. Even an innocent foot traveler like me is not allowed to get anywhere near. I'm still a bit surprised by the lack of rigor in the inspections, for, while the soldiers were busy blocking me from entering the pass, a half-dozen trucks went through without being stopped. I'm no specialist, but in my opinion the *paşa* should be a little more concerned about a truck driven by a suicide bomber that, filled with explosives, would reduce his HQ to dust, and less about an innocent foot traveler, whose bag is easy to check.

The *paşa* chose to take up residence near where I was planning to spend the night, in Sansa. All I can do is longingly watch out the window as we drive along this magnificent route, which my boots won't have the privilege of treading. I ask the driver to drop me off after we've passed the HQ, but with his index like a windshield wiper that says "no," he makes clear that he's sticking to the stout soldier's orders.

When I set my feet back on the ground, I've unintentionally traveled much farther than planned this morning. The next city that I expected to reach two days later is now only a few hours' hike distant. Between here and there, there's no village where I can stay. So I decide to push on all the way to Tercan (*ter'-djan*), which will mean a forty-one-kilometer (26-mile) walk, not counting the truck ride. So much for an easy stage.

As I'm hoisting my backpack onto my shoulder, a horse-drawn cart with two men and one woman on board comes trotting along the road toward me. Behind it, the mountain ridge offers a sumptuous backdrop. Naturally, I want to preserve this scene for all eternity—and I do—by taking a photo with the cart in the foreground. Furious that she didn't have time to cover her head with her scarf, the woman spits as they go past me. Her image belongs to her alone, and I have stolen it: I will try to remember this in the future. But between those who want a photo and those who see it as theft—or even rape—how am I to tell the difference? This is one of many things I have yet to learn.

Even before reaching Tercan, the pillars of an old bridge dating from the twelfth century and were not knocked down is a promising sight. Have authorities here been more careful to preserve the treasures of the past? Tercan is the city of "Mama Hatun." She was quite a personality. In this male-dominated country where being born a woman is considered a calamity, in 1191, Mama Hatun inherited the principality belonging to her father, İzzettin Saltuk II. This Turkish Joan of Arc led an army against the Ayyubid invasion. For a period of ten years, she had to fight, weapons in hand, to defend her position, which her hot-tempered nephews wanted to wrest from her. El Adil, the sultan who ruled Syria and Egypt at the time, tried to find a worthy husband of equal rank for her. In vain. No one was eager to be under the thumb of this firm-handed princess. In the meantime, she had several buildings erected that are, even today, considered some of the most outstanding examples of medieval Ottoman architecture: a mosque, a caravansary, and a hammam, and, later on, the most grandiose and original of all: her mausoleum.

Mama Hatun disappeared one day in the greatest of mysteries. Was she assassinated, or locked up by her nephews until her death? Was she even inhumed in the edifice she had so beautifully built for herself for that very purpose? No one has the slightest idea. Her marble catafalque also disappeared, which Evliya Çelebi, the great Arab traveler, was able to admire when he passed this way in the middle of the seventeenth century. Although the mausoleum is typically closed, I'm fortunately able to visit it. The small building consists of a circular wall inside which were constructed twelve niches or *eyvan*; these are sepulchers for Mama Hatun's inner circle. In the center, a small tower, capped by a *meçit* (small mosque), holds, in its basement, the false sarcophagus designed as a replacement for the original. It's all capped by an umbrella-shaped roof divided into eight sections, every other one indicating a cardinal point. The entire ensemble exudes exquisite harmony. After a long search for the keeper of the keys, I succeed in touring the caravansary. Its restoration is almost complete. Small in size, it nevertheless has two immense vaulted stables. The hammam built by Mama Hatun has been less fortunate: Turkish concrete has once again left its mark.

From Tercan to Aşkale, the journey affords neither surprises nor lunch. A very intense storm blows in, but Lady Luck is in my corner. Just as I start to be completely drenched, an abandoned tunnel provides me with shelter where I wait for the sun to return, drying my gear and snacking on a few pieces of dried fruit and a hunk of bread. I must look just like a homeless person. Despite all the exercise I get each day, these light meals are all I need. I'm expending a huge amount energy—my pack is no feather on my back—and yet one full meal a day is enough. Caravan travelers, for their part, generally carried water skins and a little dried meat. They found everything else they needed in the caravansaries.

Is it because I visited Mama Hatun's monument? I can't help but notice that Turkey's women figure prominently in my thoughts. The feminist "revolution" initiated so magnificently by Mama Hatun was nipped in the bud. But that hardly diminishes what she accomplished.

In the male-dominated Middle Ages, how could an army have agreed to be led by a woman? Everything in this country's religion and culture represses girls and wives. The country's as-yet-insufficient economic development allows it to get by without their help and keeps them from having any domestic or political power, under the full financial control of men. They are refused education and culture. Of course, legally, men and women are considered to have equal status. The country has even had a female prime minister. But in villages and Turkish households, I've been able to observe the extent to which women remain subcitizens: exploited at will, hidden, and clothed according to rules dictated to them starting at a very early age and that repudiate their bodies. Of course, in large cities, I saw young women who had apparently broken this dress code, wearing European-style clothing, a tangible sign of independence. How long, though, will it take for these winds of reform to reach the villages of Anatolia?

Besides Mama Hatun, other women rulers have left their mark on the history of this land. But that was under the Eastern Christian Empire. Helena, Irene, Theodora: each had a great influence on her time.

Helena was an innkeeper's servant, sufficiently crafty to seduce the emperor Constantius Chlorus. Their son, Constantine, rather than lazing around in Rome, founded a city on the site of former Byzantium and named it for himself: Constantinople.

In the eighth century, Irene reigned over the Eastern Empire for nearly twenty years as her son's regent. When he was of age, assuming the power that was his right, this delightful mother had his eyes gouged out and enjoyed, as the result of this infamy, five more years as ruler.

It is said that Theodora was of very loose morals before she married Justinian, Constantinople's greatest emperor. Having become an irreproachable spouse, she even gave her husband a lesson in power. When he planned to flee when an especially violent revolt had sparked a bloodbath in the city, Theodora told him, in essence: "When you have worn purple (a symbol of royal power), you should be prepared to be buried in it." They stayed put, overcame the revolt, and would later die in bed.

These three women, it's true, were Christian. Mama Hatun's accomplishments are all the more impressive in that she was born in a Muslim land.

Each day, I am appalled by the fate of Turkish women living in villages. They're programmed from birth to be self-effacing and to work hard. I've noticed that when I take pictures of children, little boys are delighted and turn to look at the camera, while little girls hide behind the boys. The daughters of Fazil, the villager I met on the morning of June 16, are not allowed to continue their education past elementary school, as their brothers do. They, too, hide so as not to be photographed. And, at the very heart of village life, they can only enter the mosque if they take up their assigned place: behind men. This kind of education works: before long, women freely and rigorously apply to themselves the law imposed on them from childhood.

I've fortunately encountered some exceptions. The granddaughters of Behçet, the old wise man of Hacıhamza, seem to be exempt from these rules. But I dined alone with him, glimpsing his wife only before I left, when she said "farewell" from the balcony. In Istanbul, and in Turkey's largest cities, most young women who went to school and then on to college hold the same professions as men and enjoy equal status. But they're the trees that prevent us from seeing the forest. Turks are very proud of having granted women the right to vote in 1934. And that year, indeed, nearly 5 percent of elected members of parliament were women. But the proponent of reform, Atatürk, died four years later. Ever since, the status of women has steadily declined. Today, thirteen out of five hundred and fifty elected members of parliament are women.

Turkish tempers flare if you tell them that in their homes, women are second-class citizens or even second-class human beings. But in practice—and in villages—that's how it is. They're the ones pulling weeds on their knees in beet fields, making bread and cooking dinner in the shadows, wiping their children's backsides while their husbands reinvent the world in the teahouse or seek salvation at the mosque. An association called Ka-Der has been founded in Turkey, seeking to prepare women to assert themselves politically. These women made a tremendous observation: interest and participation in political life are functions of education. Access to parliament hinges on a university education. But who's going to send them there? For the moment, kept in ignorance, indoctrinated, monitored, and dominated by their men, Turkish women stand no chance of gaining independence. Each time I attempted to broach the subject, I ran into a wall of silence. And with respect to the Kurdish part of the country, I was warned for my own security: do not speak to women.

As I walk toward Aşkale, my heart goes out nevertheless to the women with whom I was able to exchange a few words: the joyful ladies carding wool near Ilgaz, and Şükran, the Caucasian who cooked *börek* for me. And I often think of Kürşat's little sister, who gave me such a big, spontaneous hug in Tosya.

The city of Aşkale, once located along the Silk Road, has lost even the memory of this past. The hotel, located over a teahouse, ranks solidly in the top three of the filthiest I've ever seen. I grope around for ten minutes searching for the switch for the light in my room. I finally find it . . . at the other end of the hallway. But I'm so tired that I'd sleep on a pile of garbage if I had to—which, in fact, is not far from the case; I've just walked three hundred and forty kilometers (211 miles) in nine days without getting any real rest. Today, once again, I must have logged my forty kilometers (25 miles). If I were reasonable, I ought to stop for a few days or shorten the stages. But that ever-present force keeps urging me to walk, and to walk some more. Each day, I come up with excellent reasons to keep going. Since this morning, I've felt as though I've entered the home stretch: after tomorrow morning, in theory, I'll be in Erzurum.

It's a city I'm drawn to like a magnet. From the outset of my journey, so as not to trigger disbelief among my interlocutors, I stopped saying I was headed to Tehran. I told them Erzurum was my final destination. And now I'm almost there. This accomplishment is like wind at my back. But I won't cover the sixty kilometers separating Tercan from the largest city in Anatolia all at once. I've done some foolish stages over the past nine days, and the results are in: I can't handle it. So I'm going to stop in

Aşkale (*ash'-kah-leh*) tonight (thirty-eight kilometers/twenty-four miles) and tomorrow in Ilıca (*uh'-luh-djah*). Then, all I'll have left is a twenty-one-kilometer (13-mile) leg. Especially since the final stair I have to scale to heave myself into the city is a high one, given that I start at 1,300 meters (4,265 feet) and end at 1,800 meters (5,900 feet) with, between the two, a mountain pass at over 2,000 meters (6,500 feet).

The one thought that helps me keep walking is that I'll soon be able to get some rest in a comfortable hotel room. I truly sense I've reached the end of my rope. The filth and lack of comfort in the hotels in Aşkale and Tercan did me in. And in the pitiful state in which I find myself, I don't want to ask for room and board from private individuals, as I don't feel up to the three or four hours that I'd have to devote to the duties of stardom. Being popular is no easy matter: you always have to please your fans, and you could actually wind up enjoying it, in which case, all of a sudden, you'd find yourself stuck with obligations that you always loathed; in a word, you could become completely enslaved if you're not careful. And then, to make yourself likeable, you have to feel good. On top of it all, even though I don't really want to admit it, I'm still traumatized by the way the inhabitants of Alihacı brought out the army, while putting on a good face and assuring me that they appreciated having me as their idol. The episode gave me a new perspective on the virtues of Turkish hospitality. A hotel, apart from all its filth, lets me feel I'm in a familiar and relatively safe place.

Aşkale-Ilıca, my next-to-last leg before Erzurum, is off to a bad start. My joints hurt; I feel a constant pain in my left thigh. My body, for the first time since finding my rhythm, has started protesting. I promise myself, without too much confidence, that I'll take a day off each week from now on. Exiting Aşkale, I leave the newly constructed highway heading east and take the old road. There are a lot of potholes and few cars, plus an occasional tractor: it's the kind of road I like, and, to boot, it heads through a landscape of pastoral majesty. This is the steppe with its wide-open spaces, where not a single tree is visible on the horizon. With the elevation and the sun, it's delightfully cool, the weather splendid. I forget my hardships for a while. Herds of cows and flocks of sheep process over the hills. I had read that the Turks sacrifice two and a half million rams each year for the feast of Kurban Bayrami. And I wondered where they came from. Here they are, by the thousands, clinging to the slopes, specks moving across the soft green steppe, watched over by teams of shepherds, backed up by their fearsome Kangals.

At Kandilli, two societies, one civil and the other military, exist side by side without mingling. Under broad hangars, armored cars and all-terrain vehicles are lined up in perfect rows. A nursery school was even built for the military's offspring; the other children, the village kids, are deeply engrossed on the square in a soccer game that's being played with a tin can.

Shortly thereafter, I'm battered by a violent storm. I go for shelter under a small bridge that allows herds of livestock to pass beneath a rail-road line. How thrilling to watch the long veils of rain sweep over the gentle hills. The clouds are so low that the black sky seems to fuse with the green grass. Less than an hour later and back on the road, I see another squall coming my way. It's still far off, and I look for anything that might provide cover, but there's nothing. Not a single tree, not even a wall, and the railroad track is far away, meandering down in the valley. For fifteen minutes, I'm dowsed with an ice-cold shower, and it even starts to hail. My big waterproof poncho, snapping in the unstoppable gusts of fierce wind, is of no use. In just a few minutes, I'm drowning beneath a shell that's supposed to provide protection. The cold rain runs down my neck, making my pants stick to my legs, and trickles into my shoes. I'm wallow-ing in water; the hailstones sting my face and hands. Finally, the storm moves off. A dark veil, a wall of water pursues it across the landscape. And out of all this, in the lowlands, near the river, emerges a train, as if coming out of a tunnel. The temperature has plummeted. I try running to warm up, but it's no good; my clothes are soaked, and I'm chilled to the bone.

In the past, caravanners covered the bundles of goods with special cloths made of wool and other animal hair, tightly woven and covered with fat. The silk and paper, the dried fruit, and all of their precious and fragile goods were thus protected throughout the journey. They also knew how to use herbs to keep insects from nibbling away at their earnings. I've heard that in many Turkish villages, these herbs are still used. Basil, for example, is grown in leftover pots to keep away ants and insects.

Five kilometers from Ilıca, probably brought on by the cold or perhaps by some poorly washed apricots as well (I had been told: only buy fruit that you have to peel!), a sudden and violent bout of diarrhea wrings my stomach. Where can I go to relieve this sudden urge out here on the boundless steppe? I'm not about to put my buttocks on display in a land where just exposing your lower leg is considered a violation of common decency. I manage nevertheless, by way of clever calculation and sprints that have less to do with my fitness and more to do with sheer necessity, to protect my privacy in a small depression in the terrain, or among the tall grasses.

I hope to reach the stopover very quickly, so I can rest up in an inn, but one of the locals I meet up with dashes my hopes when he tells me that there's no hotel in Ilıca. Can I stay in someone's home in this condition? I have a hard time picturing that. My spirits down, it takes me over an hour to travel the final kilometer, making ten emergency stops to pull down my pants. I enter the city taking baby steps, stiff from having to squeeze my sphincter shut.

Just to be sure, before looking for somewhere to stay, I ask around. Hallelujah: there is a hotel in Ilıca after all. Hallelujah once again: it's also clean. Located atop a bakery, a wonderful scent wafts through it whenever batches of bread are pulled from the oven. I pay extra to have a room for two all to myself. There's no shower, but there is a hammam across the street. I'm there in no time flat and gleefully take a dip in the large circular pool. The color of the water in which a good twenty of us are steeping suggests that it hasn't been changed since the days of Atatürk. But pleasure precedes hygiene, as any child will tell you. Feeling relaxed once more from the bath, I wolf down a *çorba*, then head up to my room.

In the morning, my diarrhea has been cured. The Ilıca-Erzurum stage is one of the shortest that I'll do since the very start: twenty-one kilometers. It will be a simple formality, a walk in the park. As I leave the village, what's like a two-lane highway runs east, straight as an arrow. It's the only access road to the big city. The series of storms of the past two days have cleansed the air. The sky is crystal clear, engendering a certain lightheartedness. The plain is so flat that, near the sign indicating that the city is eighteen kilometers away, I can already distinctly make out Erzurum's houses backed up against the mountainside. It's as though I were already there.

That is, unfortunately, without taking into account how tired I am, how weak I feel after yesterday's bout of diarrhea, as well as a total lack of motivation. Whenever I'm just about to reach a goal, I lose all interest in it. It's the next one that motivates me. Erzurum is about halfway between Istanbul and Tehran. Over the past few days, I've looked over the information I have on Iran several times, and I've already given some thought to how I'm going to tackle the second half of my trek.

Erzurum keeps running away from me. I think that, although it's the shortest stage, it's the most difficult one since my journey began. I walk slowly, arduously. I feel crushed beneath my pack. The city seems to take malicious delight in running farther away every time I think I'm almost there. After three hours, my legs giving way beneath me, I can go no farther: I sit down and fall asleep with my back against a chain-link fence. I empty my water jug and nibble on the dried fruit I have left. Once I've regained my strength, the city seems farther than it ever was; the warm, blurry air makes it float above the horizon, as if it were only a mirage. That's what it's truly starting to become for me. Three hours later, I finally reach the first buildings, which belong to Atatürk University: several concrete cubes planted on lawns that irrigation trucks rescue every morning from burning to a crisp. Male and female students, some wearing chadors, wander about campus walkways, a book under an arm, or hunched over under the weight of their backpacks full of knowledge.

People ask me questions. I'm not very talkative today, so they decide to take me to the tourist office, which, when I finally see it, is of hardly any interest to me. I'm keener on getting rest than obtaining information. But since it was destiny's wish, and since, for the time being, I have almost no willpower at all, let's go. Perhaps I'll glean something that reinvigorates me. Muhammet Yokşuk, the director, a big man, says the same thing I've heard everywhere else. "The Silk Road? No, I don't have anything on it." But he's interested in my travels and asks a thousand questions, so I share my story. As I talk, he places several phone calls. When I've finished and am ready to leave, he motions me to come back.

"Your story is unique. I just called several journalists for a press conference."

A few minutes later, correspondents from the three national newspapers ask questions, take pictures, and even film me. All three promise there will be feature articles in tomorrow's editions, and a telecast on local TV.

Muhammet, delighted that I was willing to endure all the trouble he put me through, proves very helpful and shows me where I can find a recently opened hotel. He assures me that I'll find it comfortable and not too expensive. I walk there taking baby steps. At first glance, there's nothing special about the city. Stone and concrete buildings, five or six stories tall, line wide avenues crisscrossed by a steady stream of pedestrians. The hotel is as promised: new, clean, functional, and reasonably priced. It's also in keeping with the others, since a pipe spews water out onto the tile floor. In my entire journey across Turkey, I cannot recall a single bathroom where there wasn't a gurgling leak somewhere. After a long shower, I plop myself down onto the bed and sleep until nightfall, wanting to visit the city at its best. In summer, cities in the Orient only reveal themselves in the evening. In the lower city, dominated by the well-preserved citadel, hundreds of shops show off their treasures in the dim light of miserly lamps, more suited to vigils or discussing private matters than to conducting business. It takes traveling to the Orient to understand that business here, having been conducted for two thousand years, is based on the art of conversation. Here, each time a customer enters a shop, the merchant looks as much forward to the joy of a good discussion as to any financial gain. When I started traveling the world, I was captivated by the game that merchants in the Orient play with each potential buyer: a game of cleverness, seduction, high diplomacy, craftiness, and tactics often worthy of the greatest strategists, which Westerners tend not to like, in the name of the sacrosanct principle of openness, or *transparency*, as it's called today. But upon closer consideration, it's in this face-to-face, person-to-person experience that souls reveal themselves, trustworthiness or treachery is expressed while looking each other in the eye, business between beings takes place *in the light*.

Muhammet Yokşuk put me in touch with a French professor at Atatürk University. Mehmet Baki arranged for me to meet with three history professors interested in the Silk Road. Selahattin Tuzlu wrote his dissertation on the caravan route between Trabzon, on the Black Sea, and the Iranian border, from 1850 to 1900. Mehmet Tezcan is interested in the Silk Road from the third century before Christ to the third century after. Finally, Dr. Kevan Çetin has limited his research to a great caravan market in the center of Turkey—Yabanlu, near Kayseri—during the Seljuk period. Leaving our three-hour-long conversation, Mehmet, who provided the simultaneous translation, is exhausted. We were so impassioned by the topic that a national television crew, which had come to interview me, tiptoed out, not wanting to disturb us.

The journalist left me a note indicating that he'd come back to my hotel tomorrow morning. In the evening, I realize that he won't have time, since that afternoon comes the announcement of the verdict of Öcalan's trial. The leader of the PKK is sentenced to death. Westward, among the Turks, people must be celebrating. Eastward, among the Kurds, people must be weeping. Here, in Erzurum, in this place straddling two worlds, the news puts people in a stupor.

I'm not surprised by the verdict. Everyone was expecting it. Öcalan's trial traveled with me throughout my voyage, for it began just as I was setting out. Every day, in restaurants or at people's houses, I was able to see the face of the PKK's leader in front of the judges, protected from a possible gunshot by bulletproof glass. Obviously, I didn't understand the commentary. But more than once, the images were sufficiently explicit for me to realize that television wasn't erring on the side of excessive objectivity. I remember them showing a lineup of the men killed in PKK attacks: when a close-up of each face was shown, it changed into a huge blood stain showing the date on which each one died. On the other hand, I never saw anything on the burning or bombing of Kurdish villages by the Turkish army, whose purpose is hardly to conduct humanitarian work. And during the trial, the daily presence in the courtroom of the mothers of soldiers killed in combat, each with a photo of her child pinned to her breast, did little to ensure that debate would remain civil.

How are the Kurds, whose territory I'm preparing to enter, going to react? After having observed a truce for the duration of the trial, is the revolutionary party going to launch a series of attacks? Are the Kurdish villages I'm about to visit going to boil over? Unsure about the situation, I decide to remain an extra day in Erzurum as a cautionary measure. It will help my worn-out body recover, too.

I dine at the *Guzelyurt*, the best restaurant in town, with Huseyin, the friend of a friend from Istanbul. He's a pharmacist here. He's about fifty years old, with an open and warm personality. A lover of pleasures and of gambling, Huseyin doesn't abide by the prohibition on alcohol, but he's still a man of great faith. Half in English, half in Turkish, our conversation centers, of course, on Öcalan's sentencing and the status of the Kurds. Huseyin orders a bottle of Turkish wine. Tasting my first glass of a liquid high in tannins and slightly too acidic for my palate, I realize that I haven't had a drop of alcohol since I left Istanbul, with the exception of Blue-Eyes's whisky, which I gulped down joylessly.

As we are bidding each other farewell, Huseyin utters a phrase that is, to put it mildly, surprising, given what he said during dinner: "I believe in two things, my God and my Army." From this perspective, he's aligned with the vast majority of Turks. I've already expressed how positive the image of the army is here, except for the youngest generation. I don't know exactly why this is. It's true that, led by Atatürk, the army gave the country back its soul and its pride when, at the beginning of the twentieth century, the "question of the Orient" was raised, and Europe was preparing to divvy up the spoils of a Sultanate in disarray. Is this where the Turks' veneration of soldiery comes from? Or does it have its roots further back, in the military traditions of the Ottoman Empire? Or further still, in the bellicose past of the nomadic tribes that came from the far reaches of Mongolia? Whatever the case may be, respect for the

military is everywhere. God, the State, and the Army: for many, they are
one and the same.

At the post office, I pick up my mail, including what had remained
undelivered in the lockbox in Suşehri. On the other hand, a box of ten
rolls of film has vanished. The man at the window tells me a story, and,
as usual, I understand nothing, except that the package was supposedly
returned to France. When I finally pick it up in Paris, only three rolls
of film remain. The others vaporized. Fortunately for me, after running
around to every photographic shop in the city, I manage to find five rolls
of the type that work in my camera.

I also use this unplanned downtime to assess where things stand in
my journey. Arriving in Erzurum, I've traveled one thousand four hundred and fifty kilometers (900 miles). I've covered just over half of the
Istanbul–Tehran route. And I'm approximately ten days ahead of the
schedule I established before setting out. From a physical standpoint,
on which the rest of the journey hinges, things are almost perfect. My
boots have done quite well on their diet of tractor grease and are now
getting along marvelously with my feet. I've lost three kilos (6.6 pounds)
in a month and a half. I've had to tighten my belt three more holes and
have gained muscle mass, especially in my legs, thighs, and shoulders.
My resting heartbeat is fifty-six beats per minute, and its rhythm of
between eighty and ninety during exercise is proof that I'm in great
shape. I have to simply be careful not to overdo it to avoid chronic
fatigue. My recovery times, almost immediate, are evidence that from
a physical perspective, I'm working out like an athlete getting ready for
the Olympics.

The cultural and historical aspect of my journey is not as satisfy-
ing as I'd hoped. My inadequate understanding of the language is a
real handicap with respect to gathering information. But the strong
relationships I've managed to establish, especially with families who
took me in and who, speaking the language of the heart, had little
need for vocabulary and syntax. And in the end, that's all that matters to me.

I also capitalize on these two days off to "improve my look." My pants and vest—worn from all the rubbing, soaked day in and day out with sweat, and rinsed a thousand times but still dirty—are in tatters. But since none of the clothes I find are as comfortable, it's Zühtü Atalay, a joyful tailor who is delighted by my traveling attire, who mends the most visible tears. Plead as I may, he refuses to take even a small coin in payment. All he wants is to hear about my journey; and so, for a good half-hour, that's what I do.

Two of the three news stories written by the journalists never appear in print for lack of space. Öcalan's conviction is the big news. The newspaper headlines confirm what one academic I met on campus told me: "The press wanted his hide, now they have it." In this country where democratic traditions have not yet been permanently established, where political structures are weak, he told me, the press "invents" public opinion at will. Eight columns wide, in block capitals, the papers don't beat around the bush: THE DEATH PENALTY FOR THE TRAITOR; THE MARTYRS CELEBRATE; THE BABIES' REVENGE, proclaim the headlines, accompanied by photos of a dead baby, women dancing for joy at the rendering of the verdict while hugging the photos of their sons, or of soldiers' funerals, their coffins cloaked in the red flag stamped with a crescent. It all smacks more of revenge taking or a settling of accounts than an act of justice. The authorities did, nevertheless, attempt to adhere to the rule of law, concerned about the reputation of the Turkish brand on the eve of a fresh request for membership in the European community. But all of that hardly makes me feel any better knowing that, starting tomorrow, I'll be pushing into a territory where traditions of violence go as far back as anyone can remember.

I'm at once worried about getting caught up in this cycle of heightened debate that might be sparked by the verdict, and eager to see and hear for myself the Kurdish point of view. For up till now, I've only dealt with Turks, whose views on the matter amounted to a simple finger gesture pretending to slit someone's throat.

I check over my gear, buckle my pack, hop in bed, then sleep a dreamless sleep.

On July 1, I leave Erzurum on a highway heading east. War is in the air: on the right and on the left, there are nothing but army camps. Over here, men are training, shouting in guttural voices behind a palisade fence. Over there, other men are running obstacle courses. Farther on, they're doing maintenance work on their trucks and armored vehicles. The roads seem to be traveled by army vehicles only.

After walking ten kilometers, I veer south on a dirt road that was once the Silk Road but that has now been abandoned for a brand new paved road. I'm back to peace and quiet . . . and a new army base with chairlifts behind it. Is it a place for soldiers to relax, or a training base for the mountain division? I ask the grunt on sentry duty about it, and he calls over a ranking officer, whose only answer is a blunt order to keep on walking. Here, everything is "classified."

The road rises to a mountain pass at 2,000 meters (6,560 feet). I victoriously hold out against two soldiers who try their damnedest to give me a ride in their truck. People here are decidedly obsessed with lending the solo hiker a hand. After the pass, a stunningly beautiful valley, enlivened by a small river, offers me the shade of a willow grove: an ideal spot to stop and have a snack. Beyond, the road continues on, paved with loosely interlocked stones on which the old iron-rimmed wheels of chariots have left their marks. This road, like most caravan trails, was used as a strategic road all the way up to the last war. The army maintained them to carry its cannons and wagons full of supplies and munitions, should a conflict erupt with Persia or Armenia.

On the hillsides, dozens of abandoned bunkers cover the meadows. They all face the northeast, a reminder of the days when Turkey was one of NATO's forward military bastions. At the West's front line, the country stood at the ready—albeit not overanxiously—for the Soviet ogre to invade. The Russian danger has passed. The bunkers, now useless, were left to the winds of the steppe; never again will thunder rumble from their gray, wide-open mouths. I discover several masses of flowering rhododendron. Michèle Nicolas, a researcher in ethnobotany at the

CNRS,* told me that the Turks call honey made from the nectar of rho-dodendron and azalea "mad honey." It's said that Xenophon's army was defeated because his soldiers had partaken of it and were unable to fight.

The wheat is still green here, the result of the region's elevation. At noon, in the deserted village of Korucuk (*koh-roo-djook'*), I walk in circles in the small streets lined by earthen houses. The roofs are circular, and they, too, are made of soil. A few thin weeds have sprouted from them. A woman lets me glimpse part of her nose and chador from behind a half-collapsed wall. I head in her direction to ask whether there's a store in the village. But when I draw near, she disappears.

After a fruitless quest, two young, timid girls show me where the *bakkal*'s shop is, a windowless earthen building that I'd mistaken for a barn. The door is partially opened. I give it a push and discover three men in the shadows. The grocer has nothing edible to sell me. I'm finally persuaded to take a can of juice. They ask me to tell them about my jour-ney. One of the men is the imam. He goes out while the *bakkal* spreads a piece of cardboard on the ground, performs his ablutions, and spends a long time in prayer. As I'm about to get going again, the cleric invites me to have lunch.

During the meal, he and the *bakkal* speak only about religion. The *bakkal* wants to know what my religion is. I answer him with a little white lie, saying I'm a Christian. His lips curl in disdain and, I suspect, in disgust, as though I had said, "I am the devil." The imam knows nothing about the rites of Catholicism, and he asks me about them. I answer as best I can. While walking with me to the edge of the village, he tries to convince me to convert to Islam. If I were to tell him that I'm an agnostic, he'd be horrified. I noticed, for the first time since I began entering people's homes in Turkey, that there was no portrait of Atatürk on the wall.

* TN: CNRS—France's *"Centre national de la recherche scientifique,"* or National Center for Scientific Research.

Pasinler is a town known for its thermal baths. The hotel, catering to spa-goers, is comfortable. I'm unfortunately not able to take advantage of the water—which, I am told, is quite miraculous—for tonight is women's night. High above the town, one of three walls of the former fortified castle has been cobbled back together. A modern must: the crenellations were rebuilt in cement masonry. The effect is bizarre, like a papier-mâché stage set, only looking real from several kilometers away. The bakeries of Pasinler sell a peculiar kind of bread, like a soft, flat baguette over a meter long. I tucked one away in my pack, and it lasted me several days.

The following day, I decide to do an in-depth exploration of the Kurdish homeland. I haven't had much news, but Öcalan's sentencing doesn't seem to have resulted in any serious incidents. My understanding is that the affair had the effect of sparking a polemic within the PKK itself. Öcalan, during the trial, indicated that he was ready to seek a negotiated settlement to the Kurdish question, going so far as to consider asking his supporters to lay down their arms. Some are heeding his suggestions, advocating an end to hostilities in the hopes that their leader, whom they fondly refer to as *Apo* (Uncle), might be granted some measure of clemency. Hardliners, on the other hand, point out that the man was drugged and undoubtedly manipulated during his trial, so no one can take his orders seriously. For them, the guerilla war has to be stepped up and brought to the country's largest cities. They claim that only a renewed offensive would allow them to negotiate from a position of strength so as to help Apo avoid the worst. Images of attacks in Istanbul and Ankara are already flashing across television screens.

Heading south out of Pasinler on a small dirt road that runs straight across an irrigated plain where early season fruits and vegetables are grown, I'm hardly reassured. But I want to see, to know, to touch the land of the Kurds. My first observation is that agriculture is the prevailing activity here, but that it's carried out using antiquated tools. On Pasinler's public square, I noticed more horses than tractors, and out on the plain, I see nothing but carts. The women and some of the men I come across are working the ground hunched over—I'm certain, though, that they see me—and they don't return my greetings. I tell myself that it's going to be tough making contacts, and I tackle the steep climb, somewhat on my guard.

Yastıktepe is a mountain village that rises in terraces for one kilometer on both sides of the road. Half curious and half afraid, intent on covering as much distance as possible since I have set a far-off target, I decide to traverse it without making contact with the inhabitants. I have to avoid saying anything, not even hello, as that would be to open the floodgates for questions. So I do my best to return their glances with a smile, but one that's not too approachable. There they are, ten, then twenty, then thirty, just standing there silently, watching me as I approach. I come up Main Street, avoiding the puddles of water or horse manure that have, in spots, turned the ground into sticky mud. I reach the village's very last houses, but then, huffing and puffing, a man comes galloping in my direction and catches up to me. He's very angry:

"Where are you going?"

Obstinate, I keep right on walking, but I have little choice but to answer him.

"Payveren."

"That's the wrong road."

"But my map shows that it is to the south."

"Yes, but you're wrong. Anyway, come have tea."

"But I'm in a hurry, Payveren is far . . ."

"Come have tea!"

The invitation is nonnegotiable. His tone may not be aggressive, but it's firm. The rascal pulls me by the sleeve. As we head back down, he holds onto my arm to make sure I won't get away. A veritable committee of somber men is there, waiting for us. The rascal introduces himself. He's the *bakkal*, and he invites me into his store. The usual interior. Very little in the way of foodstuffs, but three benches. Here, as elsewhere, you go to the grocer's primarily to talk. The committee piles in behind us. A tall boy prepares the tea. The mood lightened up as soon as I set down my pack. Certain, now, that they'll have answers to their questions, they're happy and smile. They address me in Turkish but discuss among themselves in Kurdish. When I discover that it's the grocer's son who readies the tea, they laugh, since, with his twelve children, the *bakkal* is not about to prepare the tea himself. They offer to take me to Payveren in a tractor, since to cars the road is impassable. I turn them down, but, before leaving, I ask them if they'd like me to take their picture. All the men present walk outside. Some of them don't want to be in the photo and go their way. They all wave good-bye to me until I finally disappear. This first contact in a Kurdish village is encouraging. No one brought up Apo, no doubt as a matter of prudence.

The high trail is difficult to follow. I was told to go "straight ahead." Except that, every two kilometers, there's a damned fork in the road. It's the perennial question: straight ahead to the right, or straight ahead to the left? My only option is to inquire, should I be so fortunate as to run into a peasant farmer, since they are few and far between at these altitudes. After walking for about one hour, a man on his tractor towing a trailer of milk jugs banging about, making rhythmic metallic music, confirms what I was beginning to sense: I'm going in the wrong direction. At the first fork, I should have gone straight left. He offers to take me back there.

We're rolling along a road cut through the rock, near the edge of a precipice. The jugs are bouncing about with renewed vigor, making a charivari to wake the devil. There's no point trying to converse. While still driving, the man turns around in an attempt to reposition his seat cushion, which has slipped. My eyes follow his, for the cushion in question is covered in a stylish silk cloth that doesn't match the rest. But as he keeps fiddling with his seat, I look back and scream. The road suddenly veers to the right, so we're headed straight for the abyss. As soon as I scream, the man, even before turning back around, instinctively turns the wheel hard to the right, in the mountain's direction. The front left tire nearly goes over the edge.

His legs like taffy from the fright, he stops his doggone machine. He slowly turns to look at me. His eyes are full of terror at what might have been. His face has gone white, and I'm probably as ashen as he is. Then, all of a sudden, we burst out laughing. A hearty, liberating laugh;

a resounding fit of laughter that echoes back to us. Then, as our hilarity finally dies down, there's silence once more. We look at each other, then at the road, and then at the ravine where death was lying in wait, one hundred meters below, in a jumble of craggy rocks. And once again, we erupt in a fit of laughter. Good God, life seems wonderful when death, an idiotic death at that, has brushed past us. But what death isn't stupid?

We say nothing as the man puts the engine in gear and starts his tractor of doom rolling once again. At the fork in the road, I'm happy to get off and feel the solid ground beneath my boots. Still a little too shaken from the scare to start right back out, I sit down and let a good quarter hour go by. The path heads down into the valley then traverses a hamlet made up of a handful of sad-looking shacks. A man is shearing sheep in the shade of a high wall. Some snotty kids stop their games and stare at me. My reckless tractor driver told me that the people living here are Shiite Kurds. I decide to cut across the fields, since, a distance off in the valley, I spot the paved road I'm looking for.

My map shows that I have to take a drivable road to the east. Eureka! I find it, but then, three kilometers on, two schoolteachers in a car tell me that I've once again gone off course. They offer to give me a lift to the right road. In their view, the Kurds are very angry. Since yesterday, there have reportedly been several attacks, and a veritable arsenal of armaments was found in Istanbul. They beg me to be careful and warn me that should I come across an army patrol, they'll prevent from traveling the route I mapped out from one village to the next all the way to Ağrı (*ah'-ruh*).

The dirt road near where they drop me off climbs along a gentle hill. With sweeping motions, men are mowing grass by hand, and children, in the stream, are looking for crayfish while keeping watch over a few cows and horses. How could there be danger in such a bucolic setting, where cilantro and licorice grow on the wayside?

Around five o'clock, some beekeepers from the Black Sea, of whom there are many in this region, hail me. "*Gel, çay!*" One of them beckons me into the portable hut they live in. Six loaded rifles are mounted on a

rack. We walk around the outside of the tent. A fearsome Kangal, ears
and tail cut, is chained nearby; at first it growls, then barks ferociously at
my approach. I keep my distance. They tell me that they let the dog run
loose at night:

"The terrorists can come, they'll find someone to talk to," the older
one tells me, his face as wrinkled as a baked apple. This will be his last
season at high altitude.

I'm starting to tell myself that the least I could have done was buy a
gun in Erzurum.

The village of Payveren is two kilometers farther. It suddenly comes
into view as I round a bend. The earthen houses tucked away against the
slope are grouped around two white buildings the setting sun has turned
pink: the mosque and the school. On which door should I knock? Before
leaving, I'd gone to see a representative of the Kurdish community in
Paris; he, too, gave me a warning: "I'd feel better if you'd board a bus in
Erzurum and not get off until you reach the Iranian border. But I suppose that's not what you plan to do?" I'd confirmed that that was indeed
the case, and, after I explained that I wanted to avoid the main road and
get to know the villages, he continued:

"All right. In Kurdish villages (he drew me a sketch), you'll see that
one house is larger than all the others. This is the ruler of the village.
Knock there. If a woman answers the door, simply say, "I want to see the
master," and nothing more. In his house, you'll be safe. And tell your
host where you're headed the next day. There's a distinct possibility that
he'll let the entire clan in on your journey. That way, you'll be more or
less safe. And above all, don't forget: never speak to women!"

I look around for the largest house in Payveren. There isn't one. Proof
once again, as if I needed it, that reality likes to throw you off track
and defy whatever you think you know about it. For after all, in Paris,
things seemed simple: the ever-so-simple landmark of "the large house"
where you'll receive a warm welcome and where any difficulties that lie
in wait down the road will be resolved was a nice thought, easy to keep
in mind whenever I felt worried. But here I am, and Payveren—no doubt
the exception that proves the rule—has decided to mess with me. After

many unanswered questions, I get a taciturn fellow to agree to take me to the *muhtar*'s house. His shack is no different from any other, with a satellite TV dish on the roof. I knock. A young pregnant woman opens the door. I ask to see the master. Without saying a word, she goes back in the house. Several moments later, a string bean, hairy as a monkey, stumbles out. His face is bloated and his eyes cloudy. Is he still asleep, drunk, or stoned?

CHAPTER XI
. . . AND THIEVES

The man, perhaps in his early forties, is at least twenty centimeters (8 inches) taller than I. With his disheveled mop of hair, his three-day-old beard, and tufts of black fur poking out of the open collar of his shirt, he's the spitting image of an Ostrogoth. He immediately barks: "Papers, papers!"

I take out my passport, which he pockets without even looking at. Then, he opens the door, which serves for two houses, and his invitation to step in is more like a shove. We set foot in a vast reception room. I'm surprised by the comfort of the dwelling, which is out of keeping with the appearance of these Kurdish houses. On the exterior, they're cubes of gray masonry, without any visible windows, covered by a flat, dirt roof overrun with sunbaked weeds. The interior is cozy. The carpet and paintings give it character, and a small window lets in muted, yet sufficient light.

Is it distrust or fear, or perhaps discomposure due to some unknown alcohol or drug? In any case, my host is agitated, nervous. I think back to my arrival in Arif's house. Is this guy going to do like him and call the *jandarmas*, before even knowing who I am and what I'm up to? Against the backdrop of civil war prevailing here, and especially after Öcalan's conviction, I'm not surprised that people would seem nervous. But I'm confident: I'll fill him in, we'll have a conversation, he'll calm down, and everything will work out fine.

No sooner have I set down my pack than the man grabs it and tries to open it. He probably has the same fears as the villagers in Alihacı.

For him, this unfamiliar object must conceal a weapon or some untold danger. I'm ready to reassure him, but I won't let him rummage through my things: that's something I can't stand. So, to gain his trust, I start taking out the little plastic or canvas bags, one by one, announcing what they contain: clothing, first aid kit, food, sleeping bag. He has sat down on the ground next to me and takes a quick look at all my "treasures," then sets them down nearby, barely paying attention to them. Once I've emptied out main compartment, he wants to see what's in the side pockets. I empty them as well. The first object I take out is a ballpoint pen. He quickly pockets it, saying, "for me." At best, I find that his reaction is lacking in courtesy, but, then again, if he wants it, let him keep it. My knife goes down the same path, but this time, I take issue. I need it, it could prove handy in case I'm attacked or have an accident. But not wanting to provoke the beast, I take from the pocket my battery-powered lamp—which has never worked—and hand it to him.

"Not the knife, no. But you can have this."

Just as he's about to snatch it, I step back, asking first for the knife. He regretfully hands it over, then examines the lamp, which he tries in vain, and for good reason, to get working. I explain that the batteries are dead and that it needs new ones. But while he's greedily examining the object, the mystery suddenly clears up. It seemed to me that the fellow was a little too young to be the *muhtar*. All those I met until now were mature men, sometimes even quite aged. And his behavior—the proof is right in front of me—has nothing to do with his fear of terrorism: he wants my knife and my pocket lamp.

"Are you the *muhtar*?"

"No, my brother is the *muhtar*."

"Where is he?"

"In Erzurum. He'll be back this evening."

"So give me back my passport, I'll show it to him when he gets back."

"No, tomorrow morning."

And he goes back to toying with the pretty little—albeit perfectly useless—lamp. He wants to know what else is in my pack. But I put an end to inventory taking, glad that I didn't open the pocket with my camera. Now that the search of my bag has come to an end, he puts his hand in one of my vest pockets. I quickly pull away and scowl. I try to act tough and intimidate him, but I know all too well that I'm at his mercy. All the more reason why I have to assert myself. I put everything back in my pack, despite his protests, reassuring him all the while. When his brother is here, I tell him, he'll be able to look through everything. I wish I had first asked about the scoundrel's identity. I also realize that he has brought me into the *muhtar*'s house, but that he lives in the adjoining dwelling with the pregnant woman I saw a short time ago.

He sits down a short distance away, takes his lamp and pen out of his pocket, and caresses them with such pleasure that his face lights up with glee. His wife, glaring at me and full of curiosity, has entered the room and begins to make her way over to me. The scoundrel gets up, shoves and jostles her, trying to force her out. She resists. He gives her a poke in the shoulder, and she finally decides to back away. Over the next two hours, she comes back ten times, and each time he chases her away just as viciously.

"Is that your wife?"

"Yes."

"Why do you hit her?"

He doesn't answer but goes over to my gear. Everything is finally becoming clear. He's not drunk nor drugged, he's mentally unstable. It remains to be seen whether he's a gentle madman or a malicious madman. He gives me the willies: no doubt because he's so big, but especially because of the hazy look in his eyes. And the brutality with which he treated his wife could, if I'm not careful, be used against me, too. And I'm trapped here, stuck for as long as I can't get back my passport.

An old woman comes in. He treats her with great respect. It's his mother. In Kurdish, he sums up for her everything I told him about my journey. In any case, that's what I imagine he says. She doesn't try to talk to me, and recalling what I was told in Paris, I refrain from saying anything to her. Two kids, about twelve years old, exploit her entrance by slipping in, too, silently planting themselves in a corner. Once his mother has left, the macaque goes over to the children and shows them the "treasures" he managed to get from me. One of the kids wants a lamp, too: do I have any others? No.

The brute takes my passport out of his pocket and hands it over to the other kid. I realize that the reason he hasn't looked at it yet is that he doesn't know how to read. The kid tries pronouncing the foreign words. I go over to the kid, putting on an air of innocence:

"Do you want me to show you where the stamp from the Turkish police is?"

He doesn't say yes or no, but I authoritatively take the document from his hands. I show him the stamp in question, then the colorful page containing the Iranian visa. Now's my chance: it's all or nothing. I close the passport shut and slip it posthaste into my pocket, and carefully button it closed. The macaque rushes over.

"Give."

"I'll give it to the *muhtar*. You're not the *muhtar*."

He's furious but makes no attempt to take it by force. I breathe a sigh of relief, since, in a confrontation with an athlete like that, I stand no chance whatsoever. Now I need to get out of this trap. I go back to my pack, hoist it onto my shoulder, and head toward to the door.

"I'll be back this evening. If your brother's looking for me, I'll be with the beekeepers at the entrance to the village."

"No, stay."

My departure throws him into a panic. He puts his hand in his pocket and takes out the lamp.

"Here, I give it back to you, but stay. My brother won't be long."

I give it some thought, for I have to be careful not to make a false move. Here, I feel threatened. But the risk is very different from what I went through in Alihacı. The Kurds won't call in the army. The relationship between the army and the villages is too adversarial. At Yastıktepe, my first Kurdish village, and here too, there are no portraits of Atatürk, which were everywhere I went until I entered Erzurum. From now on, if I have any trouble, I'll have to settle it with the villagers themselves. If I go now and hang out with the beekeepers, I'm going from the Kurdish camp to the Turkish camp. And, by refusing his hospitality, I'd be rubbing the *muhtar* the wrong way. He is, beyond any doubt, a respectable and respected man. I cannot hold him responsible for the odd behavior of his crazy brother. Ultimately, even if I were to seek hospitality from the beekeepers, I'd be safe for one night, but what about the next? I think back to what the Kurdish gentleman told me in Paris: from one hamlet to another, everyone knows everything. It would be impossible for me to get through the other villages if I lose face with the *muhtar* here.

After all, the vital thing for me was getting back my passport. And as soon as the brother returns, everything will be fine. I must therefore be patient and wait. I set my bag back down. The rascal breathes a sigh of relief. But he's clearly angry with me. But I think I can handle the situation: with the pocket lamp he gave back to me, I have something I can trade with, and I ought to be able to soften him up.

In the hours that follow, the usual scenario unfolds. The village elders are first to come see the foreigner, since they have plenty of time. Then the community's prominent figures. One of them is quite young, about thirty-five, clean-shaven and wearing a three-piece suit. He's a bit fat, whereas all the others are lean country folk, their faces worn by the harsh weather. I have no trouble figuring out who he is: he's the imam. The macaque plays the ringmaster, running about, disappearing, then coming back with more curious villagers. Every able-bodied person in the village has soon squeezed into the room. The memory of Alihacı haunts me. What are these men thinking? What do they want from me? They're friendly to me and ask about my journey.

Those sporting caps traditionally worn by devout men congregate about the imam, whom they treat with the utmost respect. After having said nothing for a long time, he asks me a hundred questions about my journey, religion, profession, and sources of income. As soon as he speaks, the faithful all nod their heads in agreement in a display of support. As if, after all, there were two camps: his and mine. I get the sense that I can't expect anything from these people, although they don't appear hostile. Our two worlds are *too far apart* from each other. It's now dark out. Once again, worry has set in. The *muhtar* is still not here. In his absence, I'll be all alone tonight with that horrible macaque, and I don't have a very good feeling about that. Anytime I say something, he throws a greedy glance at my gear, sometimes brushing it with his hand as he walks by, as if wanting to reassure himself that it's still there. The man is clearly mad with greed. And no doubt simply mad. When the villagers start singing the praises of my big boots, which, after one thousand five hundred kilometers, seem to have at least that many left to go, he says, with a big, worrisome smile: "They are mine." Ill at ease, the men look away. I've been warned: he won't stop at just the pocket lamp.

At eleven o'clock, I'm quite certain that the *muhtar* will never come. The macaque brings in a carpet. The imam and four men recite prayers while the others, paying no attention to the ritual, continue their conversations. Now very dubious, I'm wondering why they didn't go to the mosque to pray. And yet I realize that Islam is a very flexible religion: the temple can be wherever the faithful find themselves. Then, little by little, the men get up and leave. Around midnight, everyone has left except the imam. The madman goes to get yogurt, bread, and cheese, and we have dinner. He then sets some mattresses and blankets on the bunks. I glance over nervously at him. And with one pronouncement, the imam reassures me.

"I'm sleeping here."

Everything is becoming clear. Although the imam told me that he lives next door with his wife and children, if he plans to sleep here, it's to protect me in the absence of the *muhtar*. It's proof that I am indeed dealing with a man suffering from mental illness. Fear prevents me from falling asleep. I occasionally drift off for a few moments, but then I wake back up in a start. The madman, rolled up in a blanket on the carpet, is fast asleep. The imam is snoring.

At 5:00 a.m., I'm woken by the first ray of light, since I'm already on the qui vive anyway, and all I can think of is freeing myself from the macaque's clutches. But I cannot violate the sacrosanct laws of hospitality, so I have to wait for breakfast. While the madman gets it ready along with the women, the imam questions me for a long while on Catholicism and Christian rites. I answer as best I can, nimbly thumbing through my pocket dictionary in search of the religious terms that—a true curse—are words I haven't learned. Breakfast resembles dinner: bread and cheese, washed down with tea. Coarse food and exhausting work: it's no surprise that no one is overweight here, as in Turkey's west.

I'm about to leave when the imam stops me:

"Don't go: the dogs have not yet left with the flocks. You'll be ripped to pieces."

I'm chomping at the bit. We sit in total silence. I feel despondent, as I'm in a hurry to get a move on. The macaque is going around in circles. He can no longer bear it, he asks me to give him back the lamp. I hand it over to him with as friendly a smile as I can muster. I hope that that will calm him down for good, but I doubt it.

Finally, around seven o'clock, I have permission to leave. The shepherds and their flocks have headed off for mountain pastures. The village is deserted. I wasn't able to fill my water bottle last night as I typically do and let the purification tablets take effect through the night. I therefore head to the spring. Meanwhile, the imam seizes this opportunity to ask me more questions about my religion. I have no trouble pretending not to understand what he's saying, for my mind is elsewhere. What awaits me in the next village? I sense some imminent threat. If he only knew just how little I really care about all his questions on the comparative virtues of the world's different religions! I'm eager to get away from the fear that has gripped me since last evening when I knocked on the madman's door.

When that macaque of misfortune who'd gone off into a barn a little while ago comes back to join us, a wave of fear paralyzes me. As if I weren't terrorized enough already, he tells me he's going to walk with me.

And in his hand, he's holding an ax, as sharp as the one that I saw in the skilled hands of Hüseyin while he carved his pitchforks, or Mustafa the carpenter, as he sharpened his ax with love. I throw the imam a frantic glance. But there's no help coming from that quarter. He holds out his hand, saying that he's delighted to have met me, then quietly walks away, his hands in his pockets. He likely stayed with me last night to protect me, because no one wanted a foreigner to be robbed or harassed in the village. But were that to happen outside his fiefdom, he could care less.

The madman is beaming. He knows that, as soon as no one can see us, he'll be able to steal whatever he wants from me.

I try not to panic. With the weapon he keeps waving in front of me and his obvious strength, I wouldn't stand a chance. In the face of irrepressible desire, what's one man's life? For this fellow, nothing.

If I acted on impulse, I'd drop my backpack and take to my heels. But where would I go? There's a tractor in front of the *muhtar*'s house. With a spin of the wheels, the madman would catch up to me. Eager to make his move, he invites me to get going. While stowing my brimming water jug, I try to come up with a plan. How can I gain time, get out ahead of him, and away from danger? Suddenly, I have an idea. Last night, when I told him I was headed back to see the beekeepers, he went to pieces. Why not try that again?

"I promised to say good-bye to my friends the beekeepers," I tell him. "I'm headed there first, and when I come back through town, you can join me."

Frustrated like a little kid, he nevertheless seems to buy into my crazy idea. I immediately put on my pack and start going. My beekeepers have already been out working for a long time. I give them a nutshell version of last night's ordeal and ask them to confirm what I'd already guessed:

"Is it true that the *muhtar*'s brother isn't quite right?"

They mime an answer that is unambiguous. So I tell them about the ax, and how he wants to come along with me.

"Head back the other way. If he comes by here, we'll try to stop him."

No sooner said than done, and I hustle. I don't think I've ever walked so fast. From time to time, I stop and listen, ready to hide should I hear the sound of an engine. In the hamlet I traversed last night, I hand out some candy to the children. A tall man who says he's the *muhtar* wants to see my passport. Are my problems going to continue? Full of apprehension, I hand it to him. He fingers through it, then hands it back to me, satisfied. That reassures me, as I'd begun to think that courtesy might be a thing of the past. A half-hour later, I'm back on the paved road, and I stop a truck headed to Pasinler. Only when we drive off do I feel I'm finally out of harm's way.

I ask the driver to drop me off near the banks of the Aras River that, further on, serves as the borderline between Iran and Turkey and then between Muslim Turkey and Christian Armenia. In the seventeenth century, Muslims feared that their Christian enemies might sully the river's water. For that reason, they drank from their cisterns only. On the other side of the river, the Christians feared the same thing and only drew water from their wells. Today, terrifyingly polluted, the Aras would poison everyone irrespective of their religion and would populate both Heavens and both Hells in short order.

On the other side of the river, I'm back on State Road 100. We're fifteen kilometers from Pasinler, the city I left yesterday morning. The forty kilometers I covered yesterday and the ten kilometers this morning have therefore come to naught since I'm now practically back at my point of departure. But it's a privilege to still be alive and in good health. Why should I complain?

Farewell Kurdish villages. If one day I return, I'll try not to come alone, and I'll try to avoid picking the week your idol is condemned to death. I decide to stick to the main road while cursing myself: in Yastıktepe, people warned me—either miming a rifle or a finger across the throat—that I was headed straight toward the terrorists. And the first beekeeper I met, the one who offered me a glass of *ayran* yesterday morning, was concerned whether I was armed. So I was perfectly well aware. But no, I had to press my luck, invoking my guardian angel, naive as I am. One of these days, if I keep demanding the impossible, my little angel's gonna leave me high and dry. Whatever happens, as a big fan of westerns, I tell myself that the next time I watch one in which a gunfighter kills a cowboy just to steal his boots, I'll be reminded of the scoundrel I met in Payveren.

The spot where the truck dropped me off along State Road 100 is called Köprüköy (the bridge village). And a bridge there is indeed: an old, very beautiful stone bridge with eight arches. No longer open to traffic, it once linked the two halves of a village straddling the two banks of the Aras. Then, for a reason no one can quite explain, the villagers relocated three kilometers away. Today, the structure now only connects one field to another. As I'm looking it over, a man rides by on a bike. He's a tourist, and he's laden like a Silk Road camel. He yells something to me that I can't make out and just keeps on going. Solid proof that he's a foreigner. Farther along, a family is seated on the grass for a picnic lunch. The couple and their two children are in European dress. The man tells me that he's a *jandarma*. His wife is stunningly beautiful. They invite me to partake in some vegetable-and-meat *börek*. The whole event feels so pleasantly rural and amicable that it makes me forget my awful night. In the river, wet up to their midriffs, women and children are dunking large carpets that they then vigorously shake out or scrub and then spread flat out on the stones along the bank for them to dry in the sun. The children horse around, splashing one another; their mothers scold them. These rustic, peaceful scenes are comforting: come now—yes, I had the misfortune of falling upon a half-wit, but that's no reason for me to lose my sunny disposition! But no sooner am I back on the road than dark thoughts begin once again running through my mind. What rotten luck! One of the most interesting regions I'm traveling through is Kurdistan. And here I am, like a common tourist, forced to walk along a road that is as impersonal as it is international.

I don't recall the scenery between Köprüköy and Horasan that day. Anger drives me forward, each step of the way. And I travel the twenty-seven kilometers lumbering gloomily, my shoulders hunched, looking at my feet.

At my hotel, I snap out of my anger only to wade right into a dreary bout of depression. The strain was too much. Suddenly, finding myself alone is a crushing burden. I'm only two hundred kilometers from the border that I was really looking forward to crossing. And now, doubt and fear have clouded everything. Fear. Unreasonable fear. I'm not afraid of the PKK. I know that its political activists can be brutal, even murderous. But their actions are predictable. The PKK could, strictly speaking, lock me up and use me as a bargaining chip. That's a risk I'm willing to take. But I refuse to bear the risk of a crazy man who wants to kill me just to steal my shoes. Of course, I'm aware that these poor people, lacking everything, are mesmerized by the more or less glitzy wealth, the moneyed splendor that the West flaunts all over TV. It makes these poor people dream and leads the weak-minded to give in to impulses of unfettered greed.

And yet, like them, my skin has been baked by the sun; like them, I wear clothes with a few holes in them; and all day long, I struggle under the weight of my load as they struggle under that of their bales of hay. But whether I like it or not, we are from two different worlds. I represent Europe and its riches, its cars and its jewels, its McDonald's, and its movie stars. In my backpack, which I'd prefer were transparent, they imagine a thousand treasures. Not one day goes by without someone asking me how many cars I have, what my salary is, or without someone guessing how much money they think I have, since I can travel, whereas they . . . For millennia, they have seen wealth parade by in big bundles on the backs of camels. On my back, although it's small and modest, there's also a bundle. But it's another thing to imagine it might be full of gold. And in these regions, far from everything, the sometimes-murderous game of cops and robbers is still going on. Here, or in Iran, am I going to run into other madmen? With the spell of bad luck that seems, of late, to be right on my heels, it's quite possible. For the first time since my departure, I regret having gone it alone. In spite of my fatigue and yesterday's sleepless night, it's late into the night when I finally fall asleep, and I wake up after only four hours of fitful sleep.

From Horasan to Eleşkirt, there are seventy kilometers and not a single hotel. I get going without really knowing where or when I'm going to stop. Around noon, while I was resting by the roadside having just come over a small mountain pass, a cyclist appears, looking to me like the twin of the one yesterday, but this one stops. He's English and hails from Liverpool. A little later, a couple of other riders catch up to him. These three young men, whose combined age is probably just a little more than mine alone, are on their way to New Zealand, where they hope to arrive for Christmas. They camp, which explains why they have so much gear. The bikes disappear quite literally beneath the saddlebags and bundles. There's a certain family resemblance with our tanned skin, sun-chapped lips, and the quiet jubilation that springs from well-tuned bodies. Each morning, they tell me, they ride anywhere from sixty to eighty kilometers, then rest in the afternoon when it's hottest out. I take their picture, they take mine and then get back underway, carried off at top speed by the downslope. Exchanging a few words with these kind, jolly fellows has pulled me from my unhappy thoughts. Just now, I regretted traveling alone. But after they leave, I reconsider. Yes, they're on one hell of a trip, making one-of-a-kind memories. But that's where the me-and-them parallel ends. On their bikes, in their tents, they see only part of the country they're visiting, mostly its scenery. Trapped within the language they share, lying in their tent, they are less exposed than I am to the danger of being robbed, but they interact very little with locals. They're discovering the world, whereas I'm confronting it through my own experiences.

Today, all the car and truck drivers want to give me a ride. It's as if word had gotten out. One bus driver stops, yelling, *"para yok"* (it's free). A father and his two sons who drove past me back up in their van. They offer me snacks while getting me to tell them about my voyage. The father recites a long speech to his sons that I interpret as the defense and illustration of the virtues of hard work. He points several times at me, and his sons gaze at me as though I were in the process of being canonized. Then, when they finally give up trying to get me to accept a ride, they head off, waving at me as they do.

It's very hot out. One T-shirt dries on my pack while the other gets wet on my back. Out on the steppe, dozens of flocks graze under the shepherds' watchful eye. When I'm close enough, one of them runs up to me to ask a few questions, then goes back to the others to fill them in. I wish I were a dragonfly so that I could drop in and hear his version, the questions that are sure to be asked, and the answers that the little shepherd, building on his interview, must be tempted to invent.

Kurdish villages blend into the natural surroundings. Their walls are made of stones excavated from the mountains and have the same color; the earthen roofs planted with grass blend in with the prairie. All of the houses and stables—which resemble one another—face south. The houses have few windows and the stables have none, so as to better with-stand the heat and cold. Hamlets are typically located on the edge of a plain, slightly terraced up the hillsides. Before them lies the cropland. Behind them, the pasturage. In this land ravaged by hordes of warriors for three millennia, the mountains' proximity provides a refuge. On the road, there are more soldiers than ever. In the hills, armored vehicles take up position, monitoring dozens of kilometers in every direction. A tractor is towing a trailer containing three large metal beds. In the front of the trailer, a special seat has been constructed for the grandfather, a handsome, hieratic old man protecting himself from the sun with a wide, black umbrella he holds straight up as if he were doing a sword salute.

By the time I reach Sac Dağı (*sadj dah'-uh*) pass, at an elevation of 2,300 meters (7,550 feet), I'm drained. A young shepherd comes over to me and offers me a drink.

"If you want," he adds, "I'll bleed a calf, and you can drink his blood. That will give you strength."

And as he says this, he mimics having large pectoral muscles. I give him my sincere thanks and do a poor job holding back a shiver of disgust.

On the other side of the pass, the small village of Aydıntepe would be perfect for a stopover, if it weren't for the memory of Payveren, which dissuades me from seeking hospitality. There is indeed one large house, where, I imagine, the lord resides. But I lack the courage. Farther below, the road plunges into a deep gorge. It's late: for my safety I have to stop walking. I therefore opt to stop a long black car, which already has five men in it. I've barely settled in when the driver, a solid fellow whose face is dashed with a large black mustache, says, in a voice pierced with polit-ical passion:

"What do you think of Öcalan's conviction?"

Good grief! This is no time to answer carelessly. Are they Turks or Kurds? I get myself off the hook by asking a question of my own:

"I'm a foreigner and don't know much about the situation or the region. Isn't this conviction going to cause trouble around here?"

The answer, which I have a hard time understanding, is spoken in a rather reassuring tone. But suddenly the term "Turks" is pronounced, and the man who says it slides his finger over his throat like a knife blade. Now I know. Their expressions are stern. Well dressed, they're no country yokels, and they don't look like businessmen. Having worked for fifteen years in political reporting, I recognize their kind: they're militants. Possibly members of the PKK. I'm dying to find out, but how should I ask? I try to sound as innocent as possible:

"Do you know any people with the PKK? I'd like to know what they think about all this."

The question ushers in a deep freeze in the passenger compartment. After a few moments of silence, the driver points to the cliffs:

"There is gold there!"

I obviously stood no chance of getting a reply, but at least I tried. I take a stab at the gold story:

"So why don't you mine it?"

He holds his finger against his throat:

"The Turks won't allow it."

Many throats are cut with gestures in this car. And I see the same sign again later on when, in the city suburbs, we drive past some army barracks. Turned toward the road, dozens of tanks display the black, menacing hole of their cannon. My five rascals, as soon as they see them, in a collective gesture, slice their carotid arteries with their index fingers.

In Eleşkirt, the five cutthroats get out and go over to a group of men—other cutthroats?—waiting for them in lively discussion. As they bid me good-bye, they say something nice about Danielle Mitterrand.* I'd give anything to be fluent in Turkish and be able to chat with them, but I carry only a few lonely words in my bag, just enough to thank them for having brought me here and wish them a good evening.

---

* TN: Danielle Mitterrand (1924–2011), the spouse of former French president François Mitterrand, is sometimes referred to in Kurdistan as the "Mother of the Kurds" for having championed their cause on several occasions: in 1986, she came to the defense of Mehdi Zana, the mayor of Diyarbakir, sentenced to a fourteen-year prison term for having given a speech in Kurdish. In 1988, she pleaded for international intervention when Saddam Hussein's forces attacked Iraqi Kurds. She traveled to Kurdistan several times, most recently in 2009 for the opening of a school in Erbil that bears her name.

The only hotel in Eleşkirt, located above a service station-restaurant open all night, is, needless to say, very, very noisy. But I'm so far behind on sleep that I go to bed before it's dark out and I sleep straight through till five o'clock. When I rise, I empty a fair amount of my gear out onto the bed, keeping only the essentials, then get back on the road. A truck heading to Erzurum to deliver wood takes me back to the spot where I was picked up yesterday evening in the Kurdish limousine. I know how odd this way of doing things may seem. But I want to be clear: this defile along the Eleşkirt road that I'm already acquainted with after having traversed it twice, in a car yesterday evening, now in a truck this morning, I have not, in fact, truly seen: I want to experience it on foot, at eye level. And indeed, when I do, it appears quite different to me: it's larger, more majestic, more impressive. In a word, more real. Grain of sand by grain of sand, the river was thinking big as it hewed a bed out of the rock into which the road has now slipped. A rider on a fine white horse waves at me before turning into a kind of narrow corridor that weaves its way through the cliff. Three kids I give some candy to head off to work, each holding a billhook. The youngest, about ten years old, is mounted on a donkey, starts whining, acting quarrelsome. I tell them I have nothing else to give them, having lost the small bag that contained my little buttons. But the kid keeps on grumbling and grows bolder, repeating louder and louder: "*para, para, para.*" And when I ask him what he'd do with it, he mimics smoking. So I answer him by mimicking empty pockets and leave them high and dry, furious at my refusal. A few hundred meters on, the English cyclists pass me up, loudly ringing their bells and waving their arms. They must have bivouacked at the entrance to the defile and woke up late.

As I exit the gorge, I take a break and contemplate the scenery. To my right, a poor Kurdish village, just like all the others I've seen over the past two days: a few houses with rust-colored walls, sheep returning from pasture, not even a mosque. To my left, overhead, an army garrison guarding the entrance to the defile. Clean, new buildings covered in fresh sheet metal, flowerbeds, and the usual rows of tanks. Behind the barbed wire, soldiers stand guard bearing assault rifles across their chest.

My eyes behold *The Castle* by Kafka. Two worlds that either ignore or confront each other. And for those who may wish to "climb up" to the castle-garrison, the sight of all the menacing muzzles of rifles and tanks does little to foster dialogue, on one side or the other.

I walk along effortlessly. My backpack is light. The deep, post-Payveren depression I had fallen into melts away under a sun already high in the sky. Here and there, young boys are watching over their herds, throwing stones at the stray cows, coaxing them to rejoin the main group. Once again, I come across a construction site for the gas pipeline. Here, it's nearly completed. The backfilled trenches have left a trace of fresh dirt that looks like an open wound running across the steppe. The natural gas flowing in these big black pipelines—so large I can almost stand inside them—will go to the Ankara region.

Several dozen kilometers to the south is the huge Atatürk Dam, which people tell me is the largest in the world. Other dams, twenty-two in all, are almost all situated in the same zone. They hold back the water of two rivers that witnessed the birth of the earliest civilizations, the Tigris and the Euphrates, and form the GAP (*Great Anatolian Project*). The electricity they produce is routed to the industrial West. In Kurdistan, wealth only passes through. If some share of the jobs and revenue don't stay put, the army will be guarding the narrow passes, pylons, and pipelines until the end of time.

Upon my return to Eleşkirt, a crowd is gathered around a man covered in blood and terribly banged up. A car ran him over: they're waiting for the ambulance while speaking about the accident vociferously and waving their arms. But I'm certain that the reckless driver will get off scot-free. Every driver in Turkey, as I've said before, is entitled to spill blood in the country's busiest streets, most peaceful roads, and bucolic byways!

The next day, up early, I've traveled for ten kilometers or so when a minibus full of passengers comes to a stop alongside me. A man lowers his window. I'm about to state that I prefer to walk, but he smiles and says, in my native tongue:

"*Tu es français.*"

"Comment le savez-vous?"

"Des gens me l'ont dit . . . De quelle ville?"

"Paris."

"J'ai travaillé à Créteil. Tu connais Créteil?"

"Oui."

*"J'y étais en même temps que Mitterrand. Tu as connu Mitterrand? Et Danielle? C'est une amie . . ."**

Danielle Mitterrand is as loved by the Kurds as she is hated by the Turks.

Having left Eleşkirt around 5:30 a.m., five hours later I'm already within sight of Ağrı, lurking on the plain off in the distance. But it will still take me at least two more hours to reach the city's center. The road leading in is reminiscent of certain villages in Normandy: houses with small yards all lined up alongside the road, standing with their backs to the fields. As I walk, I slide my hands under my backpack, which has regained all its weight, to help alleviate the friction on my shoulders. In so doing, I notice that the backside of my pants has ripped through. I doubt the poor thing will make it all the way to Tehran. With two safety pins, I attach a t-shirt onto my pack as a screen to cover up my brightly colored boxer shorts that must be visible through the gaping hole.

As soon as I find a hotel, I start an urgent search for a tailor who can do a temporary fix. I also make some large withdrawals from my bank account and convert my last Turkish liras to dollars. I'm afraid I won't be able to exchange money in Doğubeyazıt (*doh-hoo-beh-ya-zuht'*), the last city before the Iranian border. I also buy a long-sleeved shirt because you don't trifle with the ayatollahs. A banner is stretched over the street advertising an Internet café. I make a mad dash to get there, but it's occupied by painters who inform me it won't be open until the following evening, provided the work is complete and the paint dry. Tomorrow

---

* "You are French." / "How do you know?" / "People told me . . . From what city?" / "Paris." / "I worked in Créteil. Do you know Créteil?" / "Yes." / "I was there at the same time as Mitterrand. Did you know Mitterrand? And Danielle? She's a friend of mine . . ."

evening, I'll be long gone. I'm told there are none in Doğubeyazıt. I don't
expect to find any in Iran. So here I am, for a full month at least, cut off
from my friends and family, as well as from the news.

I spend July 7 resting and mostly getting ready to cross the Iranian
border. As at the outset of my journey, my natural pessimism hits me
like a wave. I hear that the border-crossing formalities are long, cum-
bersome, and complicated. So I start letting myself get carried away
by unanswerable questions that only serve to put into words the dull
misgivings now engulfing me. For example, how am I going to communicate with the Iranians? As though I'd never given the problem
any thought. Or, how am I going to manage with a map with a scale of
1:3,000,000, barely good enough for motorists? I suddenly fear being
condemned to stick to state highways, which I utterly despise. Another
source of anxiety: I have no arrangement, as in Turkey, with an Iranian
bank, so I'm going to have to move about with large sums of cash with
me. I'm decidedly much too unreasonable, and I reprimand myself mer-
cilessly. The only pat on the back I give myself is for having resolved my
visa problem thanks to my forced marches. It's valid until July 29: I'll be
at the border on the eleventh, and in Tabriz between the twentieth and
the twenty-fifth. I'll be able to extend my visa there. I study the possible stages on the other side of the Turkish border. If all goes well, at an
average pace of thirty kilometers (19 miles) a day and stopping one day
per week, I'll be in Tehran by the end of the first week of August, the
fifteenth at the very latest.

My pants were ripping all over the place. The tailor—a veritable art-
ist—had to sew on at least nine patches. But with what results! Imagine
a Harlequinesque garment, with a subtle blend of colors ranging from
the ochre of the savannas to the golden beige of the dunes, a model that
our noble fashion designers in the West would most certainly want to
copy, were it, by the most unusual of circumstances, to fall into their
hands. Long live Turkey's creative little tailors! I've now earned the right
to rail against so-called "adventure" clothing, barely designed to with-
stand parading about Paris's Left Bank bistros. My mind is made up: I'm

going to buy a new set of clothes in Tabriz. In preparation for the border formalities, I have some ID photos made along with some copies of my passport, as I'll be asked to provide these in hotels. It's cold and rainy in Ağrı; recurrent icy downpours wash over the city. The downtown seems to be of little interest, and, despite several attempts, I fail to engage any-one in conversation. Mistrust or indifference?

So I leave Ağrı with no regrets. Instead of continuing along State Road 100, I've decided to try one more jaunt into the Kurdish coun-tryside. Last night, I told myself that I couldn't leave Turkey without having established some connections with the countryfolk of this region. My adventure in Payveren was pure bad luck. I have to stop imagining that all the *muhtars* will be out of town and replaced by their deranged brothers. Out there, behind these barren hills, I'm going to meet some warm and generous countryfolk, like so many I've seen up till now. More careful now as the result of my misadventures, and in order to enjoy both the pleasure of meeting people and the security provided by a hotel, I've identified a route that travels cross-country and taking me into villages but that doesn't lead me too far from the next city along the highway, where I'll sleep tonight free of fear.

Confident and reassured, after leaving the city, I take a dirt road soggy from the past few days' rain. I wade through a field of slippery, clayey soil. A *jandarmas's* car, skating through this cesspit, comes to a stop. The officer asks to see my passport. The usual routine. They go their way, and so do I. As I lose sight of the last few houses, I catch up to a young man coming back from the city with his groceries. We come upon one of those cursed forks in the road. To the right or to the left? "To the left," he tells me; whereas my compass tells me it should be to the right. But he must be correct, he knows. We walk for about one kilometer. Then the road turns into a two-track, and then finally a footpath that vanishes into the prairie. Not so sure, I stop:

"This isn't the road to Eskiharman."

"Yes, yes, it is . . . and hey, do you see that house over there? That's mine. I'll make some tea for you."

"No thank you. I'm going to Eskiharman, and this is the wrong road."

"Do you want to buy this bread, or these cigarettes?'

So that was it. He dragged me here to get money from me. If any doubt remained, his next question sweeps it away.

"The money you have, is it marks or dollars?"

I laugh at his naive question. On the front porch of his house, another scamp about his age appears. He hails him and invites him to come over. I make a quick U-turn, for, if I stay here, with two against one, I'm in danger. He doesn't try to follow me, but the other man runs after me for a little while. I stop, ready to confront him. He must have been convinced by either my determination or my walking stick, for he wisely ends the chase.

I'm back at the fork in the road and forge ahead. Three or four kilometers farther, a car driven by two young people stops.

"What are you doing here? It's dangerous. There is 'terror' ahead."

The driver offers to provide me with dinner and a place to sleep in his home and suggests I hop in his car. But his village is too far off my path. So that he doesn't press the issue, I tell him that when I reach his village, I'll stop by to see him. They take off again. A little later, a taxi stops. The driver gets out and comes over.

"Where are you going? There is no road farther on."

I show him on my map the path that I intend to follow. He doesn't know these roads. His passengers are telling him which way to go. They told him to ask about me and are ready to pay for my journey if I want to join them. Once again, I refuse, and the taxi drives off.

Finally, I can enjoy some peace and quiet, the steppe, and the rolling, barren hills. The road, full of ruts, dawdles along through the hills. Another fork in the road, but this one appears on my map, and I head due south. The same map shows that, very soon, one or two kilometers on, a path will take me east, back to the highway. But as much as I walk along looking for it, I can't find it; there's neither path nor road, only fields of grain and pastures grazed by livestock. In an electric company jeep, four men confirm what I already know: there is no road. Once again, my map has betrayed me. It shows, about five kilometers away, a small village and a secondary road heading from it to my destination. It will make for a long detour, but let's give it a try.

As soon as he sees me, a young cowherd on horseback comes galloping in my direction, passing me by while shouting a sonorous "*salamalek*," then rushes off toward the village. Well, people will know I'm coming. Indeed, as soon as I reach the first house, a group of children escorts me. I haven't bought any more candy, so I don't have anything to give them. A ruffian, stepping out of a stable, a bucket in his hand, hurries over.

"Where are you going?"

"To Taşlıçay (*tash-luh-chai'*). There must be a road this way if I'm to believe my map."

He reaches out to see my map, takes it, and, without even looking at it, stuffs it in his pocket.

"I'll come with you to Taşlıçay."

"OK, but give me back my map."

"When we get to Taşlıçay . . ."

I'm instantly on my guard. The city is thirty-some kilometers away, and I can't imagine that this fellow will just drop what he's doing and travel that far for the simple joy of accompanying me. The way he swiped my map makes me suspicious. About twenty-five years old, short, stocky, and fidgeting, the fellow has a plaid shirt he has probably worn every day for eons beneath a sweater studded with holes. One of his shoes is on its last leg, and he has tied it up with string like a rump roast, so the sole doesn't slip off for good.

I keep telling him, to no good, to give me back my map.

I have no choice but to follow him, and that way I'll find out what he wants from me. The kids behind us are snickering. They already know what he's up to. The rascal, waving his arms, steers me between two houses, then leads me toward the steppe. There's no sign of a road, just a kind of crevice in the flat landscape with a few small live oaks growing at the bottom. I stop dead in my tracks.

"Where's the road?"

"Over there, farther on . . .," and he points to the horizon, out beyond the pastures. At the same time, he picks up stones and throws them at the kids, yelling at them to clear out. He asks me what I have in my pack.

It's now obvious that he's intent on robbing me by leading me into the ravine, where no one can see us. The kids stay far enough away so as not to get hit with stones but stay put. They don't want to miss the show, and—who knows?—they probably hope to come away with a few scraps of loot.

Paying no attention as he insists that I follow him, I head back toward the village. I realize that as long as there are witnesses, he won't dare make a move. Increasingly jumpy, the man tries to hold me back by the sleeve, swearing that the road is this way. Some women have come out onto their doorsteps. They're amused by the spectacle and are probably wondering how Mr. Jumpy, as I call him, is going to swindle this tourist. As I make my way back to the road—this is becoming a habit—I angrily curse myself. Once again, I walked straight into a booby trap. And I can't say that I hadn't been warned. There has been one sign after another since this morning. Now I'm trapped. There's no "village lord's house" here, only a dozen poor shacks, more like huts than houses, nestled in a low spot in the terrain.

I have to quickly come up with a solution. If I head back toward Ağrı the way I came, then, in the solitude I hiked across this morning, I'll be handing this ruffian exactly what he wants: a secluded spot where he can plunder me at will. So long as I remain in sight of the villagers, I'm more or less safe. I recall that, on my map, two groups of houses were rather close to each other. I climb the small incline heading south. From the top, I spot the other hamlet, about two kilometers away. I immediately decide to go for it. It might be worse over there, but Inşallah! To make matters worse, it's in the exact opposite direction to the one I need to travel, since the rest of my journey is to the north. But right now, the urgency is to escape the danger posed by this man. So, with a decisive step, off I go, and the fellow gives chase at a pace to match mine. My decision to make a run for it was motivated by another idea that came to me. Should it come to a power struggle, I'll at least have a chance to get away. If I stay put, as demonstrated earlier by the behavior of the women and children, village solidarity will play into his hand. Rather than one burly fellow against me, there'll be ten.

This is really not my lucky day. No sooner have I walked a hundred meters past the last house than a young man runs up to join us. Friend or foe? He must be seventeen or eighteen years old. He has an open face and greets me with a friendly smile. I especially take notice of his handsome, honest eyes, and I convince myself no treachery could ever come from someone like him. Although they're speaking Kurdish, it's clear that Mr. Jumpy is trying to persuade him to help him out. The other, on the other hand, seems to be trying to calm him down. He speaks to him in a calm voice and doesn't shout. Changing tactics, Mr. Jumpy, who's walking next to me, suddenly reaches his hand into my pocket. I block his arm and with a heavy shove send him to the other side of the path. Adrenaline courses through my veins, and I'm ready to pounce on him, outraged as I am. Fearing that I'll strike him, Mr. Jumpy keeps his distance. So, the young man, with his index finger at his forehead, motions to me that "he's crazy." You'd damn near think I'd become a magnet for village idiots.

Dropping the idea of fighting, I press on. Mr. Jumpy, a little subdued in the face of my determination, has gone over to the young man. He takes my map from his pocket and shows it off with pride. I've noticed on many occasions how this mysterious object holds something magical for these simple country folks who've never seen one. While for me it's purely of practical value, for them, it is a book within their grasp, since even people unable to read can decipher a map by identifying surrounding cities and villages. I've closed the gap between me and my thief. Paying too much attention to his loot, his guard's down. I suddenly snatch it out of his hands. His eyes flare with rage. This time, we're going to come to blows. But then no, since, just at the right moment, the young horseman I saw earlier comes riding up at a full gallop. He's a robust fellow riding bareback on a handsome dappled horse. Mr. Jumpy speaks to him in Kurdish. I avail myself of this brief respite to tuck my map safely away in my pocket. And once again, I ask myself: friend or foe? Unfortunately, I quickly have the answer. He speaks only to Mr. Jumpy and ignores Honest-Eyes. His first sentence lets me know where things stand.

"Your pack is heavy, I'll put it on my horse."

They take me for a complete imbecile. But the horseman's arrival isn't helping my situation. Given that I'm in good physical shape, I stood a fair chance of escaping Mr. Jumpy. I could keep him at bay with my stick, as I did with the Kangals! And walking at full tilt as I'm able, I could have exhausted him rather quickly, because, young though he is, he hasn't been training like I have. But now that he has the young rogue to back him up, I'll have to kiss that stratagem good-bye.

During this time, I've made headway, and we're midway between the two hamlets. I'm very focused, tense; the rush of adrenaline nearly has me running. I'm not afraid. I'm simply furious. First with myself, then with the local culture, according to which there's a fellow ready to rob me in each village. The horseman speaks rather crudely to Honest-Eyes. He clearly is trying to get him to go back to the village. I have no intention of letting my only ally get away. I go over to him, put my hand on his shoulder, and say "*arkadaş*" (*ar'-kah-dahsh*) (friends). He smiles at me, but he's clearly somewhat worried, for the two rogues will make his life miserable after today's events.

Mr. Jumpy keeps trying new tactics. He pretends to have a painful headache, and, saying that he needs to find something to help, he tries to open one of the pockets of my pack. A little later, he slowly nudges me toward the horse, and the horseman comes near, probably getting ready to jump me. I move away. A tractor towing a trailer comes toward us in the direction of the village that we left. If it's going beyond it, I'm saved. The man driving it looks friendly. I raise my hand and he stops about twenty meters (66 feet) or so away. I run toward him, but as soon as I'm about to put my hand on the trailer, he starts back up. Clearly, my two rascals must have motioned him behind my back not to give me a ride. I'm out of luck. I start back up toward the small town, which is now not very far away. The horseman, a little sharper than the other, realizes that if I make it to the hamlet, I just might get away from them. He tries a ruse.

"There are terrorists in that village. We'll protect you as you travel through, and afterward we'll show you which way you need to go."

The way I need to go is right here, to my left. But to head that way with an escort like this, risking it in the countryside would be suicidal. I pretend to go along with the idea. I have to reassure them and get them to drop their guard.

In front of the second shack, a man lethargically digging up his yard takes advantage of our arrival to take a break and watch us. I suddenly turn in his direction and ask him where the *muhtar*'s house is.

He turns to look toward the road leading west along the side of his house and begins to raise his arm, then suddenly stops. Behind me, Mr. Jumpy must have motioned him not to say anything. So he says nothing, but the initial gesture was enough. I turn onto the road heading west. This is clearly the right thing, because the three dodgy customers, after a few steps, stop, then watch as I move away. One hundred meters farther, to two unschooled little girls standing hand in hand, I repeat my question. They giggle and point to the house right in front of me, behind a wall closed with an iron gate. Back in the distance, the two clowns haven't budged. When I knock at the door, they turn back and head off. I feel a huge relief. If they didn't think I'd find an ally in the person of the *muhtar*, they wouldn't have fled. So there's a decent chance I'll be in good company.

In the courtyard, a young, veiled woman is busy washing clothes. She is in her early twenties and has twinkling eyes. The *muhtar* is not home, but I can come in.

What am I going to tell these people? As I go up the stairs leading to a veranda, which opens out onto a large room, I cobble together an explanation. I don't want to cause an argument by accusing Mr. Jumpy and the horseman. After all, nothing happened, and they'd find it easy to categorically deny all my accusations. The relationship between two villages so close to each other must be good, and a foreigner, if there were some conflict, would surely serve as an excellent scapegoat. But there's no way I can keep heading south; that's not my road. If I return north, I'll have to go back through Mr. Jumpy's village. I have to therefore return to Ağrı as quickly as possible and, this time, stick to dreary State Road 100 to limit the risks.

In the vast room that—as always in these houses—serves as the living room, the reception room, a room for just passing through, and a meeting place, ten women or so and just as many children are seated on cushions filling the air with their chatter. "Above all, don't speak to women" was the recommendation of the Kurd I met in Paris. But how, in the present circumstances, can I do otherwise, since there's not a single man? A rather heavyset woman steps forward: she's the *muhtar*'s spouse.

"I'm lost. I want to return to Ağrı, but I'm too tired. Can you call a taxi?"

"Of course," she says, asking me to set down my pack, while offering me some tea.

I agree to everything, I'll go for anything, provided they don't throw me out of the village with an escort of thieves. A young boy picks up the phone and turns to me gesturing comically: the telephone is out of order; there's no dial tone. No problem, I'll wait for it to come back. The women form a circle around me and ask me to tell them about my odyssey. I take my time, embellishing the story. But I avoid mentioning this morning's two hoodlums. The plump woman, waxing eloquent, tries to tell me about life in this microcosm, managed by her husband. The bulk of her lesson escapes me, but I understand that most of their husbands work in Germany and return only once a year.

Little by little, in this pleasant gynaeceum, I let things go. I'm transported back to the warm, soothing environment in which childhood revels for a time and that is so very comforting, as long as you don't fight it, to experience once again as an adult. Time passes slowly, the telephone remains silent, everything seems to be put on hold. As we are finishing our tea, the dial tone finally reappears, and the outside world reasserts its rights. They translate for me. It's all set; a car will be coming, but not right away. I'm in no hurry. A young man of about thirty, radiating authority and righteousness, joins the group. He's the son of the house, Selattin Akbalik. He asks me to tell him about my journey and wants to know all about Paris. The women, at all times efficient, capitalize on the opportunity to prepare a meal. Growing bolder, I offer to take a picture of all the women present. I expect them to turn me down, at least some of them, but they surprise me, and they all agree. The women of Doğutepe (*doh'-hoo-teh-peh*) definitely enjoy liberties that, in Turkey, I've only observed among city dwellers. The moral of the story: when man is away, woman feels she can fly.

Selattin and I allow ourselves to be served by the rotund woman and her daughters—it only takes two men to reestablish subjugation—a meal of diverse vegetable dishes that are both delicious and filling: rice pilaf with caramelized onions, incredibly flavorful eggplant, and this yogurt that would delight any palate . . . True comfort food that melts in the mouth, food made for childhood. Yes, women definitely know how to work magic.

When we've had our fill, Selattin asks me to step outside the room with him, since the women want to eat and we cannot be with them during their meal. I follow him out onto the veranda, where, as though in a smoking room, we continue our conversation.

After the "second service," one of Selattin's sisters comes to ask her brother something in Kurdish, which he translates for me: the women want me to photograph them again. I'm delighted to be able to do this for them. With great seriousness, they go back to the same places that they had assumed for the first snapshot. Does the order in which they stand correspond to some hierarchy that exists among them, to an age spectrum, or are they simply taking up position based on the affection they have for one another? I noticed earlier how important their positions seemed to them, and I admired how quickly it all took place: they made me think of a group of young boarding school girls out on a field trip who've been reminded to get back in line and who silently comply, frightened like baby chicks. After all, this camera, even if they boldly confront it, must nevertheless seem to them like some magical box in secret league with some kind of sorcery. And, as everyone knows, when the devil's close at hand, it's best to obey and lie low.

Around 5:00 p.m., the *muhtar* and his brother-in-law come looking for me. They'll taxi me to Ağrı themselves, provided that I pay for gas, since it's very expensive. We fill up in town, and they warmly thank me, whereas I'm thinking how I'll never be able to thank them enough for having saved me from the damned booby trap that, stubborn old ox that I am, I walked straight into.

So here I am, back at my starting point and, this time, definitively cured of my desire to go off on little excursions into the villages. Tomorrow, reconciled with State Road 100 that I've been snubbing for the past one thousand six hundred kilometers (990 miles), I'll begin the final kilometers that will lead me to Iran.

CHAPTER XII
DOWN ON HIGH

It's Friday, July 9, and in front of the door to my luxury hotel, passengers are getting on a bus headed to Doğubeyazıt, the border town. Just for a second, I want to hop on board. The banditry to which I almost fell victim yesterday shook me more than I can say. This is because, more than just the events, the atmosphere of mistrust and the fact that I constantly have be on my guard are sources of discouragement and disillusionment. I'm tempted to drop the whole idea. Stirring up dark thoughts, I teeter between despondency and anger. Quite simply, I have no desire to get back on the road. I walk toward the highway, but I've lost my nerve. In a *lokanta*, and even though I just ate a copious breakfast at the hotel, I have them bring me a piping hot *çorba* in which I dip half a hunk of bread. My father used to call this a "*soupe de maçon*" (a mason's soup). Made right, it was so thick a spoon would stand straight up in the bowl. That's what I busy myself trying to do. I have the sense that I'd do just about anything to waste time, like the class dunce in the morning before heading off to school. I'm in a rotten mood as I leave the restaurant. The temptation to take the bus disappeared as I watched it drive off. The sun is barely above the horizon. The happy owners of automobiles are busy washing them like they do nearly every day. It strikes me that they'd be well advised to save water, rare as it is here. I tell myself that if they spent less time washing their cars and a little more time scouring their washrooms, there'd be a little less showing off, but improved hygiene. Farther along, yet another army garrison gets me thinking that if the money spent on tanks were instead used to build farming schools for

Kurdish children, they'd be more willing to use their pencils than their fathers' rifles.

I'm sore at the whole damn world. The weather reflects my mood. The ground is soggy from yesterday's rains. To make matters worse, a pain from nowhere, in my left leg and ankle, is making it tough to walk. Looking down at my shoes, indifferent to the scenery, I push on, while images from yesterday parade before my eyes, and I'm completely obsessed with those of the horseman and the thief with one shoe tied up in string. Add to this my anxiety about crossing the border into Iran, and my mind goes wild with all the troubles that lie ahead of me. Why would the situation be any different there, in an even poorer country than Turkey? Swarms of mosquitoes in the marshlands and thirst in the arid deserts lurk ahead. Will people there, too, take me for a millionaire, a Martian, or perhaps a terrorist? My eyes on the pavement, I don't even look up at the trucks honking just to have a look at this madcap's face, or who offer, waving their arms, to take me on board.

What am I doing here? Around the world, in Europe, in the United States, in the Alps or in the Rockies, there are fairy-tale settings, just as beautiful as those here, where walking is a pure joy. There are other legendary roads where you can wander without risking your hide with every step. I vaguely regret not having chosen other itineraries I considered. The Pan-American Highway, for example, in the footsteps of the Inca, or the long walk of America's pioneers heading to the legendary West on the Santa Fe Trail. Why did I opt for this country, where my life is at risk? What is the meaning of this journey as the prospect of arriving safe and sound is seeming increasingly unlikely? After all, I'm under no obligation to be here. I didn't undertake this journey for financial gain or in a spirit of competition. My pension is enough for me to live comfortably, and, were I to return home tomorrow, no one could throw stones or hold it against me because I chose not to die in Anatolia. Often, when taking side roads, as was the case on several occasions, I was well aware that I was getting lost so as to best go in search of myself, to see what I was made of. Isn't this an illustration of what Josée said to me jokingly before I set out, that my project could be boiled down to the formula: *"Here's to the two of me*"? But there are stupid gambles. As it has been unfolding over the past two weeks, isn't this journey one of them? And though I'm not adverse to the thought of losing myself in strange lands, since Erzurum, I've had enough keeping company with so many crackpot or half-wit oddballs.

And then walking, marvelous walking, performs its usual miracle. As my muscles begin to warm up, my flow of bile dries up, and my anger subsides. After two hours on the road, I turn around and see Ağrı's rooftops shining beneath the rising sun. To my right, five or six kilometers as the crow flies, I catch sight of the village of Bezirhane, where I had such a tough time yesterday, flanked by my two bandits. From here, it doesn't look all that terrifying. Looking at it on the brighter side, the results of my outing, after all, are not so dark. I was the target of three attempted robberies, but in each case, my lucky stars allowed me to escape unharmed. I lost a full day in Payveren and another in Bezirhane. And so what? I'm not in that much of a hurry. I have all the time in the world, because, on top of it, I'm two weeks ahead of the travel schedule I'd set for myself. I'm in top physical shape, and the pain that popped up this morning in my left leg vanished after the my first few steps. Yes, I came close to being robbed yesterday, but I also had the distinct privilege of spending several hours chatting with Kurdish women who kindly treated me with motherly love. How many people can say that? Bezirhane and Payveren hardly represent all the other villages in Kurdistan.

As for whether my presence here is appropriate and how likely it is that I'll reach my destination, I think back to the answer Monique gave me, on the Way of Saint James. Unlike me, she had embarked on the pilgrimage for religious reasons. "You have better reasons to walk than I do," I told her, "since to touch the tomb of Saint James is for you a meaningful objective. As I am not a believer, for me the Cathedral of Santiago de Compostela is not a goal." "But the goal of reaching Compostela is not so important to me, hardly any more than for you," she answered. "For all of us, it's not the goal that matters, but the Way."

The Way . . . Is there one more fabulous, more legendary than the very one I am traveling? Where else in the world could I be as much at one with all those who, for over two millennia, walked before me on these rugged pathways across Anatolia? Their route is my route; the risks they faced, I face, too.

Little by little, good spirits return, and, when a truck and then a car stop to offer me a ride, I turn down their invitations as lightheartedly as I did before. Little by little, too, my eyes have risen from the asphalt to gaze out over the short grass, which, like a soft, silky carpet of long wool, hugs the hills and glows tender green in the sunlight for as far as the eye can see. The dream is back.

I think about all the Turks and all the Kurds who offered me their soup and sometimes their bed, let alone their time. The memory of these fraternal gestures makes my heart beat just a little faster, and not because I'm walking. Yes, I've been through some dark days since setting out, but so very few compared to all the bright, beautiful times spent here in Turkey, this country that I'll soon be leaving. Selim, the philosopher; Mustafa, the *bakkal*; Hikmet, the student; Şükran, the hostess; Behçet, the old intellectual; Arif, the peasant; and all the others: you are my friends. Extraordinary friends. Friendships for a day, and yet strong and solid as though tempered by time. I'd never experienced that before: that friendship and love are not the work of time, but the result of a secret alchemy; and that eternity has nothing to do with how long something lasts, either. Every pilgrim, it is said, returns home transformed. My Kurdish and Turkish friends: as a pilgrim of fraternity, I will return home holding your smiles and farewell embraces close to my heart.

Walking along, I lunch on some bread and cheese while over the billowing hills float the faces of these fortuitous friends. As I cross over a low mountain pass, I'm awakened from my dream by a sonorous *hello*. A cyclist has snuck up on me and comes to a stop. His bicycle is barely visible under the saddlebags, and the cargo rack is bedecked with a floppy sausage and a spare tire. The man, not much older than twenty, looks at me with a smile. He's blond, tall, and athletic. He's wearing round glasses that give his laughing eyes an intellectual look, eyes protected from the sun by a golfer's cap. His face and arms, those of an adventure traveler, as well as his legs protruding from his cycling shorts, are the color of burnt bread. His loud laugh resounds in the narrow ravine of the mountain pass. I walk over to him while he laboriously gets off his bike, stiff from the position that he has apparently held for several hours.

His name is Toralf Benz. He's a young German who set out from Berlin in the hopes of reaching Sydney to attend the Olympics. A death in his family forced him to make a week-long round trip back to Germany. All the way to Erzurum, he traveled with a friend, the one I spotted while I was on the Köprüköy Bridge. They will meet back up in Iran, in Isfahan, a city known for its carpets and its one hundred and thirty palaces. He speaks excellent English. We walk side by side, letting loose a flood of words, all that we've been holding back for a very long time no doubt. Toralf will return to Europe, completing his round-the-world journey, but he's unsure yet whether he'll travel across North or South America. He has plenty of time to think about it before reaching the shores of the Pacific. Aside from English, he doesn't speak any of the languages of the countries he's crossing, and the vocabulary he knows is generally limited to a handful of words. From time to time, he's lucky enough to run into a Turk or Kurd who used to work in Germany, with whom he can converse.

Around 3:00 p.m., we're in the little town of Taşlıçay. This is where I stop, while Toralf continues on. Since we still have a lot we'd like to share, I invite him to lunch. The city center is situated off the highway. There, a restaurant owner treats us to a most welcome *tas kebab,* and we swap travel stories. This young athlete's goal seems most of all to achieve the feat of strength of traveling around the world. These young people, in my view, are quite audacious. But aren't I, too?

Time catches up to us, and Toralf has to get going. He wants to make it to Doğubeyazıt, or at least somewhere as near to the city as possible by tonight. I take his address because I want to know how his trip "round the Big Blue Marble" turns out, and I promise to send his parents the photo I take of him standing, smug and with a handsome smile, beside his bike.

We part and bid each other happy trails in front of a young Turkish man who teamed up with us because he wants to practice his English. There's no hotel in Taşlıçay. Once again, I'm going to have to go begging for hospitality. The young Anglophile has an idea. He asks me to follow him and leads me . . . to the *jandarmas*. The officer he introduces me to tells him in Kurdish how one should proceed. And that's how I wind up in the office of the regional officer, the equivalent of the *préfet* (prefect) in France.

İsmail is a brilliant and overworked young man who takes the time to listen to my story. His coworkers clearly admire and respect him. He also enjoys the authority that all government employees in this country enjoy. Especially since managing a region in Kurdistan for Turkey's central government is a highly political—and risky—position. Considering that the PKK will target anything representing the government in Ankara, including schoolteachers who come to teach Turkish in Kurdish villages, it's no secret that revolutionary militants would love to target this building.

As elsewhere, I said that I was a retired schoolteacher. İsmail issues orders, and without any fuss, they move me into a kind of very clean and newly built hotel for teachers. The *jandarmas*, İsmail's offices, and the teachers' residence are all in close proximity to one another. It's no coincidence: safety is a constant concern, and the fear of attacks is ever-present. It's the weekend, so only a few teachers are in residence. I'm given a brightly lit room and access to the showers. In the evening, I go for dinner in the restaurant located on the building's ground floor, and İsmail, who's meeting a few of his coworkers there, greets me and asks whether everything's working out. Once again, he must have issued orders, because the server refuses to let me pay. I spend a pleasant evening in the lobby. People are either playing chess, *stira*, or cards. Most of them, though, engage in the nation's favorite activity: conversation.

One of İsmail's coworkers, who has a good command of English, corroborates the claim that there's gold in Kurdish soil, but that, inexplicably, the central government refuses to mine it. He also confirms what I already know: PKK hardliners would prefer that their leader be executed.

For when he called for his troops to lay down their arms, the organization split into two factions: the doves and the hawks. The hawks refuse
to give up the fight. We agree on the idea that Öcalan's execution would
be a political error, for the immediate result would be to pull the rug out
from under the supporters of a negotiated solution and once again rally
the revolutionaries—the hard-liners as well as the moderates.

It's the first time I'm able to have a dispassionate conversation with a
Turk on the issue of the Kurds without the inevitable finger across the
throat to end the debate. On several occasions over the past few days, I
spoke about the Öcalan affair with Kurds and have been surprised by
their answers. Young and old, men and women all agree on one thing:
they don't approve of the PKK's violence. I'm not naive: if they were
members, they wouldn't have said so anyway, but they wouldn't have
criticized its politics. On the other hand, all of them, without exception,
expressed their support for Öcalan. "He is our president" was the phrase
employed most often.

The Öcalan affair continues to be a source of embarrassment in the
country's political arena. The army and along with the vast majority of
Turkish citizens are demanding his death. But the Kurds are united in having self-identified with Apo. What's more, European countries are asking
the Turkish authorities to show leniency in their conflict with the Kurds,
especially since several atrocities carried out by the army and the *jandarmas* in mountain villages have scandalized Western opinion. To execute
Öcalan would, therefore, satisfy the Turks and the army but would stir
things up in Kurdistan and prevent Turkey from entering Europe. There
must be days when politicians in Ankara regret ever having captured him.

The conversation with İsmail's colleague focuses for a long time on
the obvious urgency of stimulating the local economy. He explains that
some programs are already underway, such as trout farming. Trout farming is great. But, as I see it, the focus should first be on modernizing
agriculture. A difficult task, especially since the army is doing everything
in its power to empty out villages in the mountains so as to gain greater
control of the territory where the terrorists are reported to be, as the saying goes, "like fish in the sea." Which brings us back to trout . . .

One anecdote underscores for me that, even for enlightened minds like those I'm rubbing shoulders with here, age-old traditions carry a lot of weight. The opportunity arises for me to tell how, at the start of my journey, I tried to pay for my stay at Nevzat's house, and how his daughter Şükran walked in on us while we were talking. Catching me with some banknotes in my hand, she turned red with anger and questioned her father: "You didn't take any money, did you?" They all burst out laughing. They laugh so hard that it's obvious I'm missing something. I ask what they find so funny about the story. "Because the man listened to something a woman had to say" is the unanimous response.

Translated into plain French, they tell me that this man is a "*couille molle*" (limp-dick). So for them, a man can do whatever he wants, even if that means violating the taboo against accepting money from a guest. His wife and his daughter must accept his actions without saying a word, even if they are forbidden. That's how it is: women are not to judge men. On the other hand, men have the right to dominate, contradict, and judge women.

Here, as elsewhere, I'm received with great generosity, the kind reserved back home for distinguished guests. Turkey, a place I will soon be leaving, has taught me the meaning of one of its language's most beautiful words: "*misafir.*" In French, too, I like the French word "*hôte*" and the halo of mystery surrounding it: does it refer to the one whose honor it is to receive (the host), or whose pleasure it is to be received (the guest)? What better way to show that the success of one's welcome depends on both parties? But in my many travels, I don't think I've ever encountered as much warmth, as much naturalness about opening one's house to others as I have in Turkey. In the villages, I was always struck that host's pride was something all the villagers shared in. In our "civilized" countries, this way of welcoming a guest has little by little been forgotten or perverted. We still welcome our family members and a close circle of friends. As for anyone else, there are houses for that purpose called hotels, all the more impersonal in that they are international. The Texan, French, or Japanese traveler wants to feel "at home" whether in New York, Buenos Aires, or Bangkok. As for those we actually welcome into our homes, if they are in our close network, then it's most often within the framework of a "quid pro quo" (hosting you is something I "owe" you) or for some well-defined purpose: "come on over for the weekend, we'll discuss the matter." An open door, without any expectation of reciprocation, or a reward, without any preconditions, is now just a rare holdover from the days when the country wasn't so prosperous. Is it still possible in our societies back home to welcome others to our table for the simple pleasure of discovery, exchange, and conversation? I would have my doubts had I not experienced firsthand such warmth in French and Spanish homes while hiking the lengthy Road to Santiago. While for us back home that remains the exception, here in Turkey, it's a way of life.

This is why the Kurdish activist whom I met in Paris recommended that I seek hospitality in the house of the master of each village, as he remains the guarantor of time-honored traditions. To betray tradition would have terrible consequences for his public image.

When I wake up, day is breaking. The road is long to Doğubeyazıt, the last city before the Iranian border. It's over sixty kilometers (37 miles) away, and I have no desire to do another take of my previous long-distance feat. I'd like to try to cover as much ground as possible even if it means, as has now happened twice, having to hitch a ride in a car or truck in one direction and then in the other the following day. So I quickly get up and cinch up my pack . . . but I cannot leave. For security, all the exits are locked. I silently search the entire building up and down, looking for a way out, but it's no good. The rooms are located on the second floor. A first door blocks access to the staircase. And I would bet that the door opening out onto the street is also locked. I bide my time for a while, but no one gets up. After searching for over an hour, I finally discover an emergency stairway in back of the building. It's accessible through a small window. It's hard getting my backpack through, and I have to really struggle. Just as I'm almost through, the man who helped me get settled yesterday opens the door for me. We go for breakfast. We chat. When I depart, it's already 8:30, and my plan to cover a lot of ground falls through, having lost three precious hours, the very ones when the temperature favors fast, comfortable walking. So I proceed unhurriedly, part of my energy having been sapped by my forced captivity. One of the teachers told me yesterday that in the small spa city of Diyadin there's a hotel, so that's where I'll plan on stopping. The landscape varies little. This is still the steppe, a place of far-off vistas on which the clouds cast fast-moving shadows that climb to the mountaintops. From time to time, a few houses are a reminder that people live here. A farmer working in a field with his son tells me that in the village I see off in the distance there's a church, because it was once inhabited by Armenians. After they left, the building fell into ruin. Such churches were sometimes converted into mosques, as was the case of the Hagia Sophia during the Ottoman conquest of fifteenth-century Istanbul.

The exterior architecture of Kurdish houses is very different from that of Turkish houses, but both bear witness to the same history. These populations have preserved in their culture the legacy of their nomadic ancestors. Everything is reminiscent of a tent. First and foremost, the single main room that serves as the greeting room, the dining room, and the bedroom. The other rooms are secondary and soulless. In this room, unusual because of its furniture, the carpets and pillows on the floor and on the bunks, the custom is to eat while seated on the floor . . . nothing has changed, except that stone walls have replaced canvas or felt. In most houses, there's no more furniture than there would have been in their ancestors' tents. The Turks do not see anything sacrosanct about the family home. When a house falls into ruin, they get a new one, as though they were abandoning one pasture and extinguishing the campfire before folding up the tent so as to set it up farther away. And the housing complexes, the towers, and high-rise blocks that I saw as I left Istanbul have the same fascination for the masses as they once did for our rural populations who left their old village farmhouses for the concrete housing projects of Paris's suburbs and their oak beds for Formica sideboards, without a tinge of regret.

A society stuck in time? Not exactly. Information society is rife here. And this change is visible in every home, for one very specific piece of furniture has made its appearance, identical everywhere. It's a large sideboard with a glass-enclosed upper section containing a few photos or trinkets. The lower section contains the household dishware. And in the middle sits the television, the reason this piece of furniture was purchased; but the remote controls are kept within easy reach of the head of the house. Oral transmission, the importance of the spoken word, is still at the heart of Anatolian culture and has easily blended with modernity, embodied in the cell phone, which Turks call a "pocket phone." The success of Internet cafés is the result of these same mental processes.

As for social organization, in Kurdistan more than elsewhere, whether in terms of the relationships among men alone or the status of women, it has maintained the hierarchical and clan-based structure of ancient tribes. It's only in the larger cities, in well-educated families, that the influence of Western culture has changed ancestral traditions. People sit around a table to eat and sleep in a room reserved for that purpose. And the bonds that ensure submission to the "lord" are relaxed among the undifferentiated masses of city centers, such as in Ankara, İzmir, and Istanbul.

This morning, in my mind, I am already in Iran. Two weeks ago, a truck driver told me that the border was closed. Why? The fellow couldn't say, but he was very assertive. In Erzurum, over the Internet, I asked a friend in Paris if she would look into it at the Iranian Embassy. They told her very graciously that the information was false. So my mind is at ease with respect to that matter: Iranians, irrespective of their political concerns, want foreigners to visit along with their dollars, and so they keep their borders wide open. In a Turkish newspaper lying around somewhere, I saw a photo and a headline related to Iran. Something's going on there, but I don't know what. I'll find out when I get there.

As is often the case in Anatolia, the city of Diyadin is a distance from the highway. It can be reached by taking a road running southeast. At the turnoff for this road, an ultramodern hotel complex is going up for the spa-goers who want to avail themselves of the hot sulfur water springing up from the ground. Unfortunately for me, it's not finished. So I continue on to Diyadin, reaching there around 4:00 p.m. It's a small city with dirt streets scattered with manure. The hotel, whose exterior appears dirtier than most, has been closed for a long time. I go into a neighboring teahouse to have a glass of juice and glean information. A schoolteacher—yet another one—comes over to talk. He tells me that if I'm interested, five kilometers to the southeast there's a hotel with its own sulfur spring spa. I'm hungry, so I decide to first go in search of a restaurant. No need to spend much time looking: there's only one. Stepping into the dark, one-room restaurant where several men are seated, my foot slips out from under me. Encumbered by the weight of my pack, I narrowly avoid falling. The floor is made of rough-hewn wood planks covered in a greasy layer of an unknown substance that you have to skate through if you want to keep your balance. I've never seen a restaurant so squalid, but who knows what I'll see between now and my journey's end? And, in any case, it's not like I have a choice. In the hope that greater attention is given to the food than to the housekeeping, and once again placing my trust in my lucky stars, I order an eggplant ragout that—lo and behold—isn't bad. The question now is whether my stomach will tolerate it.

As usual, the figure of five kilometers is very approximate, as it takes me nearly two hours to get there. Along the way, to my surprise, I see a car stop, and out of it steps the *muhtar* who, the day before yesterday, drove me back to Ağri. He asks me many questions as though we were old acquaintances and can't seem to let me go. He's a friendly man, and I tell him, as best I can, what a pleasant time I had in the heart-warming gynaeceum and the interesting conversation I had with his son.

Along the road, in several spots, wells are being drilled. The local water is reputed to heal skin ailments. I see an enormous pipe hiccuping as it spits steaming, yellow water in spurts out into a field. A pipeline under construction will soon carry it to the nearly completed resort near the state highway.

The spa consists of two small resort houses, one private and the other public. They're surrounded by one or two stone structures and a dozen round tents forming a kind of temporary encampment. What the schoolteacher from Diyadin grandly calls a "hotel" is in reality a single, windowless room, with cold, wet fieldstone walls that the wind passes right through. They crammed in four beds, whose sheets might, at one time, have been white. Three of them are occupied by men already fast asleep even though it's still light out. The manager offers to rent me the fourth at a perfectly prohibitive price.

Just as I'm about to begin negotiating, four men beckon me to come over. They're the electric company employees I ran into just before my last encounter with thieves. We drink some tea. They tell me that they've come to bathe in the miraculous water and invite me to join them. The spa is a small structure built around an open-air cement basin about four square meters in size.* In it, splashing and jostling one another, are nearly thirty strapping lads, like herring in a barrel. There are no changing rooms; everyone just hangs their clothing on nails mounted on the walls around the basin and bathe in their boxers or briefs that they then let dry by simply slipping them back on. The water has the same brown color that I've seen in many hammams, when it's saturated with too much accumulated dirt. It's boiling hot. After ten minutes, we're asked to get out, since there's only one basin and it's the women's turn.

Getting out of the bath, my new friends introduce me to a young man, Yakub, who runs a small shop under a canvas tarp. During the season, he sells juice and cookies to spa-goers arriving in a steady stream of small buses. He's a happy businessman. He has one associate and an assistant, a university student who works with him during summer vacation. They have a lively business. Given the elevation, the season here lasts three months. Before and after, snow and cold take hold of the premises.

"And what do you do the rest of the year, Yakub?"

"Nothing, I work on my car and visit friends."

What a fortunate man, for whom three months of work provides enough income to get him through an entire year.

The young Yakub, who returns each evening to his home in Diyadin, offers to let me spend the night in the tent where his shop assistant and associate sleep. It's very roomy, and they have an extra mattress and large blanket. For dinner, his shop assistant takes out some split pea soup from

---

* TN: The size of a square about 7 feet on each side.

a small freezer set up in a corner and drops it into boiling water. With a little water drawn from a pump and a bit of bread, we dine as we watch the last spa-goers shiver as they climb out of the sulfur bath and back into their minibus. Sundown sets the far-off hills on fire, offering a fabulous show. We go to bed as soon as it's dark out.

I fall asleep quickly but am wakened by the cold. I had completely forgotten that we are at an elevation of over 2,200 meters (7,220 feet) and that night is ice-cold. I quickly take my sleeping bag from my pack but can't seem to warm up. I tremble for hours until finally, I remember that, at the bottom of my bag, I had stowed a survival blanket just in case. I had never used it. Why am I so absent-minded? In the dark, so I don't wake up my hosts, I wrap myself in the thin plastic film and then slip once again into my down bag, pulling the blanket over me. I finally warm back up, but I foolishly spend three hours shivering and by the time I fall asleep, the sun is already coming over the horizon.

Our camp comes back to life, the minibuses that spill out streams of spa-goers shortly after dawn drive me all too soon from my at-long-last-warm bed. We're nibbling on hunks of bread that we wash down with tea when I have to make a run to the bathroom adjoining the hot water basin. I make a return trip, my backpack cinched, just as I am about to leave. But I don't see any reason to be worried. It's the third time since leaving Istanbul that I've come down with a case of the runs. In two days, I'll have forgotten all about it.

When I begin to walk, the sun is already high. The traffic is relatively light. I'm already looking forward to the pleasures that lie ahead. In a few kilometers, ten, perhaps twenty, I'll have my first glimpse of Mount Ararat. In the Middle Ages, Armenians had the custom of making the sign of the cross whenever this sacred mountain came into view. The reason is that there is an enduring legend that it was on the slopes of this ancient volcano, whose summit reaches 5,300 meters (17,400 feet), that Noah's Ark ran aground. Several scientific expeditions claimed to have found vestiges of the sacred ark, but each time the wooden debris was dated, their hopes were dashed. Nevertheless, a small village on the Russian side bears the name of Nakhitchevan, which, in old Armenian, means "People of the Ship." Personally, I rather like the idea that Noah ran his Ark aground at the foot of this sea of marvelous blue mountains.

The road ahead gently climbs to a mountain pass topping out at 2,500 meters (8,200 feet). I try to ignore that dinner and breakfast have begun to dance a crazy waltz in my unhappy intestines and try to concentrate. But, between my belly and my head, it's a lopsided contest. What's going on in my tortured bowels outweighs my every thought. Fortunately, the road is built on a kind of embankment, such that, on either side, I can duck out of the view of the passing cars and trucks to relieve the severe bouts of colic, which force me to make increasingly frequent sprints, at the end of which I drop my pack—and my pants—in a mad panic. I've never had such a severe case of turista. The road continues to climb, and I find it harder and harder to walk. A severe headache grips my forehead. I blame the sun, which has grown fiercer, and I put on my hat. It makes no difference. All told, in the six- or seven-kilometer climb to the top, I have to stop nearly ten times to relieve a bout of diarrhea that's knocking me out. The headache was the harbinger of a fever that soon has me shivering in spite of the heat. At the summit, a small stone structure shelters a group of soldiers. Two Kangals are chained outside. One soldier, hidden behind some sandbags, sees me and hails their commanding officer. The officer, a young man with a shaved head, intrigued by my getup, shouts to me in a voice blending both amusement and curiosity: "*Gel, çay!*"

Even though I still have a long way to go before Doğubeyazıt, I'm quick to take up his invitation. I feel terrible, weak and incapacitated, and the fever is getting worse. The soldiers invite me out of the sun, into a kind of blockhouse. It's a strategic location. From here, they can monitor the road below for ten kilometers or more from west to east. Before entering, the officer points to the cloudy summit of Mount Ararat. But I'm barely listening, and I have no desire whatsoever to contemplate anything, for I feel utterly awful. I plunk myself down onto a bench and wait for tea. The officer and I are seated at a small pedestal table, while over at the central table, several soldiers are busy carefully cleaning their weapons, which they've disassembled and whose components glow in the dim light. The officer has a good laugh when he hears that I've come from Istanbul. He says to himself that as soon as he saw me, decked out as I am, he took me for a strange bird, and in that he was not mistaken. Ah, ah, ah! Istanbul! Tehran! I don't understand a thing he says, except that he finds me an inexhaustible source of mirth and that there are "problems" in Iran. But none of that alarms me. I've seen my share of "problems" from day one. A few more no longer frighten me. On the other hand, for the moment, I'm cold and I'm sweating, both at the same time. When a soldier brings me some bread and cheese, I feel like throwing up. I have a very hard time convincing them that all I want is to drink a bit of very hot tea. Little by little, after many cups of the beneficial liquid, my discomfort fades.

I really have no desire to get back underway; I want nothing more than to lie down and sleep. But first, I must answer the eternal question, "*güzel, Türkiye?*" (is Turkey beautiful?)—the question is asked with such intonation that it demands an immediate answer. I reply that, of course, Turkey is "*çok güzel*" (*choke gu-zehl'*) (very beautiful). The expression works in Turkish like "*very nice*" in English. A kind of all-purpose "open sesame" that punctuates statements and can be used to answer almost any question asked, and when associated with one's index finger pointed at just about anything, it can fill awkward voids in difficult conversations. As soon as I stepped foot in Turkey, it became clear that if there were one expression to learn, this was it. But is it because I'm a little cranky on account of the turista that's bothering me? I hit a sour note in my reply. Yes, Turkey is beautiful, but, I tell him, it's too bad the country's in a state of war.

The young officer gets up to be more persuasive and assures me that they are surrounded by enemies. The Armenians, the Iranians, the Iraqis, the Greeks, and the PKK: everyone is out to get them.

I'm aware that the border with Armenia is indeed closed and that the traditional enemy of Turkey is still Greece. As for the smoldering conflicts with the Iranians and Iraqis, they're the by-products of the fight against the PKK, the Turks accusing their neighbors of harboring Öcalan's militants within their territory. The Turkish army, moreover, does not hold back and from time to time asserts that it has the right to pursue them beyond its own borders, a practice that doesn't help relations. That's the situation outside the country; domestically, the PKK is everywhere, there are snipers in the mountains and bombings in the cities. I imply that when you're on such poor terms with all your neighbors, you may be partly responsible. That puts a damper on the conversation. The soldiers, all Turks, then want to know what I think of Öcalan's conviction. I scandalize them by predicting that it's unlikely he'll ever be executed.

"But he's a child killer!"

What army hasn't killed children? If we start judging generals for all the atrocities committed by their armies out in the field, many heads have yet to roll. But I don't want to argue. So I tone down my antimilitaristic remarks. In the heat of the discussion, which might have, at any moment, turned sour, I somewhat forget how terrible I'd been feeling a short while ago, and the cool of the small structure along with the tea have revived me.

How I wish I were more fluent in Turkish! I could, for example, tell these slightly naive grunts what I'd been told in Istanbul. Namely, that they should read a recently published book titled *Le Livre de Mehmet*.[*] Mehmet is a common first name and designates the average Turkish soldier: in English it might be called *The Soldier's Book*. Written by a female journalist, Nadire Mater, it's a series of interviews with around forty men who were drafted and fought in the war against the Kurds, especially as *jandarmas*. What these draftees reveal is enlightening. They're mistreated by their officers and poorly fed, while the sons of good families—thanks to people they know—avoid the drudgery and slaughter: that's just the backdrop. As for the horrors they face each day: the massacre of civilians on the simple suspicion that they belong to the PKK, the forced evacuation of villages that are then burned to the ground as soon as the last inhabitant has been ousted. And I could go on with this unfortunately now well-known list of the sophisticated forms of cruelty whereby the weak are made to suffer at the hands of those who, thanks

---

[*] The book was in fact banned by the Turkish government at the end of 1999, and its author risked prosecution for "damages to the armed forces' morale."

to the uniform, think they're strong. But I keep all of that to myself and simply nod in response to the many considerations my officer insists on meting out to me.

He's interrupted by two rascals in rather unusual garb. They're local peasants. Over their jackets, they've donned a kind of vest with many pockets made of camouflage canvas similar to what soldiers and *jandarmas* wear; pockets that turn out to be bursting with rounds of ammunition. The men are backup soldiers whom the army trained in the villages and who are reporting in. I recognize the same model rifle that the man in Alihacı was waving around in front of my door. Pointing at them, the officer tells me that there are "good" Kurds, and these two are proof of that. I can't understand the ensuing discussion between the officer and the two backups. And since I'm feeling better, I leave them behind.

The sun is ablaze as I step back out of the small, thick-walled fort. The road leads gently down toward a valley in which a river is napping. I'd like to do the same. Off in the distance, Mount Ararat is shrouded in mist. It'll take me four or five hours to get there. I have to stop to relieve myself several times over the course of the next two hours. My water jug, because of my persistent thirst, is almost empty, and I try to hold off from drinking the last few drops. I put my jacket back on because the fever's back and I'm shivering despite the harsh sun. I dip my hat in the river several times. The sun is beating down so hard at this altitude that in just a few minutes, it's dry. When I stop beside the road and set down my pack to rest, I miss the cool air of the little fort that's no longer in sight.

My legs are increasingly weak. In an attempt to regain some strength, I try to eat a bit of bread. But just the sight and smell of it is unbearable and makes me queasy. As soon as I get back on the road, I stop once again on the berm. My teeth are chattering. The pack weighs tons. I set off yet again but notice that despite all my efforts to walk straight, I'm zigzagging down the flat road that, off in the distance, leads to a low mountain pass. Cars and trucks are fortunately few, as they could easily mow me down. I stop once again and start to crouch to take a seat when my legs, all of a sudden, decide they can no longer hold me up.

When I regain consciousness, I'm lying by the side of the road, face down against the thick grass, and I'm pinned beneath the weight of my pack. For how long was I unconscious? I'm unable to get up. With tremendous difficulty, I undo the straps so that I can break free from my gear. I sit in the grass. My head is spinning. When I try to pick up my hat, which had fallen, I realize I'm no longer able to walk. I'm going to have to flag down a car and get a ride to Doğubeyazıt.

It's one of those small buses that provide connecting services to cities throughout Anatolia. It stopped a few meters away. The young boy helping the driver opens the back door for me. I drag my pack over; the kid grabs it and sets it on the back-row bench, and I get in next to it. The little steward eyes me intently: I must have an odd look. A practical fellow, he reaches into a box, pulls out a plastic bag, and hands it to me without a word. He's just in time: I bury my face in it and throw up, hiccuping as I retch. Then everything disappears into a pleasant haze. When I finally regain consciousness, we're in Doğubeyazıt. The minibus has pulled up alongside a sidewalk. The passengers have all disembarked, and the boy is standing in front of me, saying nothing. I hand him a banknote worth one million Turkish liras. I try to get my pack out of the minibus and have almost managed it when he comes over to lend me a hand. He helps me lift it so that I can get a strap over my shoulder. The vehicle's parked just outside a three-star hotel with a freshly painted facade. I go in.

My room costs seven million liras. It's the first splurge of my journey. The lobby exudes bourgeois respectability. But from experience, I know that appearances can be deceiving. The prudent thing to do would be to first take a look at what they're offering for that rate, but I'm unable, sensing once again that I might lose consciousness. An employee is given orders to take me to my room. Short on luck, the elevator's not working. I let my pack slip off my shoulder and motion the young man to take it, as there's no way I would be able to carry all that weight up even a single step. He casually grabs it but has to make a second attempt, as he was expecting it to be lighter. On the second floor, which I'm able to reach after several stops in the stairwell to catch my breath, he opens a door. As soon as I walk in, I can hear the leak hissing in the bathroom, but my focus, right now, is to get some sleep. I close the door behind the young man and make a mad dash for the bathroom. Diarrhea and vomiting: I'm emptying everything out. Finally a truce, and I head over to one of the two beds and let myself drop. One of the bed's legs snaps off. I'm shivering. To warm myself up, I take the blankets from the second bed and pile them up on mine. The one I've lain down on feels like it's going to collapse every time I move. I could care less, though, and fall asleep.

For two days, all I can do is run back and forth to the bathroom. I have nothing left in my belly, yet endless contractions wring out my intestines. It isn't long before I notice blood in my stool. In disregard of all the rules concerning food safety—which up till now I've tried the best I could to follow, although present circumstances suggest that I failed—I slake an unquenchable thirst from the tap. Ten minutes later, I return this water to the toilet bowl. A leak in a pipe attached to a wall has flooded the bathroom floor, such that each time I go in, I take an ice-cold footbath.

The first morning, I asked the young employee who came to make my room to buy me some cooked rice from a restaurant nearby. I also asked for a phone in my room. He forgot. The next day, since he didn't come to clean the room—he must have forgotten that, too—I risk a quick venture down to the lobby and back to ask once more for rice and a phone. I have to be quick about it, as another urgent need comes over me, which has to wait nevertheless for me to make it back up the stairs at the speed of a disabled old man. All my strength has left me. About midafternoon, the young man brings me the rice that he most likely cooked himself. He has no trouble remembering to charge me for it at full price. I grumble, but I'm at his mercy. His rice is tasteless and crunchy. I barely have the time to down two spoonfuls before I spit them back up. My stomach is on fire. Each time I go to the toilet, the pain is unbearable. I complained to the management about the pitiful state of the bed and the leak in the bathroom. The flippant young man offers to give me a room on the third floor. Why not the fifth? I must be the only guest in this hotel. I give up on the idea of heaving myself up an extra floor, certain that I'd never be able to get back down. So be it, I'll put up with the footbaths.

On the other hand, I put up a fight to get a telephone, which finally arrives in the evening. We struggle for an hour to install it, since the cord lacks a male connector. And the wall jack is located behind my bed, meaning it's very hard to get to. After endless fiddling and failed attempts such that the whole dreadful time I want to kill him, the bungler finally manages to get a dial tone by shoving two stripped wires into the jack. On the first try, the bed moves and the wire falls out, and we have to start over. After he leaves, as soon as I lie back down, the wires come undone. I have to choose between sleeping or placing a phone call.

My confidence in Anatolian medicine is very limited. From deep within my bag, I pull out a small "*IMA*" card—*Inter Mutuelles Assistance*—insurance coverage for the duration of my journey. After wearing myself out in my struggle to get the dial tone back, I manage to get through to them. They ask me to give them my number, and they'll call me back. A few minutes later, the flippant young man knocks on my door: there's a phone call for me, but the wires have slipped out again, and they can't patch the call through to my room. We fiddle with the wires once more. The doctor who returns my call for a telephone consultation is a woman with a very reassuring voice. Her diagnosis is clear, unambiguous, and final: amebic dysentery. It's a hard blow. From what I know, this is no minor illness. It once terrorized armies in the field, often killing more men than the bullets. The pleasant voice tells me that I have to take a particular medicine right away that contains a miracle molecule—offhand I can't recall its name—and that's sold under three different brand names, which I jot down. I'll be able to find one of the three. It's too late in the evening for me to go out looking for it now. I'm also dreading to have to make a trip downstairs and, even worse, to climb back up. I try to laugh at myself and at my sudden weakness, whereas, just two days ago, I felt invincible. I overcame a foot infection, forced marches, Kangals, almost going headfirst over a cliff, Turkish and Kurdish bandits, and soldiers; now here I am the victim of some microscopic bugs eating away at my intestines. How ironic. Humor is an excellent remedy when we're afraid, but right now I need a good companion if I'm going to really get into it. All alone, I have to come to terms with my miserable innards and low spirits.

The next morning, I venture out into the main street, which seems horribly noisy and chaotic. The nearest pharmacist, from what they told me at the hotel, is fifty meters away. A first miracle: the pharmacist is probably the only one who speaks English in all of Anatolia. A second miracle: he has the medicine. I return to my room, completely drained. As soon as I take the second dose, the treatment begins to take effect and the diarrhea lets up a little, allowing me to get some rest. From my bed, I can finally take in the view of Mount Ararat. Those who come after me in this room will be less fortunate, since two buildings are going up, and they'll soon block the view.

Majestic and crowned with snow, the mountain is superb. In the early morning, as the sun comes up, it looks as though it's drowning in fog, lending it an even greater sense of mystery. And then, as the sun climbs higher in the sky, a veil of clouds comes to rest over its head, hiding it from view for the rest of the day. Mount Ararat is flanked by another, smaller volcanic cone that the Turks call "the mountain of a little pain." As for Ararat, it goes by the name of Büyükacı Daği (*bu-yu-kah'-djuh da'-hee*), "the mountain of great pain."

Of course, one hand on my swollen, burning belly, the thought was already on my mind.

CHAPTER XIII
THE GREAT PAIN

Feeling depressed over my illness, exhausted from my demise and from three days of forced fasting, I'm in no condition to head back out on the road. It's a feat just to stand up. How many days will it take until I can walk and carry my gear? My stomach ravaged by amoebas, vomiting, shitting blood, and mucus: I'm a complete wreck. The first thing I need to do is change hotels. In this one, where there's no food service and they force you choose between the bed and the telephone, the indifference of the extraordinarily incapable staff and the obligatory footbaths have succeeded in draining off whatever morale I had left.

In the evening, feeling slightly better, I risk an expedition out into the main street. Along with July, the tourists are now here, almost all of them English-speaking. Flaunting their tans in shorts and T-shirts, they take themselves for adventure travelers as they drive about in four-wheel-drive vehicles, packed to the roof with a jumble of camping gear and clothing. We are on entirely different journeys. They cross the country, they view it and take pictures of it . . . but never walk through its front door. Aren't I clever, bragging like this, telling myself that I, unlike them, am an *authentic* traveler! You must look like a doddering old fool, a quivering ghost, a poor soul lost in the Orient: such are the thoughts running through my mind, the lecture I give myself while stepping onto a scale that a shrewd kid has set out on the sidewalk, waiting for customers. I'm blown away by the number I read; I step off and check to be sure the device is properly calibrated. Another scale, with another boy next to it a little farther on, confirms the previous verdict: they both agree it's really sixty kilos (132 pounds). In Istanbul, I weighed seventy-four (163 pounds); in Erzurum, just a week ago, I weighted seventy-one (157 pounds), after two months on the road. So I've lost eleven kilos (25 pounds) in less than three days.

I witness a scene that for a few moments makes me forget the squeezing and stretching sensations tormenting me. On a street grocer's cart set up in front of a store window, an old man is more slumped than seated on a pile of rags that at one time must have been blankets. His body seems to lack a spinal column, and his limbs are misshapen. With a trembling finger, he follows along lines in a Qur'an written in Arabic characters, while chanting in a soft voice, paying no heed to the passers-by, some of whom toss him coins or banknotes. Under the cart, two little scamps are seated cross-legged, as snotty and brown-skinned as can be imagined, playing cards. They laugh. Suddenly, the old man slams his book shut and slaps the palm of his hand three times on floor of the cart. The two kids crawl out from their shelter, and, without stopping, which proves how much this scenario is quite routine to them, they rush to take up their posts. One pulls on the cart while the other pushes, and they drive straight into the crowd, no doubt looking for a better location unless they're taking their pious paralytic to the mosque, as it's almost time for prayer.

Before going back to my hotel, I visit another, one that's more comfortable and less expensive. I search for an Internet "café" but come up empty-handed. "No coffee here," an old Turk tells me, "only tea." In the lobby of my fake three-star hotel, I tell them I'm leaving and ask that they prepare my bill for tomorrow morning. I notice that the manager is very displeased that I'm moving, so I anticipate a monumental rip-off. Then I hoist myself up to my room, where I collapse and sleep the whole night through.

In the morning, as expected, I have to wage a minor war against the fleabag's owner, who, for lack of customers, tries to fleece those he already has on hand. The "bill" is a ragged piece of grid paper on which he has scribbled an astronomical figure. The room rate he quoted me on the first day has tripled. I placed a thirty-second call to France, but according to him, the conversation lasted fifteen minutes. On top of it, he wants to charge me for the incoming call. When I threaten to go to the *"polis,"* he cuts the charges by two-thirds. What a good-for-nothing, small-time scoundrel, and a coward when it comes to the cops: precisely the kind of human worth keeping at arm's length.

The tourists at the Ararat Hotel are for the most part from Europe or America, shows-offs given to flaunting their Ray-Bans and safari hats and who don't speak a lick of Turkish. Seeing that my look is completely different, I draw the sympathy of the staff, who are friendly to me, even pampering me. After checking to be sure there's a telephone meter, I call my children, and then the *IMA*, to let them both know I've moved. A doctor calls me a short while later to ask how I'm doing: "You'll need several weeks before you can start walking again," he tells me. "In our opinion, you should be repatriated. We're going to call our contact in Turkey, who will get in touch with you."

I hadn't ruled the possibility out, but it's a heavy blow. It's true that my condition, at best, won't let me get going again for another two or three weeks. I'm only a normal day's walk away from the Iranian border, which is to say, thirty-five kilometers (22 miles), but what is in store for me there? Without a more detailed map, not knowing where the villages are, the only way for me to proceed is to walk from city to city. That means stages of at least forty kilometers (25 miles). In my condition, that's unimaginable. And then there's one other very worrisome problem, as it involves red tape. It's already July 14, and my Iranian visa is only valid for two weeks. Since I cannot get back on the road again before the twenty-ninth at least, I'll have to renew it. To do that, I have to go to either Paris or Istanbul, and then wait two weeks, which is the normal amount of time for it to be issued. There's indeed an Iranian Consulate in Erzurum, but there the processing time is one month. In either case, the best I'll be able to do is get back on the road around August 15, in the dog days of summer. For someone just recovering, it would be difficult to walk when the weather is at its hottest.

I don't know what to do with myself. Up till now, my routine was easy: walking, eating, finding shelter. All of a sudden, I'm faced with a great void. Common sense would dictate that I do nothing. But that's something I can't do. To kill time, stretched out on my bed, I thumb through the literature I have on Iran. I read that Tabriz, so close now at just over a week's walk away, was, at the end of the sixteenth century, the world's largest marketplace. The bazaar covered thirty square kilometers (12 square miles). Thirty square kilometers: can you even imagine? I cannot. Hard as I try, I cannot wrap my mind around such an array of stalls, heaps of treasure, piles of silk goods and brocade, pyramids of powders and spices, mountains of carpets including some of the most expensive in the world, and the falcon market—the best birds in all the Middle East; my imagination is limited by the Orient's souks that I've seen with my own eyes. By dint of letting this fairyland of shimmering colors and spicy fragrances dance in my head, I blissfully fall asleep in Ali Baba's cave.

When it's time for lunch, I attempt a quick foray out into the street. A mischief-maker accosts me, wanting to do a black-market exchange of Iranian rials for me. Unfortunately, that's hardly a concern of mine right now. In what looks like a promising restaurant, I try to get some food into my stomach. Only three bites of rice, and I have to make a mad dash back to the hotel to spew it all up. I try to drink nonstop so that I don't get too dehydrated. In a nutshell, I'm staying alive.

I finally find an Internet café. Located on the second floor of a building, it wasn't easy to see. To reach it, you first have to traverse the furniture seller's shop—he's the one who put up the money for it; zigzag your way around the beds, armchairs, and cupboards on display; and then head up a small spiral staircase in the back room. The clientele is mostly young: this is where they come to play video games and log onto hookup websites where they can chat up strangers with heady names, imagining them half-naked, lying lasciviously on silk pillows in some Western metropolis. In my inbox, I have news from my children and a message from Geneviève, a journalist friend who jokes about my sense of timing: ". . . You waltz into Istanbul for the opening arguments in Öcalan's trail, then go to Erzurum in time for him to receive the death penalty, and then onto Iran for the student uprising. It's a little too much for a retiree. When are you gonna stop *following* the news?"

Back at my hotel, I collapse onto the bed, exhausted from my expedition. A little later, I wake up from a pleasant dream and return to nightmarish reality: I'm nailed to my bed, sick as a dog, in Doğubeyazıt. It's late in the day. Will Mount Ararat, sublime and politely capped with a crown of clouds at this hour, be the endpoint of my journey? I still hold out hope. I drag myself over to the balcony and admire the view. Her Highness "the Great Pain" has pulled a veil across her face, turning a blind eye to my distress.

The telephone rings, rousing me from my contemplation. It's Doctor Günay, head of the *IMA* in Turkey, on the line from Istanbul. He has a warm voice and speaks French without the slightest accent, having grown up and studied much of his life in eastern France.

"I've taken a look at your paperwork and spoke with the doctors who handled your case. I believe there's no alternative: you have to return home. But I'm not sure how to go about it."

I'm indeed in no state to be moved. There's no way I could board a plane as a regular passenger. I can't sit upright for more than a few minutes. To get a couchette in an airplane, now that it's high season, may require waiting several days. And my condition won't allow it. Furthermore, I'd have to be taken to Erzurum in an ambulance, and then by plane to Ankara, where I'd have to change planes before continuing on to Istanbul. Going through Iran wouldn't be any easier. Chartering a plane just for me seems excessive: I still have some way to go before I'll be on a first-name basis with the Grim Reaper. Two hours later, the doctor/rescue worker calls me back and tells me that there's only one solution: to return from Doğubeyazıt to Istanbul in an ambulance. A vehicle will leave the banks of the Bosporus later tonight and will arrive tomorrow evening. Two drivers and a nurse will accompany me back, but, Dr. Günay warns me, the crossing will be difficult and tiring. I can imagine, but I don't have any other ideas, either. Especially since the pain is growing worse as the dysentery is subsiding. He confirms that in Iran there are student demonstrations and that the army's cracking down hard. So I should have no regrets, he concludes, since it would have been difficult for me to continue.

But I do have regrets. By a twist of fate, I have an opportunity to enter Iran while events are taking place that would, for me, be captivating. I have a hard time putting up with forced inaction. Lying on my bed, gazing out at the turbaned summit of Mount Ararat, I simply can't believe that this is the end—even if only for a time—of my adventure. At this hour, the ambulance must be leaving Istanbul. The countdown to the motorized return to the starting point of my Turkish adventure has begun. To keep myself busy, I reread the only book I've hardly had the time to look at and that I've been toting with me all the way from Paris: The *Lonely Planet* guide to Iran, in English.

Despite the medicine, the amoebas are still eating away at my intestines. My belly is a wound radiating throughout my body. Sleep finally comes over me, disrupted by a concert of furious barking. As soon as night invades the city, its streets become a battleground for wild dogs. Ice-cold rain falls on the deserted streets. It must be snowing on Ararat's summit. I barely sleep. When I wake up, my stomach's a little less painful. Dawn reveals the sheer mass of the snow-capped mountain looming 5,300 meters (17,400 feet) above the city. It's still early; the clouds have not yet appeared. This extinct volcano is as beautiful as Mount Fujiyama, which I had the opportunity to see last year. The majestic mass rising up out of the plain, the perfect shape of the cone, the many shades of white in which it is clothed compose one of those visions that never tire the eyes. Is it any surprise that this mountain was considered a god by those who lived in its shadow? Just to the east, Little Ararat takes advantage of the diffuse morning light, which, combined with an optical effect, makes it seem as if it were as large as the "great pain."

I walk about the city bent over, tense, and hunched up, hoping to control the wild rumpus some unknown, cannibalistic germs are raising in my tormented bowels.

On the street corners, piles of smelly garbage attract throngs of chickens and ducks that wander from their yards to come squabble over leftovers from the feast abandoned by the now-sated dogs. There's no sewer, either, and so vast pools of greenish, putrid liquid seep out from beneath the heaping piles of plastic bags, swollen from the decomposition of their contents or that have burst, spewing out frothy slime. I reach the edge of the city and contemplate Mount Ararat, whose perfect triangle stands on the horizon. It was only supposed to be a signpost along the way, but today it's a wall. I gingerly walk back toward downtown. Businesses are already open, even though it's not yet the break of dawn. Here, as throughout the Orient, shops open onto the street, and the goods for sale are piled up outside, for all to see. The few cars driving about at this hour stir up clouds of fine dust that floats down onto the stalls and sneaks in the open doors. I feel small, miserable, and dirty, both inside and out, just like this city at the edge of the world. Bouts of nausea have me afraid I might throw up right in the middle of the street. Still, for nine weeks now, filth was part of my daily routine, and I was never turned off by it. Here, I find it revolting. But could this intense feeling of disgust simply be due to the unbearable thought that today's the day my adventure comes to an end?

Back at the hotel around 7:30 a.m., I manage to swallow—and keep down—a few cups of tea, and I even chew for a long time on a small piece of bread. How will I get through the day? I cannot stand the idea of just sitting around waiting for the ambulance to pick me up. Because I am tormented by the pain, time seems to drag on forever. But whenever it subsides, the second hand of my watch suddenly seems to speed up. As if to hasten the arrival of that damned ambulance that, alas, will mark the end of my dream and of my walk toward China for a long time to come.

Since I can't walk, I'll have to sacrifice some of the tourist's must-sees. There are three local attractions here. First, Mount Ararat, of course. But the army has all but forbidden access to its slopes ever since the start of the war against the PKK. Next, the "Meteor Çukuru" (*choo-koo-roo*). It's located about thirty kilometers from the city, near the Iranian border. I'd planned to make a side trip along the way. In 1920, in what was already a desolate landscape, an enormous meteorite fell here, leaving a huge crater sixty meters (200 feet) in diameter and over thirty meters (100 feet) deep, the world's second largest. There, too, the army has put up so many hurdles that visiting it is unpredictable. The war with the Kurdish rebels has ruined a once-thriving tourist industry, based on these two attractions. But in any event, the mountain and the crater are much too far afield for me to even attempt visiting them.

That leaves the third local marvel, and that one's within my reach. Five kilometers from the city, towering over the plain, stands one of the most beautiful architectural treasures of the entire country: the palace-fortress of İshak Paşa (Lord Isaac). This was a family affair. Begun in 1685 by a *paşa*, it was completed a century later by his son, who gave his name to the edifice. The castle guarded the eastern entrance to Turkey, defending it against the armies of the Persians, Armenians, and Russians, who relentlessly laid the region to waste. From time immemorial, insecurity was the rule here. The men lived in the hills, safe from those wielding sabers. Before the establishment of the Republic, Doğubeyazıt did not exist. At the end of the 1930s, the new regime having better secured its borders, it went in search of the region's inhabitants living high in the mountains and low in the valleys, and they were then resettled in this city, created out of thin air.

The expedition promises to be risky. So I load up with toilet paper and negotiate my trip with a taxi driver. We come to the agreement that he'll drive me to the palace without taking any other passengers; he'll wait for me while I'm there and will drive me back here. Unable to sit, I lie down on the back seat, and off we go, but not before I ask him to do his best to avoid potholes. He reassures me in the half-amused, half-outraged way of someone who's not about to be told how to do his job. But not even a hundred meters into the journey, I have the unpleasant feeling my body's about to explode. It's too harsh an ordeal. I ask my disappointed driver to take me back to the hotel. I lie down and try to sleep. The second hand seems to stand still.

A little after twelve, I'm feeling better. Unable to stay put, I go back outside. The same taxi driver is still there. Can we try again? He agrees.

This time, he drives very carefully. I try not to howl at every jolt over the bumpy road leading to the palace. As soon as we arrive, I bolt out of the taxi and dart into the bathroom belonging to the restaurant that overlooks the edifice, while my driver sips tea. Then I begin my tour, taking small steps, blocking my sphincter, and squeezing my buttocks as much as my sore muscles allow. I won't see the gold-plated doors that were carried off by the Russians and are now in the Hermitage Museum in St. Petersburg. The three hundred and sixty rooms that made up the palace have mostly collapsed. Elsewhere, vast areas are off-limits to visitors because the marvel is literally being rebuilt. The ringed minaret, made of rows of red and white stones, is in good condition, as is the adjacent *türbe* (mausoleum). I'm fortunately the only visitor, and so whenever the need is so urgent that I can't make it back to the restaurant, I'm free to leave a little souvenir in one of the palace's remote corners. One less enduring than the words "Mehmet loves Fatime" engraved in a heart on one of the palace's soft, chalky walls.

Despite the passing years and how weather has taken a toll on the stone, what remains unchanged is the palace's extraordinary viewpoint looking out over the plain. I stand and get lost in dreams for a moment as I survey the vast territory stretching beyond the fortress walls. Often, in moments like this, from atop the mountain passes I'd just climbed, I'd be preparing to savor close-up all the beauty spread out at my feet. That has all changed. I'm unfortunately going to head back down in a car, time is now running short, and with it the pleasure of taking in the sights at my own pace. I scold myself: after refusing for all these weeks to climb into a vehicle, I need to be careful not to develop some form of *autophobia*.

When I walk tight-stepped out of the palace, my faithful driver is waiting for me by the front door. On the way back, sympathetic, he stops near a grove of hazelnut trees so that I can relieve yet another crisis of my tormented bowels. Time has flown by. At the hotel, weary from the expedition, I doze off. The excursion was painful, but I managed to while away this seemingly endless day in a rather pleasant way.

In the evening, around ten o'clock, the ambulance has arrived. The two drivers and the nurse look exhausted. Without the slightest appetite, I watch as they wolf down some dish that I don't recognize, and then we agree on the plan. They'll get some sleep for three or four hours, then we'll leave at three in the morning. The nurse, who looks a little hard to please, pinches my skin. "You're dehydrated, you have to drink, and drink a lot." I'd very much like to comply, but I explain that because of some blockage probably caused by the pain, I've hardly urinated all day. "Drink, and you will pee." That's the young lady's injunction, and so, on that highly encouraging note, we wish each other good night.

A 3:00 a.m., as I make my way downstairs, the large ambulance's engine is already warming up, filling the hotel courtyard with the nauseating odor of burnt diesel fuel. They get me settled in on the gurney. The nurse takes up position on a seat nearby. To say that I'm in high spirits at this point would truly be an exaggeration. I had sworn not to get into a car during the journey until reaching Tehran. And now here I am, my belly on fire, shamelessly about to retrace my journey in reverse on four wheels. I think back to the driver who, just before Suşehri, offered to give me a ride in his ambulance and how I told him in what was, at the time, an ironic and brash tone: "Not yet. Maybe later on." Well, here I am, and I'm not about to brag or crack jokes. As I very carefully set my rear end on the mattress, I promise myself to return here, sometime very soon. Overnight, I went back over my calculations: back in Paris, after three weeks or perhaps a month to rest up and regain my strength, I can get to Erzurum by plane, hop on a bus to the very spot where I left off, and continue my journey as if nothing ever happened. I even see an upside to this: this unexpected delay will allow me to cross Iran in the autumn, once the hottest weather, which would have meant nothing but suffering, has passed. But, try as I might to look on the bright side, none of that is a done deal, and I'm unable to rid myself of my bitterness at having to undergo medical evacuation.

The start of our journey through the city's rutted dirt streets sets me moaning. My abdomen is as hard, bloated, and painful as it's ever been since my bout of dysentery began, and, when the wheels drop into the potholes, violent jolts make all my muscles go rigid, as if I were being struck by bolts of electricity. The ambulance moves along fairly slowly, zigzagging to avoid ruts, but these streets are but a gigantic minefield. After only an hour on the road, the grueling shocks get the better of my willpower. Despite my heroic desire to suffer in silence, I yell out each time a more dramatic bump shakes my bed. The ambulance slows down. If we continue at this speed, it will take us two days to reach Istanbul.

Will I be able to hang on? I ordinarily have a fairly high tolerance to pain. But the stomachache eating away at my insides seems to have grown worse. The meltdown in my intestines has caused an enlarged prostate, and then a urinary tract obstruction. On top of all the suffering, my sense of modesty is under attack, which very quickly becomes just as terrible as my bowels. The situation would be much easier to bear if it were caused by some noble wound. If only I'd taken a bullet in a scuffle with the PKK or broken several bones falling into a ravine. Then you can go home head high, weighed down by a cast, wrapped in blood-stained bandages that you wear like a crown of laurels. But there's no bullet hole. All I've got, so to speak, is a large wound in the . . . bunghole.

We've been rolling along for a little over an hour when I decide to try to urinate, since the urge is so strong. This is compounded by the need to do, as kids might say, number two. I have to wonder how it's even possible, since I haven't digested anything for four days. The nurse, of course, has everything ready. She takes a kind of round bedpan, sets it down in the back of the vehicle, and tells me to have a go. While I am by no means particularly prudish, I'm not very keen on making a show of my privates, either. I tell her this, and she goes up front, facing the drivers. A titanic struggle then ensues. Given how weak I am, it's hard enough for me to maintain my balance standing up. But squatting, it becomes a veritable high-wire act. With the ambulance swerving back and forth, despite holding on with two hands, I unpredictably swing to the right and then to the left each time the breakneck coffin zigzags or lurches forward. And if I manage to hold myself in a steady, albeit hardly dignified, position, then the bedpan starts to move across the liner made of some sort of polished linoleum, as slick as a dance floor. I try my valiant best for fifteen minutes, and then, exhausted and humiliated, I hand the empty bucket back to the nurse and lie down, completely disheartened.

And at that point, a tussle begins between me and the nurse, one that will last for most of the journey. She insists on trying to get me to drink in order to alleviate the dehydration I'm apparently suffering from. I refuse so long as I haven't relieved my epic urge to urinate, which has caused my belly to become frighteningly swollen. After Erzurum, the road is in better condition, and the bumps become less frequent. We stop from time to time for the drivers to have tea and change positions. The nurse keeps at it, cruelly pinching the skin of my arm to prove how dehydrated I am, telling me over and over how I'm the one responsible for this vicious circle. If I drink, she says, I rehydrate myself, and therefore I piss. I'm tormented by thirst, and that makes me want to give it a try. I swallow several cups of tea and a can of juice. But nothing happens, except the pressure in my belly gets worse.

From time to time, I get up from my cot, and, my nose pressed against the ambulance's little window, I watch the very landscapes fly by that I contemplated those many days at the slow pace of walking. I recognize them, but they're not the same. A city, a village won't let you grasp it in such a quick glance. You have to approach it slowly, with love.

In early afternoon, I manage to sleep a little, but I'm wakened shortly thereafter by the terrifying feeling of being a wineskin about to burst open. Every square millimeter of the skin of my abdomen is stretched to the point of breaking. The nurse, who can't seem to take no for an answer, tells me I have to drink. I brush her off. This time, I'm not giving in. Brazen right to the end, now she won't even talk to me.

My eyes riveted on the vehicle's ceiling, rigged with hooks and cables, I try to escape from this world of plastic and chrome steel by focusing on the future. I'll soon be in Istanbul, then in Paris, and then back home. There, I'll see the faces of my children and friends once again, the restorative calm of the Norman countryside; and, in a few weeks, I will be back on my feet, ready for adventure. My Iranian visa won't pose any problems if I start the process early enough. From the very beginning of my affliction, I've clung to one idea bordering on an obsession: to pick up EX-ACT-LY where I collapsed, just before Doğubeyazıt. That road and its barren hills in front of me and behind me, the plain where the plumes of a few poplar trees were turning yellow under the heat of the sun, the trickle of a river down below and even grass of the berm where I fell face-forward: every detail is etched in my memory with photographic precision. I cling to it as if to a promise. The moment I take my first step, the nightmare that I've endured these last four days will finally be over.

After all, I really don't have all that much to complain about. I'll receive medical attention. The merchants and caravanners who fell along the Silk Road had no other recourse than to wait wherever they were, in precarious conditions, until they recovered from their illness before they could continue their journey. In a few hours, they'll be pampering me in a clinic in Istanbul; they'll get me refueled and back on my feet.

But we're not there yet. With every passing minute, I grow increasingly impatient. I start thinking what slowpokes the drivers are. When the pain becomes too much, I ask the nurse for a shot of morphine. She doesn't have any. "Buy some!" I shout. The pressure from my urinary blockage is becoming unbearable. No position—I've tried them all—provides any relief whatsoever. I writhe about on my cot, racked with pain. The nurse decides to spread an ointment over my buttocks that should calm things down. I don't really see the connection, but I'd happily let her butter my entire body if it came with the promise that I would feel better. So I ready myself to let her do what she wants despite my reluctance to show her my ass. The miracle salve fails to bring about any improvement. It's dark out. I lack the energy now even to sit up and watch the scenery. I have just one desire: to get there. "Faster, faster." I have the feeling that the ambulance is crawling along. The rescue team has decided that I'm a dyed-in-the-wool pain in the butt and no longer even bothers to answer me. I suggest that we stop in a hospital along the way, so I can be catheterized. Let's put an end to this ordeal. They try to put my mind at ease: we're almost there.

They can say whatever they want: mired in pain, I have no idea where we are; I have no idea what condition I'm in. While it was still light out, I occasionally glanced at my watch, but at nighttime, without my glasses, I no longer even have a sense of time whether standing still, calmly wandering about my body—now agony incarnate—or dragging its feet while

butchering my bowels. The increasingly heavy traffic gives me some hope
that we're nearing Istanbul. From time to time, the drivers turn on the
siren to force their way through the traffic. My belly is so taut that I try
to urinate several times without even getting up. If I could, I'd pee all
over the damn gurney in plain view of this baleful young lady: that's how
torture can destroy all sense of dignity. Two or three times, overcome, I
sink into a kind of comatose, restorative sleep, but, unfortunately, only
for short spells. By dint of twisting around, I finally hit on a less painful position—on all fours on the gurney—but I nevertheless howl with
every jolt. I've lost all sense of what's going on. Little by little, on top of
the pain permeating my intestines and bloating my bladder, there's now
another one: a burning sensation over my buttocks, accompanied by a
feeling of wetness.

The ambulance stops on the side of the road. A breakdown? No, the
nurse has stepped out, and one of the drivers takes her place. She's going
home. Is she angry with this impenitent patient, or does she think I'm no
longer conscious? In any event, she doesn't even say good-bye. I'm happy
to see her leave, because she told me she lived in Istanbul and that means
that, this time, we've arrived. But the city is gigantic. The last minutes
seem to go on forever. We cross the suspension bridge over the Bosporus.
Its siren screaming, the vehicle forces its way through traffic that's still
heavy though it's already late at night. We finally pull off the road and
into the brightly lit hospital courtyard. I'm wiped out and let them transport me on a stretcher and then onto a wheeled gurney that they shove
into an elevator. A slightly chubby blonde with thick, beautiful braids
guides my rolling bed, pushed by one of the drivers, up to a room. The
male nurse slips out, eager to get back to his own bed, exhausted by
two days of crazed driving. I explain what I'm feeling to a doctor who
speaks some English. He examines me, and, upon seeing my rear end,
he exclaims:

"What' going on there?"

I can't see, for obvious reasons.

"What do you mean?"

"You're burned!"

"They put an ointment on me."

"You're having a bad allergic reaction. Do you remember the name of the drug? It looks terrible . . ."

I've been spared nothing. A little later, one of the doctors comes back to catheterize me. A nasty moment. And then, alone in my room, I'm finally able to relax. I look up at the clock in the hallway. It took us twenty-three hours to cross all of Turkey. I now know that, after a certain level of suffering has been exceeded, we no longer fear death.

A sweet lethargy brought on by the morphine envelops me. After all the jostling on a narrow gurney, the hospital bed—although hard—seems deep and soft as a featherbed. I finally sink into a deep sleep.

It's 6:00 a.m. when I wake up. I slept very little but enough to regain strength. I have something like a hangover and the unpleasant sensation of having wet the bed. The allergic reaction caused by the dastardly nurse's ointment has bloated and blistered my skin, and nasty yellowish lymph is draining from the countless pustules. It oozed overnight and dried, turning the sheets starchy. It is incredibly unpleasant, but compared with yesterday's agony, it's only a minor annoyance. I have my optimism back and some of my sense of humor. I'm not much to look at, but I'm alive, the sun is shining, and perhaps I'll find the nurses I hear working in the hallway attractive. What a disappointment: the first person to come through the door is a short, chubby man here to do the housekeeping. His name is, of course, Mehmet, and he completely ignores me. As the days go by, he warms up, his apparent indifference being nothing more than the manifestation of his natural shyness, which I eventually manage to break through.

Around 8:00 a.m., a cadre of men in white examine me. The verdict in Turkish is translated by one of the surgeons who has a rather good mastery of French, Metin Sayan. The dysentery has caused such a violent and painful reaction that they dispense with the rest of the auscultation. They'll have to operate, ablating certain veins. Apart from that, I have a prostatic blockage—something I already knew—and an allergic reaction to the miracle ointment. The scientific consensus is that I'll need several days before I am ready to board a plane, and then I'll have the operation in Paris without delay. For now, I first have to regain my strength, because I'm too sick to endure the four-hour flight between Istanbul and France.

The medical faculty now gone, I take an emotional nosedive. An operation? That means several weeks of hospitalization and rest. After such extended inactivity, I'll be physically at the bottom of my game. During the time I'll need to recover from the surgery and then begin training again, a lot of water will have flowed beneath the bridges of the Euphrates. My plan to get back underway by the end of August on Doğubeyazıt's silken road is now much more problematic. What alarms me most is this prostate business, since next year I have to walk in the desert.

Dr. Günay—the *IMA* associate—who drops by to see me is a die-hard optimist.

"There's nothing wrong with your prostate, it's probably just a case of prostatitis, which is to say a temporary condition that will quickly return to normal. Aside from that, we'll get you back up and walking. The staff at *Vatan* (Homeland) Hospital, where you wound up, are all top-notch. I'm booking you on a flight back to Paris four days from today."

I'd like to believe that his diagnosis is correct, since I'm not too keen on the prospect of having long-term problems with my prostate. The trouble of growing old is to a large extent the result of an accumulation of little nothings, physical manifestations that on their own are by no means insurmountable. Failing eyesight, a knee that hurts when you bend it, stubborn low back pain, the last few strands of hair that fall out or go white, an arthritic flare-up . . . so many minor annoyances that pop up and punctuate the long and winding road that leads us, according to an expression I find rather silly, to our "final resting place." In my travel notebook, right where I broke off, I jot down my war plans: I go back to Paris and have my operation right away. In two months, I'll be fit enough to get back on the road. I'll have to get going no later than about September 15 so that I can be out of the mountains before the return of cold weather and the first snowfalls, since, at an elevation of 2,200 meters (7,200 feet), they come early. By the end of October, by November 15 at the very latest, I'll be in Tehran.

I receive a visit from the lovely Rabia, my Turkish friend who will soon be marrying lucky Rémi. Her friendly presence, my first interaction with a familiar face in over two months, and the opportunity to finally chat in French, all make it a heartwarming experience. Rabia tells me that her grandfather was Kurdish and that he was clan chief somewhere in the east. She, too, wants the war to end and for Anatolia's economic recovery to finally bring peace and prosperity to the region. Perhaps, I tell her, Öcalan's trial may prove to be a unique opportunity to bring the conflict to an end? But members of parliament will need to display a great deal of statesmanship and courage in order to vote against the execution of the man most hated by the Turks and most idolized by the Kurds.

While talking about her marriage, which will be held in a civil ceremony, I ask her about Muslim weddings. They're simple services that take place in the presence of three persons: the couple and a third party, a kind of witness, who can be an imam, although not necessarily. The witness asks the groom: "How much is this woman worth?" A price is offered, in gold. They're married. If the husband changes his mind later on, all he has to do is pronounce the formula "Go away" three times. They're divorced. The man's only obligation is that he must pay the price he established when they were married.

I spend my time drawing up plans for the Silk Road. Between two bursts of optimism (I'm going to shake this off and get back on the road right away, etc.) and of pessimism (you're nothing but an old man, you'll just have to settle for tour groups from now on, etc.), I let myself go in the hospital's soothing environment and start making uncompromising plans and assessments. My dysentery is due, needless to say, to having ingested either polluted water or food. I can't get that greasy spoon in Diyadin off my mind. It's now clear: the man who was supposed to clean the floor must've also been on dish duty. What I've experienced these past few weeks means that I have to be even more careful going forward.

On certain days, I clearly overestimated my body's stamina. Given the state of fatigue I was in, just about any virus or microbe sauntering about the plains of Anatolia just like me would obviously have found me rather attractive. The first amoeba walked by, and, lo and behold, I was headed to a blood wedding. I overestimated my strength. Why? Because I want to avoid growing old? To prove to everyone else and to myself first of all that I'm still a "young man"? That's possible, anything is possible, although I can attest to the fact that, if so, I was never conscious of it.

I have to face the facts: in failing to reach my destination in Tehran, I've lost round one. But the game's not over. After all, the one thousand seven hundred kilometers (1,054 miles) I covered this year prove that I'm not short on energy or endurance. I have enough left to make it all the way to China. In this long walk—this long, solitary journey—life ebbs and death flows. The former still has a few victories to glean. I know that the latter will eventually carry the day. Meanwhile, I thumb my nose at it. And I'm only at the start of a twelve-thousand-kilometer journey.

The thought reminds me of a meaningful encounter I had with a little man one evening last year along the Way of St. James, in a guesthouse, only a short distance beyond Le Puy-en-Velay. "At seventy-two years old," he told me, "I feel my abilities starting to decline. I therefore enjoy those I have left so as to accomplish the goals closest to my heart: hiking Compostela this year and climbing the Mont Blanc next year. After that, I'll do what I can." I went ahead of him until the village of Conques, where, taking a day off to rest, he caught back up with me. He had had some trouble with his shoes, which he finally resolved. He seemed to be in excellent shape. He set out ahead of me, and I never saw him again. From time to time, at an inn, I heard tell of a little old man who walked as fast as the wind.

I'd like to make it all the way to China. And I'll come back, too, for all those whom I love and for my dear Pénélope waiting for me in our small village cemetery. After that, I'll do what I can. Life lies ahead of us, not behind. Preparing for and carrying through with this journey has been a fantastic mental challenge, a new birth into a new life. For the entire one thousand seven hundred kilometers or so that I traveled through Turkey, even though I hadn't anticipated its untimely end, this journey has been absolutely amazing. From the most remote villages all the way to the university of Erzurum, I've met so many warm, welcoming people that I'm at a loss for words. My walk through this land, so rich in history, has set me right once again with the world. And all along the way, I was escorted by a host of ghosts from the past: the heroes of the Trojan War—the Golden Fleece—the Ottoman Empire—the troops of Tamerlane, that "scourge of God"—Gordias and his son, the inventors of the Gordian Knot—Alexander the Great, who sliced it in half—Julius Caesar . . . They were all there, somewhere between myth and reality, right beside me with each step and every thought. As for the landscapes, the stark beauty of these vast expanses, mountains, and chasms, of these narrow gorges and of the steppe-land that I trod with my hiking boots: it's as vivid as ever, as if permanently burned into my retinas.

However enthusiastic I am about this land's rich past, I'm more critical of modern-day Turkey. The revolution it experienced under Atatürk is now floundering, mired in a society crippled by the huge gap between the rich and the poor and by the omnipresence of religion. The rich of the country's west want to be more Western than Europeans are. The poor of the country's east console themselves with religion or guerilla warfare. The country needs a new Atatürk, but could modern Turkey ever produce one? This is, as far as I've been able tell, a society on lockdown, just as it was under the Sultan when Turkey was the "sick man of Europe." Under the weight of its inflexibility, the regime collapsed, incapable of resolving its contradictions. Today, Turkey is truly torn between the East, where it is geographically located, and the West, where it would like to be. Pulled in a hundred different directions—by its attraction to Europe, conservative society, extreme nationalism, its brutal military tradition, and a tendency to fall back on religion—the country is wavering, hesitating, trying to get its bearings.

The Turkish-speaking countries of the former USSR would constitute a region of choice for the country to expand its economy and diplomatic ties, but it does not seem to have understood this. In order to establish whether it is situated in the East or the West, Turkey must first carry out agonizing reform. Asia doesn't begin on the other side of the Bosporus, as geographers tell us. The divide exists in every family with, on one hand, men, westernized and educated, and women on the other, kept under the yoke of daily labor and far from realms of learning. There's a rift between the degree-holding women of Istanbul and Ankara, their hair blowing in the wind, and the unschooled, veiled women of the villages—whether Turkish or Kurdish—who live in a clan-based society still stuck in the Middle Ages.

The country has experienced two major events that could, if real debate were to be held within the country, guide it to redefine its positions. The first is the impact of several refusals Europe made opposing Turkey's entry into the European Community on public opinion and the political establishment. The second is Öcalan's trial. These two developments, in their implications, clearly focus the debate domestically on peace with the Kurds and externally on peace with Greece. Two of the Turks' historic enemies. The temptation to resolve these two problems through violence—the army's solution of choice—can only lead to even greater isolation and increased poverty. The fact that Öcalan has not been executed and the rapprochement with Greece after the terrible earthquake that ravaged the İzmit region in August 1999 are two reasons for hope.

Of course, it's easy for me, a Westerner detached from the historical context, to pass peremptory judgment. This is something I try to avoid, for what, in the end, can I truly comprehend? What exactly did I go looking for in those dispossessed villages? I went in search of a past that the poor themselves could care less about, because their awareness is focused on what they don't have. And what they don't have, I, a well-heeled Westerner, do have, and yet I'm trying to get rid of it.

In Room 407 at Vatan Hospital, I play the philosopher, going over my voyage in my mind, planning out the next one, and, in my school notebook, sketching out the road ahead. In leaving, I wanted to understand the world. But does the world let itself be understood? At the end of the road, will I find wisdom? Or will I still be pointlessly waiting for it to come before death grabs hold of me? As a doer both by nature and by necessity, I must seek—along this slow road I've plotted out for myself—silence, meditation, and tranquility of soul. They won't all show up at once, of course. They're not crouching in the shadows of Xi'an's high walls, waiting for my arrival to reveal themselves. They'll appear along the way—on the footpaths and roads, in the cities, with each and every encounter to come, and in the millions of steps I still want to knit together—and help me quietly set the last stone in the wall of my life.

Before me, no one ever traveled the Silk Road in its entirety on foot. At least not since Marco Polo, you might argue. But still, I don't think I'm trying to accomplish some great feat or act of prowess. Rather, I'm forcing myself to slowly digest all that my life has been. For all the time that I've been looking for myself, has this journey *revealed* me? I must humbly acknowledge that I feel that I am the same, and yet, in flashes, I sense that I have somehow gained access to the notion of *eternity*. That's a big word, you might say. But the vast steppes of Anatolia, where the eye gets lost, are conducive to daydreams in which you find yourself rubbing elbows with the divine. And there's more: if you seek, as I consistently have, to be unafraid of an occasional brush with death, if you're willing to go to the trouble to give it some thought, then the doors of the infinite will open more quickly for you.

After all these days on my own, I have some confirmation that we're only truly ourselves in perseverance, in adversity, and in the exceptional. But my stoic side has once again won out over the epicurean I'd like to be. To truly slow down, you have to give something up. I didn't give up much of myself. Even before leaving, I planned everything out: the stages, the stops, where I would go sightseeing. Today, I promise myself that, between Doğubeyazıt and Samarkand, I won't hold myself to a timetable.

Samarkand . . . just the name of that city, one that has haunted my dreams since first having read about it, gives me hope. To get there, I will once again confront the mountains of Anatolia and Iran's mosquito-infested marshlands, I will traverse Tehran followed by wild, barren deserts, and then I will relax for a time in Bukhara, where the shadows of its despotic, mad emirs still roam.

In a few hours, my plane will take me away to Paris. But my heart will remain here, in a precise location: by the wayside of the road to Doğubeyazıt, where, in another life, I fell to the ground. In a few weeks or—if I'm sicker than I realize—in several months, I'll once again leave in the sand at that spot the footprints of my trusty boots. And turning to face the east, I'll once again take up my walking stick and resume my journey. With, stretching out before me, ten thousand kilometers of the unknown.

TRANSLATOR'S ACKNOWLEDGMENTS

I dedicate this translation to my father, Stanley A. Golembeski, who proofed the first chapter several years ago. He passed away in 2018 as I was completing the final draft.

This project is supported in part by an award from the National Endowment for the Arts. To find out more about how National Endowment for the Arts grants impact individuals and communities, visit www.arts.gov.

Thank you as well to Jennifer Wolter, PhD, French professor at Bowling Green State University in Ohio and master wordsmith, both in English and French. I would also like to acknowledge a former student at Grand Valley State University from Turkey, Uğur Çakıroğlu, who kindly answered my questions on the Turkish language.

I owe a great debt of gratitude to the expert editors who proofed my translation, especially Jon Arlan and Bob Mitchell. Their constructive comments contributed tremendously to the final draft.

Above all, I would like to express my appreciation to the author himself for having set off on such an amazing and inspirational "long walk" at the age of sixty-two and—what is perhaps an even more arduous journey—for taking the time to put it into words, so it could be shared with others. Grand merci, Bernard!

ABOUT THE AUTHOR

Six days into retirement, in April 1998, depressed and still grieving over the loss of his wife, his children fully grown, Bernard Ollivier set out to hike the Way of St. James from Paris to Santiago de Compostela in Spain, hoping to figure out what to do next in life. When the journey was over—2,300 kilometers (1,430 miles) later—he returned home with two ideas: he would work with troubled teens, helping them put their lives back together through the act of walking, just as he had done for himself; and he would walk yet another of history's great roads. In April 1999, he set out to hike the Silk Road (12,000 kilometers or 7,450 miles), and, in the year 2000, he founded the *Seuil Association*, dedicated to helping juvenile offenders by offering them the opportunity to travel as an alternative to prison.

The *Seuil Association* (*Seuil* meaning "Threshold"), founded by Bernard Ollivier in 2003, organizes long-distance, transformative hikes for troubled teens (typically at least 2,000 kilometers or 1,240 miles).

Seuil works in collaboration with French Children's Social Services and the French Ministry of Justice (the Judicial Protection of Young Persons Program). Select young people facing confinement can opt to embark on long-distance treks as an alternative to prison or an educational detention center. "Long walks" are offered preventatively to other young men and women in distress as well, whenever traditional approaches fail.

Seuil—Association (Organized under French Law 1901)
31, rue Planchat
75020 Paris
Telephone: +33 (0)1 44 27 09 88
Fax: +33 (0)1 40 46 01 97
E-mail: assoseuil@wanadoo.fr
Website: assoseuil.org